Women, Revolution, and
the Novels of the 1790s

Women, Revolution, and the Novels of the 1790s

EDITED BY

Linda Lang-Peralta

Michigan State University Press

East Lansing

Michigan State University Press
East Lansing, Michigan 48823-5202

04 03 02 01 00 99   1 2 3 4 5 6 7 8 9

LIBRARY OF CONGRESS CATALOGING-IN-PUBLICATION DATA
Women, revolution, and the novels of the 1790s / edited by Linda Lang-Peralta.
p. cm.
"A colleagues book: early women writer's series no. 6."
Includes bibliographical references.
ISBN 0-87013-519-8 (alk. paper)
1. English fiction—18th century—History and criticism. 2. Women and
literature—Great Britain—History—18th century. 3. Literature and
society—Great Britain—History—18th century. 4. Popular literature—
Great Britain—History and criticism. 5. English fiction—Women
authors—History and criticism. 6. Revolutionary literature, English—
History and criticism. 7. France—History—Revolution, 1789-1799—
Influence. I. Lang-Peralta, Linda.
PR858.W6 W66 1999
820.9'006—dc21
99-050547

Book and cover design by Sharp Des!gns, Lansing, MI

A Colleagues Series Publication
Colleagues Series Editor: Robert Uphaus

Visit Michigan State University Press on the World Wide Web at:
www.msu.edu/unit/msupress

Contents

Acknowledgments

I am grateful to those who have generously given of time, support, and expertise to move this project forward. Robert Uphaus helped to shape the book and prepare it for publication. At various points in the process, Jim Aubrey, Timothy Erwin, Bill Hamilton, Tracey Schwarz, Annette Tanner, Susan H. Wood and others offered valuable editorial advice. Katherine Binhammer contributed substantially to the bibliography. Joan Griffin, Pat McAnish, and Shaun McAnish provided patient and timely technological assistance. A grant from the President's Professional Development Fund at The Metropolitan State College of Denver provided much appreciated support during the final stage of the project. Special thanks also go to John and Barbara Wertin and Catherine Lang. Finally, for practical assistance and constant support, my heartfelt appreciation goes to Tim Peralta, to whom this book is dedicated.

Introduction

To astonish by the marvellous, and appal by the terrific, have lately been the
favourite designs of many writers of novels; who, in pursuit of those effects,
have frequently appeared to desert, and sometimes have really transgressed the
bounds of nature and possibility. We cannot approve of these extravagances.

—*The British Critic*, 1796[1]

British novels of the 1790s have often
been deemed, in their own day and in ours, excessive, bizarre, or extreme. The
indictment above clearly suggests the extent to which the boundaries of prose
fiction were shifting. As the essays in this volume demonstrate, however, these
extravagant novels also dared to focus on gender, oppression, and rights in this
revolutionary period, and in ways in which many readers have found revealing.
Of course, the perspective from which we view these texts will significantly
affect our judgement of them. Traditionally literary critics who have commented
on them have been either dix-huitièmistes more familiar with Jonathan Swift,
Laurence Sterne, and Samuel Richardson, or Romanticists more at home with
William Wordsworth, Samuel Taylor Coleridge, and Percy and Mary Shelley.
Both groups have tended to view the novels of the 1790s as a literary badlands,
marked by strangely-shaped formations, a desert area generally to be avoided

for the sake of the manicured gardens of Enlightenment literature or the well-marked peaks of Romanticism. But those literary historians, feminist scholars, and cultural critics who venture into this literary territory will discover rich sources of material about a decade that offered what must have seemed astonishing possibilities. Women for the first time dared to publish books and express political views in sizable numbers, for example. William Godwin (1756–1836) dared to expound his controversial philosophy in novels such as *The Adventures of Caleb Williams*. Recently scholars such as Cheryl Turner and Janet Todd have documented the wealth of women's writings during the period, allowing us to view these texts from a unique vantage point. Our present concerns with gender, power, the body, oppression, and public and private spheres lead us to see more clearly the fictive tributaries that stream through the badlands into the river of modern novels.

As the eighteenth century waned, literacy and the novel's popularity increased. And as writers wrote more novels during this intense period of change, their texts often became vehicles for new ideas, as well as forums in which to debate current issues. Where the novel had been viewed primarily as a single genre, there occurred a "fall into Division," to use William Blake's words. This volume demonstrates that several sub-genres were evolving: romance, satire, Gothic, as well as novels of sensibility, manners, and ideas, categories of fiction that are flourishing two centuries later. Today, however, our interest in the intersections of literature and culture, including popular culture, gives us new reasons to investigate this neglected history of prose fiction. A lack of easy access to some of these novels may account in some part for their prior obscurity. The increase in scholarly and critical attention has resulted in a stream of new editions, so that they are now more readily available. Several contributors to this volume have actively been producing new editions. Shawn Lisa Maurer produced a critical edition of Elizabeth Inchbald's *Nature and Art* in 1996. In addition to her volume of criticism on women writers of this period, Eleanor Ty has edited a 1994 edition of *The Victim of Prejudice* and a 1996 edition of *Memoirs of Emma Courtney*, both by Mary Hays. Now that these texts are more accessible, scholars may reappraise their value and students may become aware of them for the first time in several generations. This formative period in the history of the novel has been revived.

Accessibility was certainly a key factor in the original production of these novels. A growing readership, made possible in part by lending libraries, created a new market for fictional texts in the late eighteenth century. High economic inflation made earning extra income through writing attractive to many women. The need for additional income certainly motivated Frances Burney, who had married a penniless French émigré, and Charlotte Smith, a struggling single mother, to provide fiction for public consumption. Selling novels by subscription, as Burney published *Camilla* in 1796, ensured a readership, encouraged writers to finish a text quickly, and provided increased income for authors. Women also felt freer to produce novels because the role of a woman writer was now not so stigmatized as before. In the 1790s, these novels often explored domestic issues, practical concerns, and social intrigues, but they also provided a medium through which women could offer a voice on issues such as oppression, rights, and revolution. During this decade, radical writers such as Mary Wollstonecraft were answered by conservative writers such as Jane "Prudentia Homespun" West. During the 1790s, Jane Austen was reading these novels, exercising her pen and her wit, and drafting her own happy mutations of the genre. Indeed, it was in reaction to the often extravagant novels Austen read that she honed her more reserved style.

In this volume, scholars from America, Canada, and England offer bicentennial perspectives on British and American novels of the 1790s, and each emphasizes the cultural relevance of the text. Several essays offer perspectives on the contemporary debates over the public and private divide in eighteenth-century women's lives and novels. Catherine Decker provides an analysis of fictional representations of women in the public sphere, for example. Decker reads the novels of the 1790s as cultural documents that reveal the ways in which social class determined how women could appear in public. Upper-class women required escorts, while lower-class women, necessarily in public more often, were generalized as prey to sexual advances. Class mobility complicated the issue, and Decker concludes by identifying seven ideological positions in the novels of the 1790s. Katherine Binhammer explores the complexities of the public and private divide in *Desmond* by Charlotte Smith, concluding that Smith posits no clear oppositions, but rather "exploits these boundaries" in order to "transform . . . the private by putting an undomesticated public firmly in place." The firm line that Smith draws, Binhammer argues, is between national boundaries. Smith emphasizes domestic space in England and political space in France as she interweaves plots, subplots, facts, romance, fiction, and autobiography. These complicated strategies result in "revolutioniz[ing] the domestic."

William Godwin's *Things as They Are; or The Adventures of Caleb Williams* (1794) draws the attention of several contributors to this collection. Carl Fisher continues the dialogue about the public sphere and popular culture as they emerge in this novel, while Glynis Ridley and Barbara Benedict emphasize its gender issues. Fisher situates *Caleb Williams* in its intense historical context, reminding us that it served as a response to anti-Jacobin texts and the increased restrictions imposed by the British government. Fisher analyzes Godwin's depiction of the power relations between the populace and the gentry, pointing out the fear of popular disorder during the 1790s. While Godwin advocated rational dissent, he feared riots as a departure from the rational. Godwin's purpose, according to Fisher, is to transport "the participants of popular culture . . . from the realm of prejudice and misinformation to the presumably more free and open air of the public sphere." Novels were ideal for promoting reform, in Godwin's view, because they reached more people than did philosophy or science texts. Godwin uses this popular form for social critique, showing that Caleb is a monster created by an ill-informed society. Godwin depicts the mob's power and demonstrates why he wants "gradual change and rational exchange rather than riot and revolution." Glynis Ridley also focuses on power and authority as she explores legal and radical language in *Caleb Williams* and *The Wrongs of Woman; or Maria*. Radical views were often summarily rejected by the English legal and political systems because the language "did not permit the discussion of abstract concepts, contained an abundance of metaphors, and . . . [was] altogether overly emotive." Ridley compares the emphasis on appropriate rhetoric in political debates of the 1790s with the transformation of Caleb Williams's rhetorical style throughout four courtroom scenes. Caleb violates both "linguistic and social norms" by ultimately "meet[ing] the Magistrate linguistically on his own terms." On the other hand, Mary Wollstonecraft's (1759–1797) Maria denies her own voice, suggesting that Wollstonecraft viewed women as existing in the margins of the legal system. The last completed chapter demonstrates "society's failure to give women a voice." The Gothic conventions that pervade *Maria* invite the inference that "true horror lies not in a recoil from the supernatural, but in the conditions of the oppressed in England in the 1790s." Wollstonecraft and Godwin chose contrasting methods of depicting legal inequality.

Barbara Benedict notes that William Godwin was reading Ann Radcliffe's *The Mysteries of Udolpho* while writing *Caleb Williams*, and she suggests that he borrowed from Radcliffe crucial techniques. Both novels share a Gothic mood, power struggle, and focus on curiosity, which opens up new possibilities for identity but also exposes the self to danger. Curiosity in 1794 meant empirical disillusionment and the importance of identity in a tense political situation. These novels present mixed messages about curiosity: it is "a trap and an escape." Godwin and Radcliffe wrote novels that appeal to those looking for philosophy or entertainment, creating products designed to appeal through instruction and delight to an audience accustomed to "buying culture." Godwin's method involves a systematic attack on ownership in the form of colonialism, inherited wealth, and physical oppression, marked by a bare minimum of physical description. On the other hand, physical descriptions abound in *The Mysteries of Udolpho*. Both novels depict not only the disintegration of individual identity but the disintegration of society.

Expanding the boundaries of the Gothic novel in response to Radcliffe's *The Mysteries of Udolpho*, Matthew Lewis, influenced by continental literature, penned one of the most extravagant novels of the 1790s, *The Monk*. Clara McLean focuses on "worming" in the novel, demonstrating that it functions both figuratively and literally. The worm emerges literally as devourer of corpses and figuratively as a symbol of unrestrained curiosity and lust. Lewis constructs a parallel between scientific discovery of truth and physical investigation of bodies, highlighting the "characteristic Gothic tension" between reason and the irrational. McLean concludes that "*The Monk* points to a dual position for the worm: at once outside the mysterious body/text, hungrily looking in, and also always already implicated within it." She interprets one passage as "an ironized defense of 'bad' reading matter, of texts that do not comply with a rising novelistic aesthetic of representational transparency and naturalness" but that offer "the pleasure of the struggle with the text." By extension the novel to some extent remains indiscernible, and all we can attempt is "to sportively take pleasure in the worm's undoings."

Eleanor Ty develops the emphasis on the female body and the resistance to boundaries as she argues that Mary Hays's *The Victim of Prejudice* "attacks the emphasis on reputation for chastity" as female virtue, an attack similar to that in Wollstonecraft's *Maria*. Ty draws on Michel Foucault and feminist criticism for her methodology, that emphasizes the power cultural scripts can have over women's lives, as Hays demonstrates in *The Victim of Prejudice*. Ty argues that this novel "demonstrates the way the female body is transformed into a feminine one by being disciplined and punished." Hays makes her rewriting of popular literature polemical by appropriating the fallen-woman genre to serve her purposes. Mary speaks in the first person, unlike heroines such as Elizabeth Inchbald's in *Nature and Art*, making a literary gesture that had political ramifications in 1790s novels. By emphasizing her heroine's "bodily experience," Hays also departs from the popular literature, which presents the fallen woman in such abstract terms that little identification can take place. Hays uses strategies to convey a more realistic account of a woman's experience. Ty employs Elizabeth Grosz's study of Western philosophy to show that *The Victim of Prejudice* "highlights the near impossibility for a woman of separating her mind or spirit from her body, of living outside codes of propriety, femininity, and chastity expected by one of her gender." Hays's imprisoned woman at the conclusion of the novel represents the circumscribed role of women, providing a powerful fictional critique of 18th-century society. Gender construction and oppression are also issues that Shawn Lisa Maurer analyzes in *Nature and Art*. Specifically, Maurer explores the ways in which Elizabeth Inchbald depicts male gender roles and class oppression in the novel, which focuses on two brothers and their sons. Because Inchbald sets up a false dichotomy between the categories nature and art, Maurer suggests that "despite moments of radical insight" Inchbald reveals her political ambivalence and support of the status quo. However, the novel offers a "powerful, and successful melding of plot and character that demonstrates the links between personal experience and institutional oppression," warranting more critical attention than it has received.

The bicentennial perspectives that form this collection offer persuasive arguments supporting the timely relevance of renewed attention to 1790s novels. Many of the issues of that decade are still very much with us. Recent dialogues about the division of public and private spheres encourage Katherine

Binhammer and Catherine Decker to reassess the gender implications for re-drawn boundaries within the novels as well as in the novelists' lives. Power relations took center stage during the revolutionary 1790s as they have also become a primary focus in literary studies in the 1990s, relations most evident in the essays on *Caleb Williams* by Carl Fisher, Glynis Ridley, and Barbara Benedict. Women novelists of the 1790s depicted the dangers to which women fell prey as they entered the public sphere, an issue we are still grappling with today according to Catherine Decker. These novels directly influenced Jane Austen, who tried unsuccessfully to publish her own fiction during this decade, and whose texts are enjoying popular film adaptations in the present fin de siècle. Our period of rapid change in which modes of communication are transforming and women are using their voices in new and powerful ways corresponds in some suggestive ways to the 1790s, making a fresh look at the novels of that decade even more necessary. The myriad sub-genres of the novel that gained currency in the 1790s have not only survived but have flourished, as Stephen King and sentimental fiction testify. We also enjoy increased access to novels, which now float before us in the cyberspace of the Internet as well as appearing in bookstores and libraries, creating new opportunities for research. We are all benefiting from a more accurate view of the history of the novel because of these inclusions. It is precisely because of their marvelous and extravagant shapes that we must turn to the novels of the 1790s as we continue to construct the history of the novel.

Note

1. From a review of *Camilla: or, a Picture of Youth* (1796), in *The British Critic*, VIII (November 1796). *Novel and Romance, 1700–1800: A Documentary Record,* ed. Ioan Williams (New York: Barnes and Noble, 1970). The review, for the most part, praises Frances Burney's novel *Camilla.*

Women and Public Space in the Novel of the 1790s

Catherine H. Decker

Is it morally right?

Is it socially acceptable?

Is it legal?

O ur awareness of some semantic differences among these three questions suggests that moral, social, and legal codes do not correlate in the world as they would in utopia. Social codes attempt to mediate between what a culture perceives as good or right and what it codifies as legal or illegal. Changes in moral beliefs are reflected in social practices and eventually codified into laws. Some laws, however, grant women a freedom that is not practiced in society or religion. This paper deals with such a "right," the right to move in public space, which is legal but often controlled or limited by unwritten social and moral constraints. Any woman who has not gone out to buy milk late at night because she is afraid of being attacked can understand this problem. Legally, she has every right to go to a public store and purchase an item at any time the store is open. However, going out alone late at night is socially suspect—the woman is "asking for trouble."

Women in the 1790s faced difficulties moving in public space that no longer exist. "Public" space is by definition open to everyone—men and women of all classes, races, religions, and physical conditions. Yet access to public space has been limited, and still is in certain ways, for women. A useful analogy might be to compare the obstacles facing a 1950s American citizen in a wheelchair and such a citizen in the 1990s. The latter individual not only confronts fewer physical challenges but is more psychologically welcomed and supported by public architecture, customs, and attitudes. Moreover, the American citizen in a wheelchair in the 1990s has more well-defined legal rights and is protected by a legal web of building codes, parking fines, and judicial precedents established in civil-rights cases. Women of the 1990s have benefited from the same kind of cultural and legal changes that have made public space more open to American citizens with physical disabilities. Yet, after studying the novels of the 1790s, I have concluded that women today are still grappling with some very real side effects of the same cultural gender biases which women of the 1790s faced. Public space is still psychologically and physically hostile to women today. A close examination of the ways in which novelists of the 1790s manipulated the cultural mechanisms that control the role of women in public space should help clarify the positions in the current ideological war over women's right to move in public space. Feminist awareness of the hostility of public space to women in the 1990s is perhaps best embodied in the "Take Back the Night" movement, in which groups of feminists gather at night to march in public space and to assert their right to do so safely.[1]

The study of the cultural conflict over women's right to move in public space in the novels of the 1790s is not only of interest to feminists concerned with using the past to change the present or even to historians seeking to understand the past. Understanding the political and polemical dimensions of the novels of the 1790s enlightens cultural and literary critics about the interaction of the novel, art, culture, and activism. Such a study can also enable us to chart more precisely the ideological positions promoted by the oeuvres of major and minor novelists of the Romantic period. Moreover, it also should shed light on the reception history of the novels of the 1790s and enable us to trace reader-responses of the past and present. Once we understand the subtle ideological stances of the novels and their relationships to general cultural beliefs, we can speculate on how these relationships might have caused the literary reputation of particular works to rise or fall.

This study is oriented towards reading texts as revealing important aspects about the world. I mean here the "world," not in the sense of discovering the actual history of real men and women, but of tracing the cultural beliefs that shaped behavior, moral judgements, and mental health in the 1790s, beliefs which are the roots of our current culture. The reading of novels as cultural documents has a long history in literary criticism, and various particular theories developed by such thinkers as Mikhail Bakhtin, Louis Althusser, Michel Foucault, Raymond Williams, and Pierre Bourdieu about culture and how texts reflect or shape culture have enjoyed vogues. The common goal of all these writers and the schools of analysis they have inspired is to classify conflicting ideological positions found in society and manifested in texts, institutions, and visual images. The language of each differs, but at heart they share a similar desire to clarify the complex underlying assumptions of a culture. This study draws on this legacy and the rich tradition of feminist criticism seeking to understand the relationship between female genetic endowments and culture—a relationship conveyed in the term "gender."

Class, Gender, and Public Space

Class was the most basic way in which the eighteenth century grouped women moving in public space. Upper- and middle-class women were expected to move in public and conduct business in public only with "appropriate" companions. Such companions included fathers, husbands, brothers, or male guardians as well as the female or male representatives of such men: footmen, grooms, abigails, maids, and companions. Lower-class women were not subject to this restraint, for economics would dictate that both they and the men who would accompany them would need to work. Moreover, lower-class women were needed as the servants and companions hired to escort middle- and upper-class women.

Lower-class women's movement in public space was controlled by simultaneous freedom to move in public space and damnation for doing so as the sexual providers, servants, and prey of culture. Roy Porter and Leslie Hall assert, "Maidservants were fair game for male advances: rakes were not the worse thought of so long as they made arrangements for any resulting bastards. Although women were often victims of unwanted attentions, many seem to have been perfectly compliant."[2] This blatant correlation of money and class with female sexual vulnerability was masked in the 1790s by beliefs in biological differences among women of different classes. Lower-class women were supposedly predisposed to promiscuity and less prone to physical and mental disorders. Some medical texts attributed this difference to the different life styles of the classes: William Buchan's *Domestic Medicine* (2nd ed., 1772) argued that the confinement of women in the home "besides hurting their figure and complexion, . . . weakens their minds, and disorders all the functions of the body."[3] Yet Buchan also claims, "women who were chiefly employed without doors, in the different branches of husbandry, gardening, and the like, were almost as hardy as their husbands" (648). Whether such a physical difference is attributed to biology or physical conditioning, the result manifested itself in radically different approaches to the illnesses of women of different classes. As G. S. Rousseau has observed: "When milady fainted or fell in a swoon, the expectation was of a complex series of ritual events and phenomena essentially different from those of the swoons of Betty, Moll Flanders, or Nan the orange woman."[4]

Because of the lower class woman's "coarser" or "less delicate" nerves, she was a more acceptable sexual victim. Conversely, the "delicate," "sensitive," genteel woman was seen as disinterested in sex and vulnerable to serious illnesses from things like a loud noise or a pet's injury. The mid-century French doctor, Jean Astruc, whose texts were translated into English and Spanish and reprinted throughout the remainder of the century, declared in his *Treatise On all the Diseases Incident to Women* (1st English ed., 1743) that female sexual desire, especially when accompanied by masturbation, caused hysteric fits, i.e. convulsions of the body muscles of the uterus, abdomen, face, and neck combined with respiratory troubles, delirium, and hot and cold fits.[5] Astruc attributes hysteria to "Acrimony of the feminal Humours of some Women, especially these [*sic*] of a bilious hot Constitution, when, for the Preservation of their Reputation or other Ends, they provoke frequent Pollutions by irritating and rubbing the Parts of Generation" (292). Hence, according to Astruc, women with delicate nerves could be overwhelmed or driven into hysteria by too much sex or even just too much sexual desire.

The sexual double standard was thus justified to a degree by this "gendering" of health. Such justification made it more acceptable for a man to vent his "natural" sexual urges on a woman of the lower classes, whose body supposedly both wanted sex and could handle the mental stresses associated with it, rather than on his "delicate," morally pure wife. Taking a lower-class mistress was in this way defined as being "sensitive" to the "delicate" nature of middle- and upper-class women. For "good" women, pleasure was supposed to come from being legally impregnated, not from sex itself.[6] This notion, new in the eighteenth century, was supposedly proven around 1780 by the Italian Lazzaro Spallanzani (1729–99). His artificial insemination of a frog "proved" female sexual pleasure was biologically useless to procreation and ergo "unnatural" (Roberts 277–8).

The bourgeoisie's efforts to elevate their social position and gain the hegemonic power of the traditional aristocracy had an obvious impact on such a system: women too could change classes in a world in which economics, not birth, determines social status. Class mobility and confusion caused women who were supposedly genetically predisposed to handle public life to be respected and women who were thought too delicate for a sexually-charged public world to be harassed. Moreover, if the equal intellectual and moral powers of "man" are used to justify removing hegemonic power from the aristocracy, such logic introduces the issue of rights for women and other socially oppressed groups.

To prevent these groups from gaining equal power, biological notions of the inequality of the sexes and races were promoted. In these larger theories of race and gender, the line between upper- and lower-class women blurred. G. S. Rousseau explains how the gendering of health in the eighteenth century likewise coded certain behaviors as biologically natural: women "were described pathologically—in the language of sickness, as victims of their uterine debility; men were assumed to be healthy . . . and became deviant only when veering from this state into nervous effeminacy" (33). In other words, "normal" women were—due to their more delicate bodies—normally ill, so that, unlike men, they were unfit for the ardors of public life.

Not only "Nature," but "God" too was recruited to demean women as unable to handle the moral and physical aspects of public life. Medical-spiritual theories of the soul and its manifestation in the nerves of the body were used to argue for women's spiritual inadequacies. For example, Antoine Le Camus

(1722–72) in *Médecine de l'Esprit* (1769) claimed to trace a link between the nerves and the soul.[7] The basic notion was that the soul manifested itself in the nerves of the body; the nerves of women were generally agreed to be weaker; therefore, their "souls" were weaker. Of course, not all saw this as medically and religiously acceptable. More common was a mind/body duality theory that the body was amoral or immoral and the soul was linked to the mind, which was thus the moral force in human beings. The same sort of biological and religious gender differences could be promoted with this understanding of the body and soul as well: women have weaker minds; consequently, they are weaker spiritually and cannot make moral decisions for themselves.

While such theories about biology and morality argued in general for women's inadequacies in public dealings, perceived differences between women of different classes supposedly rendered some women more or less fit to move in public space. The truth of women's class or birth, supposedly determined by God and Nature, is not physically revealed the way sex and race are. If class or birth were to determine if a woman was to be permitted to move freely in public space and/or to be made to pay a sexual price for such movement, it was necessary to determine a woman's social class. How one determines a woman's class or "rights" typically depended on both the physical—her clothes, her visible behavior, her demeanor—and the knowledge that can be determined about the woman's family, past behavior, and morals. The problem is of course that all of these things—clothes, behavior, demeanor, family history, morals, and, in fact, sex and race (via disguises), can be manipulated and transformed. As a result, given there is no guarantee of a correlation between appearance and truth, seven different cultural approaches existed to determine how to treat a woman encountered in public.

Before we begin to explore these positions, I want to elaborate on the difference between moral and social codes. By social codes, I do not mean merely rules of etiquette and customs associated with courtesy. The social codes of a culture are how the culture actually implements into everyday living the morality promoted by various religious organizations; modifications are necessarily required because moral codes not only conflict with each other, but frequently do not correspond with a society's legal codes. In other words, social codes are not only notions of courtesy or manners, but the general social behaviors or customs that a culture sees as "normal" or "appropriate." For example, the "don't ask, don't tell" policy about homosexuality in the American armed forces is a social code that attempts to mediate the gap between the law and morality. The social code calls for silence so that no overt legal or moral stance needs to be embarrassingly argued. The key difference between moral and social codes is that of intention and priorities; the moral code endeavors to promote truth, life, and goodness as they are best understood at any given time, while the social code balances a society's notion of truth, life, and goodness with what will en-sure the social group's physical and economic survival—in other words, practi-cal concerns about the social implementation of a moral belief.

The Seven Ideological Positions of the Novels of the 1790s

The Misogynist/Libertine Position and the Chivalrous/Quixotic Position

The two least widely held and most logically indefensible approaches to judg-ing the morals of women in public are the misogynist/libertine and the chival-rous/quixotic positions. These belief systems are held almost exclusively by men, given that the complex reality of living life as a woman would expose the unre-alistic and illogical nature of these positions. The misogynist/libertine assumes all women are, or would like to be, both active in public life and sexual provid-ers, servants, or prey. All women are perceived as desiring power, money, and sex, and therefore morally weak, vicious, or corrupt—even if they have not actually done anything morally wrong or acted to gain such money, power, or sex. Thus, no matter what a woman's behavior, motives, or appearance is, she is essentially "wrong" and deserving of the treatment generally allotted by the culture to women of low character and class.

Conversely the chivalrous/quixotic position is that of naive idealists who define all women as morally good and having good motives. Thereupon, even if a woman is doing something universally perceived as morally wrong—pros-tituting herself, stealing, sleeping with multiple sex partners—she is not evil and is to be treated with the decorum generally accorded to only middle- and upper-class women. Both the misogynist/libertine and the chevalier/quixote prejudge all women, and so avoid the issue of evaluation entirely.

Given the obvious illogic and complete social impracticality of a society adopting these approaches to dealing with women, novelists writing realistic fiction rarely bother to attack or defend such stances. Gothic novels of the time, however, frequently feature misogynists, libertines, chevaliers, and quixotes. Commonly in the novels set in Europe of the 1790s, characters are shown leaning towards such a stance, but mostly taking some more socially and logically defensible positions on women's movement in public space and participation in public life. For example, Dr. Marchmont in Frances Burney's *Camilla* (1796) comes very close to adopting the misogynist/libertine position on women's movement and participation in public life. Dr. Marchmont, disillusioned by discovering that his late wife loved another man, now suspects all women of behaving deceitfully. He is not a full misogynist/libertine because he still asserts that he believes there are some women "'who merit every regard.'"[8] Yet, Dr. Marchmont continually urges Edgar to observe Camilla for signs of her bad moral character: "'Nothing must escape you; you must view as if you had never seen her before . . . every look, every word, every motion'" (160). Later, Dr. Marchmont sums up his theory of women: "'Ask me, my dear young friend, why the sun does not give night . . . then why women practice coquetry. Alas! my season for surprise has long been passed! They will rather trifle, even with those they despise, than be candid even with those they respect'" (571).

The similarity of these two extreme positions is revealed in novels in which a character shifts from one category to the other. For example, Mr. Valmont in Eliza Fenwick's *Secresy* (1795), in a manner somewhat similar to William Godwin's much more complex Fleetwood in his 1805 novel of that name, moves from a chivalrous/quixotic position on women to a misogynist/libertine position. Valmont becomes a tyrant over his niece: "'you are not born to think; you were not made to think.'"[9]

The reality of class differences forces the misogynist/libertine in novels of the 1790s, if he would remain alive and healthy, to approach women of the middle- or upper-class differently than those of the lower class, for the men who "own" such women may have the power to enforce different, more respectful behavior. Yet, fundamentally the misogynist/libertine sees all women the same: they are all 'rakes at heart,' à la Pope, and deserve no respect. Any respect women receive from a misogynist/libertine is actually respect for the men who "own" them.

The Traditional Patriarchal Position and Its Fundamental Flaws

The crucial difference between the misogynist/libertine approach and the traditional patriarchal approach is that the latter does perceive the possibility of female virtue and does classify some women as worthy of respect. The traditional patriarchal position equates manners and morals: social codes and moral codes are the same, and, therefore, outward behavior reveals internal morality. If this position does admit there is a gap between social and moral codes, it also asserts that the gap is slight enough to be irrelevant. One fundamental flaw of this position is that manners and morals do not always correspond, and social codes may conflict with moral codes in significant, relevant ways.

At issue of course is what is meant by "moral codes." Telling lies, for example, was considered immoral in the 1790s, as it is now in the 1990s. Yet, social codes in the 1790s demanded that more truths be hidden than today's codes do. In the 1790s, a married woman who had sex at eight in the morning with her husband for the purposes of producing a child would be seen as socially wrong to respond to the question posed in public, "What were you doing at eight in the morning Mrs.——?" by saying, "I was having sex." The violation of the moral injunction to tell the truth would be overridden for the fear that it would lead to some more serious immoral acts, such as leading others to commit adultery, to have sex outside of marriage (premarital or adulterous), to have sex for reasons other than producing a child, such as for money, or to have sex with animals or children. Another reason to avoid such frank talk was the fear that it would generate, or worse, indicate, an abnormal love of sex, which would likewise lead to more morally depraved acts. (While general moral notions today are different from those of the 1790s, most people would still see having sex with animals and children as morally wrong.) The social code of the 1790s would thus tell people in the situation of Mrs.——, "Lie, because if you don't, you or other people may later commit other moral wrongs." This use of such logically flawed, "slippery slope" arguments to code social behavior as moral behavior is another fundamental flaw of the traditional patriarchal position.

Traditional patriarchal logic about women who freely move about unescorted is captured in such terms as "streetwalker," which dates to the late sixteenth century, and "nightwalker" which came into the language in the fifteenth century. Both terms are used for prostitutes and whores, and both terms imply a connection between moving in public space and female impropriety or crime. Traditional patriarchal logic can be simplified into the following syllogism: all good women are valued male property; all valued male property is kept in the home or guarded by men in public space; therefore, all good women are at home or guarded by men. Ergo, all women unguarded in public space either do not know better (because they are fools or lunatics) or do not care (because they are adventuresses, prostitutes, or criminals) and, therefore, deserve to be gulled, propositioned, or worse. As Mary Poovey succinctly phrases this: "A woman who is not 'private property' is implicitly available for public use."[10]

This traditional patriarchal attitude indicates that women in public merit condemnation or blame for not being "womanly" or "proper" women and for not behaving like "property." Such a woman is to be treated as one not worthy of respect and as guilty of social wrongs ranging from mere thoughtlessness or impropriety to more serious crimes such as prostitution or theft. This treatment creates a vicious circle, for a woman treated in such a way has increasingly fewer behavioral options open to her—a third fundamental flaw of the patriarchal position.

The woman who walks alone in public space is subject to a two-part harassment by people using patriarchal logic. First, she is harassed by acts of omission by ordinary pedestrians, shopkeepers, innkeepers, or business people who deny her both basic civilities accorded to "proper" women and the basic public services available to such "good" women. For example, shopkeepers do not want unescorted women in their stores or lingering outside them because they will either steal or discourage escorted, "owned," proper women from patronizing the shop. In Frances Burney's *Camilla* (1796), Camilla and Mrs. Mitten, although together, act unconventionally in various shops, in that they curiously look at a great number of goods but do not buy them (607–8). This odd behavior, coupled with their lack of a male escort, makes the shopkeepers suspect them of being "deranged in mind" or of being "shoplifters" (608).

Secondly, the unescorted woman in public is harassed by acts of commission—she is visually, verbally, or physically assaulted in public. For instance, respectable men and women subject the woman moving alone in public space to hostile, curious, or critical stares or may lecture or criticize the unescorted woman on her (obvious) impropriety and her implied and assumed immorality and criminality. In the *Camilla* scene discussed above, Camilla and Mrs. Mitten are stared at by all the shopkeepers on High-street (608), and one, a Mr. Drim, "made a circuit to face and examine them" (608).

In addition, more corrupt men and women may take advantage of the way in which patriarchal logic condemns the unescorted woman as "wrong"; these corrupt people prey upon the unescorted female pedestrian for money, sex, or sadistic gratification. Such unescorted women in public space are robbed, extorted, or pimped by criminals of both sexes and may be fondled, beaten, kidnapped, or raped by men. Again, in *Camilla*, Mr. Halder, Lord Valhurst, and Mr. Westwyn force open the door of the bathing hut that Camilla and Mrs. Mitten have entered to escape the stares of the shopkeepers (609, 613). Lord Valhurst tries to get Camilla and Mrs. Mitten into his carriage on the pretext of escorting them to their home, but, when a male friend of Camilla's fortuitously arrives to escort them himself, "Lord Valhurst exhibited signs of such irrepressible mortification, that inexperience itself could not mistake the dishonourable views of his offered services, since, to see her in safety, was so evidently not their purpose" (614–5). The purpose, so discretely left unspecified by the proper female novelist Burney, is to kidnap the young woman in the tradition of Samuel Richardson's *Clarissa* (1747–9).

This incident in Burney's *Camilla* does not end in sexual or physical violence because the women are now "owned" or escorted by Edgar Mandlebert, who will eventually become Camilla's husband, her legal owner. However, Lord Valhurst and Mr. Westwyn argue over Camilla's behavior so emotionally that they later duel. Lord Valhurst, Mr. Halder, and the shopkeepers have interpreted Camilla's behavior using the patriarchal code: Camilla and Mrs. Mitten's aggressive voyeurism of the consumer goods of the town and the fact that no men or servants mark them as "owned" women leads the men to conclude the women are in fact seeking to acquire something by means other than a traditional purchase. The women, according to the patriarchal code, are either mad or look-ing for adventure: to steal the goods, to acquire a man who will buy the goods for them, or to acquire the goods by earning money through sexual services.

In contrast, Mr. Westwyn reserves judgement against Camilla until he sees her response to Lord Valhurst's actions. Because Camilla is horrified at discov-ering Valhurst's intentions, Westwyn then believes Camilla is innocent despite her odd public behavior (615). Westwyn's interpretation of Camilla's behavior is typical of what I label the feminist attitude, to be more extensively defined below. Once we accept, like Mr. Westwyn, that manners and morals are not the same thing and that behavior does not automatically prove moral innocence or guilt, the entire traditional patriarchal system becomes morally questionable.

The Fashionable Patriarchal Position

The reality that patriarchal codes can be followed only on the surface and be manipulated by clever people to enable them to commit moral improprieties, while still being treated as if virtuous, is the basis of the fashionable patriarchal position. "People of fashion" is synonymous in novels of the 1790s for people who accept the cultural codes of the patriarchy only as rules, not as moral guides. Like the U.S. military policy "don't ask, don't tell," silence and concealment about the sexual realities of life is demanded, not any real moral change or sexual abstinence. In essence, the person taking the fashionable patriarchal ap-proach believes that social codes and the morality they embody need only be followed in public. Any act that enables one to follow the social code in public is morally acceptable. Any crime that can be committed in private is acceptable, for the only crime is to be caught in public.

Fashionable patriarchy was widely depicted in novels as a distinguishing mark of the aristocracy. The Enlightenment project of transferring power from the aristocracy to the bourgeoisie was morally justified by showing that aristo-crats merely followed patriarchal codes on the surface. Bourgeois men and women authors seeking to morally justify their class and their right to cultural authority would frequently attack the way "fashionable" or aristocratic society would only follow social codes in public and break moral codes in private.

Both male and female characters in novels are shown taking this position. Both are typically depicted as full of "passion" and "pride," a fatal combination that leads them to make marriages for money and power while seeking sexual gratification outside of marriage. In Helen Maria William's *Julia* (1790), Mr. Seymour is such a character who "lived in a continual plot against the rest of his species" and is described as like "a swan gracefully expanding his plumes of purest whiteness to the winds, and carefully hiding his black feet."[11] It is this desire to conceal vices that distinguishes Seymour from a man taking the misogynist/libertine position towards which he leans: "He was himself a libertine, both in principle and practice: he . . . had conceived a very contemptible opinion of the principles of the female mind" (I: 177).

While secrecy is one key aspect of fashionable patriarchy, the other major aspect is power. The more power a person has, the less secrecy is required of him or her. Elizabeth Inchbald's Lady Bendham in *Nature and Art* (1796) reveals the way the powerful victimize the powerless using this code:

Whether in town or country, it is but justice to acknowledge, that in her own person she was strictly chaste; but in the country she extended that chastity even to the person of others; and the young woman who lost her virtue . . . had better have lost her life . . . But this country rigueur, in town, she could dispense withal, and like other ladies of virtue, she there visited and received into her house the acknowledged mistresses of a man in elevated life . . . she even carried her distinction of classes in female error to such a very nice point, that the adulterous concubine of an elder brother was her most intimate acquaintance, while the less guilty unmarried mistress of the younger, she would not sully her lips to exchange a word with.[12]

The desire for society to be truly moral, not just appear to be moral on the surface while actually allowing a great deal of secret, private vice to occur (particularly among the powerful upper classes) is the basis for the last three positions I will explain, the positions that novels of the 1790s most commonly feature: the sentimentalist, the internalized/reformed position, and the feminist position.

The Sentimental Position and Its Fundamental Flaw

The sentimental position evolved prior to the 1790s as a way of attempting to combat the tendency to equate manners with morals and to judge morals solely upon manners. The sentimental position denies the link of manners and morals, but does not actually involve any "judgement" (in the sense of logical reasoning) at all. Like the misogynist/libertine and chivalrous/quixotic position, this position is both morally and practically illogical, for not only do the sentimental "judgements" of women's morality not hinge on any real attempt to determine the morality of their behavior or interior motivations and beliefs, but there is no way to insure all people would arrive at the same judgement of the same woman. Basically, a sentimentalist encounters a woman in public space and responds emotionally to her. If a sentimentalist feels a positive response to the woman's appearance, she is "good" no matter what her behavior, and, of course, if the response is negative, the woman is bad, again with no correlation to behavior or interior motives. The sentimentalist believes that his or her emotional judgement correlates with the interior life of the person, that he or she is in a non-rational way guided by physical, emotional signs in both him- or herself and the woman in question to determine correctly the moral status of a person.

The danger of making a wrong decision by this method is exposed by several novelists of the 1790s, including Burney in *Camilla*. Camilla and Miss Dennel take a walk in the moonlight and meet Mrs. Berlinton, who is out alone and is accosted by a man who makes love to her (388). Camilla's hostess, Mrs. Arlbery, tells her Mrs. Berlinton is "some dangerous fair one, who was playing upon [Camilla's] inexperience, and utterly unfit to be known to her" (390). Camilla, however, continues to excuse Mrs. Berlinton from blame and to be 'captivated' by her (426–7), even after discovering this woman is married, has abandoned her husband, and cultivates male friends "so beloved . . . and neither father, brother, nor husband" (392).

In contrast to the novels of the 1790s, the novels of the 1770s and 1780s typically promoted this position, most obviously in the immensely influential and successful *Man of Feeling* (1771) by Henry MacKenzie. But it was Jean-Jacques Rousseau's version of the sentimental position in his international bestseller *La Nouvelle Héloïse* (1761) that inspired the backlash of the 1790s against the sentimental approach: for what happens if the sentimentalist begins to "feel" that immoral things are in fact "moral"? Since to the sentimentalist moral "judgements" derive their authority from feelings, the sentimental position may not produce judgements that correlate in society or with a person's individual sense of morality. Also, it may produce "judgements" or "feelings" that challenge the very definition of morality. Mrs. Berlington in *Camilla*, a quintessential sentimentalist, eventually justifies for herself such vices as gambling and adultery.

Both the internalized/reformed position and the feminist position reject the "judgement" of the sentimentalist and the correlation of outward behavior and inward morality that occurs with the traditional patriarchal position. These two positions attempt to blend both manners and morality in making judgements about women's conditions in public. Both claimed they were promoting the best interests of women in doing so, and both saw themselves as shaping and improving the lot of women.

The Internalized/Reformed Patriarchal Position and Its Fundamental Flaw

The internalized/reformed patriarchal position rejects the idea that behavior alone determines morality, as occurs with the traditional patriarchal position (or that public behavior alone determines morality as occurs with the fashionable patriarchal position). This position also accepts that morality is not instinctive, as the sentimentalist position implies. In this position, education and the experience of living in a culture determine the interior, emotional sensations that urge to a human consciousness: "this person or behavior is good, and that one is bad." In other words, our cultural values are internalized, so what we need to do to ensure that only "good" people do things the culture labels as "good" (and only "bad" people do things the culture labels as "bad") is to accept and internalize current cultural standards.

The internalized/reformed patriarchal position rewrites the traditional patriarchal syllogism on women's movement in public space in the following way. Good women are intelligent, well-educated women who know that society believes women who move in public life without appropriate escorts are not good; good women want to *both* be good and appear good, so they follow *both* moral standards and social codes; therefore, any woman who breaks the social code preventing women from freely moving in public space is (1) not morally good, (2) poorly educated, or (3) mentally deficient.

The internalized/reformed patriarchal position shares some key beliefs with the feminist position that will be defined in the next section: (1) women are rational and moral beings, (2) education can enable women through rational thought to internally control their moral behavior, (3) women have the right to education, and (4) social codes must be redefined so women can more easily practice the key moral virtues of Christianity, such as saving lives and giving assistance to the needy. The goals of this internalized/reformed patriarchal position became more widely embraced in the nineteenth-century: middle- and upper-class women began to be granted the right to better education and to appear in public for philanthropic reasons.

The twentieth-century has continued to implement the goals of the internalized/reformed patriarchal position but has not produced a society in which moral judgements about women and the interior reality of their morality correspond because of an essential truth this position denies. This truth (which is still debated today) is that the patriarchy needs a class of women to be condemned as "bad" or worthy of being sexual prey to continue to function, and that social rules have been gender-coded and hence deviate from moral rules precisely to ensure that a large group of women are available to satisfy the sexual needs of men. Women are divided into good and bad by patriarchal codes, so that men only can enjoy sexual license. In other words, the patriarchy gives to men a permission to engage in activities unlawful/immoral to women.

Let me explain this feminist concept with a notorious incident in the legal oppression of women in twentieth-century America. A woman in a short skirt wearing no underwear was raped in Florida. On 6 October 1989, the jury revealed that they acquitted the rapist of the crime because of the victim's clothing, although they accepted that the man kidnapped the woman with a knife and forcibly had sex with her several times—a "normal," moral definition of rape.[13] The implications of this judicial decision are that women who wear or fail to wear certain clothes automatically consent to have sex with all men and thus cannot be raped. In order that society have some women who can be legally raped, certain forms of dress are promoted as "morally" bad and a sign of consent to any man's demand for sex, although such fashion decisions have no logical connection with moral goodness or evil, nor can they be seen logically as a clear and irrefutable declaration of the desire and willingness to have sex with any man.

Patriarchal codes, whether of the traditional, fashionable, or internalized/ reformed type, claim to promote the correlation of public behavior with morality. Prostitution and other crimes against women that occur in public space are theoretically something the patriarchy should discourage, but, in fact, they are a key part of the patriarchal system. It is not surprising that the official policing of prostitution started in the 1790s: in Paris in 1798 the government authorized two doctors to examine all prostitutes for sexual diseases.[14] By 1802, the Paris police registered and regularly examined prostitutes. Any woman who traveled in Paris alone risked being officially registered as a prostitute by the police.

In the novels of the 1790s, novelists and characters taking the internalized/ reformed patriarchal position call for women to be alert continuously to any way in which their behavior could be misinterpreted. This position is strongly adopted by Amelia Opie and promoted in her *Dangers of Coquetry* (1790), her immensely successful *The Father and Daughter* (1800), and such later works as "Appearance is Against Her" in *Tales of Real Life* (1813). This later tale is Opie's most explicit statement of the internalized/reformed patriarchal position. The heroine tells her husband:

> who that has once erred, can be sure of never erring again? and the only security is avoiding temptation. . . . *You* may occasionally enter the gay world, . . . but I will remain in retirement . . . and I will consider the pain I inflict on myself . . . as a just punishment for that presumption which made me, because I was conscious of my innocence, dare to set appearances and the restraints of decorum at defiance. I *know* my manner was too familiar, too inviting; I know . . . that, but for my manners neither the writer of the letters, nor *you*, could ever have admitted a suspicion of my guilt. Convinced of this, I . . . [assert] that the woman violates her duty both to society and herself, who gives any one reason to say, or even to insinuate, that APPEARANCE IS AGAINST HER.[15]

Opie's position is a blatant endorsement of the double standard and an attempt to make obedience to the codes of society a moral "duty." Women are to be indoctrinated with this notion that appearing blameless is their duty, so that, when it is "insinuated" they are to blame, they are always wrong. Moreover, women are to punish themselves for such insinuations even if they are 'conscious of their innocence' by retirement from public life. This approach denies the responsibility and participation of men in public action and that men can be bigoted judges or misogynist/libertines.

To justify this position, Opie is forced to deny the vicious circle that is created when men in power use that power to define women as bad according to "appearances" not actuality. Opie argues explicitly in *The Father and Daughter* (1800) that no good women will be corrupted by being continually treated as corrupt:

> It is the *slang* of the present day . . . to inveigh bitterly against society for excluding from its circle, with unrelenting rigueur, the woman who has once transgressed the salutary laws of chastity; and some brilliant and persuasive, but, in my opinion, mistaken writers [i.e. Elizabeth Inchbald in *Nature and Art* (1796), Mary Robinson in *Walsingham; or, The Pupil of Nature* (1798), Charlotte Smith in *The Young Philosopher* (1798), Mary Wollstonecraft in *Maria* (1798), and Mary Hays in *The Victim of Prejudice* (1799)], of both sexes, have endeavoured to prove that many an amiable woman has been for ever lost to virtue and the world, and become the victim of prostitution, merely because her first fault was treated with ill-judging and criminal severity. (I: 456)

Opie asserts that women can be "restored by perseverance in a life of expiatory amendment, to that rank in society which they had forfeited by one false step" (I: 456). But Opie's example of this, Agnes's restoration to rank, is full of unrealistic, almost miraculous occurrences and dependent on Agnes's incredible beauty, virtue, and popularity prior to her seduction.

Opie's attempt to deny the vicious circle of the patriarchy and to attack the compelling arguments of feminists in the 1790s was warmly welcomed by the reading public, which called for reprint after reprint in England and America of *The Father and Daughter*; the novel ran to ten editions in England alone by the end of the next two decades. Yet, today this work is forgotten and seems but a crude polemical attempt to justify an unjust system. In contrast, the works that in the 'slang' of the 1790s shone with feminist insights into the double standards and double binds of the period were neglected in the early nineteenth century. Today, however, these works are being reprinted, studied, and respected as many have not been since the 1790s.

The Feminist Position

While in the 1790s feminism was not a word in use or even a clearly defined concept, it has become by now commonplace to speak of the feminism of Mary Wollstonecraft or Mary Hays. Wollstonecraft's claim that both genders should be subject to the same code of virtue in her *A Vindication of the Rights of Woman* (1792) is the heart of the feminist position about freedom in public space: "I here throw down my gauntlet, and deny the existence of sexual virtues, not excepting modesty. For man and woman, truth . . . must be the same."[16] The feminist attitude towards a woman traveling alone or without the escort of a male or servant would judge the female's behavior to be moral if her motives are not vicious. The feminist attitude looks at the motive for the woman's behavior and judges it, not the behavior itself. Actions that are not blameworthy or corrupt when done by men or by women with appropriate escorts would likewise not be interpreted as wrong or immoral when done by women without such an escort. Therefore, a woman who walks in public to do something that is not blameworthy or corrupt—shopping, renting a room, visiting a lawyer, walking to a job, or visiting a friend or benefactor—would not be labeled a lunatic, criminal, adventuress, or prostitute by a character or narrator taking this stance.

The feminist position becomes more controversial when we move from evaluating to proscribing behavior. Feminists of the 1790s did not agree among themselves on how to proscribe behavior. A number of sub-positions arose, many of which are still reflected in current schools of feminist criticism. I believe that feminism needs to promote a unisex social code that combines the morally good parts of the behavioral codes associated with each sex. However, not all feminists of the 1790s or 1990s share this opinion, and that is the flaw of the feminist position. I refrain from calling this flaw fundamental because I believe that, if the position which I support is adopted, feminism can provide our culture with a social code much closer to ideal moral standards than our current social codes. But, to understand the feminism of the 1790s, we need to look at the various solutions proposed to the problem of proscribing behavior.

Does the feminist code say "obey moral codes exclusively, ignore all social codes?" Or does it say "obey social codes applying to the males?" If it says the latter, is it because (1) the codes that apply to the male sex are more closely aligned with general moral codes than those that apply to the female sex? Or, (2) is it because it is desirable, but socially impractical to follow moral codes exclusively, so follow masculine social codes because men are the "norm" of human life? Or, (3) is it because male social codes are more moral than female social codes? Position (3) of course could not be logically held by feminists who believe male social codes allow men license to oppress some women by defining them as morally evil and thus acceptable victims of harassment, robbery, rape, prostitution, or assault.

The feminist is thereupon in a double-bind: how can she argue that she should act or be treated like men are in order to be more moral when men are clearly so frequently morally wrong? Also, when morality is defined by organized religions with institutionalized sexism, how can morality be the basis for arguing women deserve better treatment by social codes? This double-bind in fact still hinders the advancement of women and divides feminists in battle among themselves: do feminists want (1) to be treated just like men? ["equal rights" feminism] (2) to prove women are—other than for a few biological differences—just like men? [feminist empiricism] (3) to prove some (or all) women are morally superior to men, so that all social codes that apply to women or that women practice among themselves should be accepted? [feminist standpoint criticism and biological criticism] or (4) to promote new standards of behavior that would combine the morally good parts of the social codes relevant to both sexes? I assert that option (4) is the only logical solution to this feminist double-bind.

A number of controversial and radical assumptions underlie this last position: (A) both men and women are capable of rational thought; (B) both men and women have internal moral motives; (C) both men and women can choose to act or not upon their internal motives (i.e. are capable of making decisions and acting upon them); (D) external, cultural codes do actually limit the capacity of men and women to act upon their internal, moral decisions; and, finally and most radically, (E) the external, cultural codes of society shape the minds of men and women and influence their sense of what is a moral, responsible choice.

There are a number of significant conclusions that can be drawn, if we accept these assumptions. One implication of notion (D) is that a woman can be forced into immoral behavior against her will by cultural codes that limit her options. Notion (E) implies that a conflict between an internal moral code and an external public code is actually also an internal conflict that can produce a paralysis of both internal and external behavior. Notion (E) also indicates the intense mental strain and paradoxes of holding a feminist (or any sub-cultural) viewpoint.

The above conclusions when applied to the problem posed by a woman moving in public space in the 1790s suggest that women treated in public as mad or immoral may become mad or immoral. In other words, the gendered social code of the patriarchy which encourages the viewing of all women who are not "owned" as becoming mad or immoral is actually what leads some women into becoming mad or immoral. To expose the way the patriarchal system "stacks the cards" against women, we need to examine women without money or social resources who need to move in public to prevent a greater evil than mere impropriety from occurring. For example, poverty or the criminal, sinful actions of others might force a woman to walk alone in public in order to not commit a more immoral crime, such as starving herself to death—a version of suicide, considered a sin—or acquiescing or consenting to having sex outside of marriage—considered in the 1790s one of the greatest sins a woman could commit. Consider how, if Burney's Camilla was indeed kidnapped by Lord Valhurst in the incident discussed above, she would have to escape with no escort at all and move through the streets alone, possibly at night, to return to her friends or family. A well-dressed woman moving alone at night in the streets would, of course, be even more likely to be treated like a prostitute than one shopping in daylight with another woman. Having a female character kidnapped in the tradition of Richardson's *Clarissa*, as Lord Valhurst tries to do to Camilla, is fairly common in novels of the 1790s set in eighteenth-century Europe. For the popular Gothics, set in Europe of the fourteenth to sixteenth centuries, such kidnappings are almost *de rigueur*.

In the 18th century, aristocratic men who kidnapped and raped women were a social cliché that was basic to the transfer of hegemonic power from the upper to middle classes, and so morally justified. The moral, domestic woman represented the values of the professional middle classes, while the aristocratic rapist represented all the vices that aristocrats supposedly both embodied and encouraged in the society they ruled. However, this domestic woman was rivaled in the popular mind by other clichéd notions of femininity: "the too public, too political, independently desiring woman of the courtly upper classes [associated with fashionable patriarchy]; the too social, 'managing' woman of the commercial and trading bourgeoisie [who apes the fashionable patriarchy of the lady with much less power and freedom]; and the labouring, sexually available woman of the servant and other lower classes [common victims of all three types of patriarchal positions]."[17] The kidnapped woman who eludes rape by her own means and moves through public space to rejoin her relatives blurs the sharp distinctions between all of these types of women; moreover, the tendency of others to see her as insane and criminal blurs the clear distinction that patriarchal approaches attempt to establish between moral and immoral women and between women of different classes. These novels, thus, present the conventional reader with an ideological paradox: an unladylike lady, one whose decision to transgress codes of propriety is based on a higher moral code. The patriarchal reader is forced to either reject the novel as unrealistic or to rethink his or her system of evaluating behavior.

When the American South wanted to arm slaves to defend the confederacy, General Howell Cobb (1815–68) asserted: "You cannot make soldiers of slaves, or slaves of soldiers. The day you make a soldier of them is the beginning of the end of the revolution. And if slaves seem good soldiers, *then our whole theory of slavery is wrong.*"[18] Let me paraphrase Cobb to indicate the polemic purpose of novels such as Elizabeth Inchbald's *Nature and Art* (1796), Regina Maria Roche's *Children of the Abbey* (1796), Mary Robinson's *Walsingham; or, The Pupil of Nature* (1798), Charlotte Smith's *The Young Philosopher* (1798), Mary Wollstonecraft's *Maria* (1798), and Mary Hays' *The Victim of Prejudice* (1799). 'You cannot treat women moving in public space and active in public life as worthy, intelligent, and moral, and you cannot treat men moving in public space and active in public life as unworthy, insane, and immoral. The day you treat women moving in public space and active in public life as worthy, intelligent, and moral is the beginning of the end of the patriarchy. And if women in public space and life seem worthy, intelligent, and moral, then our whole theory of the patriarchy is wrong.' The importance of many of the novels of the 1790s is that they call upon the reader to rejudge a way of life and guide us towards a closer alignment of moral, social, and legal codes.

Acknowledgments

Research for this paper was done in part due to a NEH Summer Fellowship at Cornell University, 1995. My thanks to the NEH for their financial support, and to Dr. Mary Jacobus, Dr. Curt Burgess, Dr. Paula Backscheider, Dr. Natan Paradise, Ms. Maureen Keeney, Dr. Olga Dugan, and Dr. Linda Lang-Peralta for their helpful suggestions.

Notes

1. A key text of the movement is Laura Lederer's collection of essays, *Take Back the Night: Women on Pornography* (New York: Morrow, 1980), especially Andrea Dworkin's "Pornography and Grief," an exhortation on why women need to march to take back the night (286–91).

2. Ray Porter and Leslie Hall, *The Facts of Life: The Creation of Sexual Knowledge in Britain, 1650–1950* (New Haven, Conn.: Yale University Press, 1995), 22–23.

3. William Buchan, *Domestic Medicine* (New York: Garland, 1985), 647.

4. G. S. Rousseau, "Medicine and the Muses: An Approach to Literature and Medicine," in *Literature and Medicine During the Eighteenth Century*, ed. Marie Mulvey Roberts and Roy Porter (London: Routledge, 1993), 26.

5. John [Jean] Astruc, *A Treatise On all the Diseases Incident to Women* (New York: Garland, 1985), 292–94.

6. Marie Mulvey Roberts, "The Biological and Ideological Role of Women in France (1786–96)," in *Literature and Medicine During the Eighteenth Century*, ed. Marie Mulvey Roberts and Roy Porter (London: Routledge, 1993), 277–78. Roberts's study, albeit focused on the French history of ideas, reveals that an international European community of scientists, medical researchers, and thinkers existed in the late eighteenth century that breached national boundaries.

7. George Rousseau, "Towards a Semiotics of the Nerve," in *Interpretation and Cultural History*, ed. Joan H. Pittock and Andrew Wear (New York: St. Martin's Press, 1991), 49, 71.

8. Edward A. Bloom and Lillian D. Bloom, eds., *Camilla; or, A Picture of Youth* (Oxford: Oxford University Press, 1983), 161.

9. Eliza Fenwick, *Secresy; or, The Ruin on the Rock* (London: Pandora Press, 1989), 6.

10. Mary Poovey, *The Proper Lady and the Woman Writer* (Chicago: University of Chicago Press, 1984), 20.

11. Gina Luria, ed., *Julia; A Novel*, 2 vols. (New York: Garland, 1974), I: 53, 54.

12. Elizabeth Inchbald, *Nature and Art*, 2 vols. (London: G. G. and J. Robinson, 1796), I: 122–23.

13. See, for example, the coverage in the *New York Times*: "Defendant Acquitted of Rape; 'She Asked for It,' Juror Says," Saturday, 7 October 1989, 6 col. 3.

14. Kathleen Barry, *The Prostitution of Sexuality* (New York: New York University Press, 1995), 91.

15. Amelia Opie, *The Works of Mrs. Amelia Opie*, 2 vols. (New York: AMS Press, 1974), II: 143.

16. Carol H. Poston , ed., *A Vindication of the Rights of Woman* (New York: W. W. Norton, 1975), 51.

17. Gary Kelly, *Revolutionary Feminism* (New York: St. Martin's Press, 1992), 15; Kelly indicates his ideas are shaped by Lawrence Stone, *The Family, Sex and Marriage in England, 1500–1800* (Harmondsworth, U.K.: Penguin Books, 1979), 404.

18. Geoffrey C. Ward, et al., *The Civil War: An Illustrated History* (New York: Alfred A. Knopf, 1990), 253.

Revolutionary Domesticity
in Charlotte Smith's Desmond

Katherine Binhammer

Charlotte Smith prefaces *Desmond* (1792), a sentimental novel set during the French Revolution, by defending her right as a female novelist to take on public and political topics: "But women it is said have no business with politics—Why not?—Have they not?—Have they no interest in the scenes that are acting around them, in which they have fathers, brothers, husbands, sons, or friends engaged?" (iii). Women's business in politics stems, for Smith, from the business of familial relations. Smith's argument follows a common trajectory in radical feminist writings from the 1790s: women's political subjectivity is a necessary antecedent to the proper fulfilment of their domestic role. Wollstonecraft, in *A Vindication of the Rights of Woman* (1792)—a text addressed to revolutionary leaders in France—makes an identical argument: "make women rational creatures, and free citizens, and they will quickly become good wives, and mothers" (250). Positing women's political role as a prerequisite to, and extension of, her domestic role was a common route used by women to declare their place in the public world of the French Revolution. Joan Landes, in her influential study *Women and the Public Sphere in the Age of the Revolution* (1988), notes the importance of the "ideology of Republican Motherhood" for women's political identity. But Landes and others have argued that the notion of Republican Motherhood, far from enfranchising women, actually facilitated their exclusion from political activity. Landes

—25—

contends that "a demand for citizenship based primarily on woman's performance of her maternal duty was easily refuted," and she traces the exclusion of women as a constitutive element in the creation of the bourgeois public sphere (138).

Recently, feminist critics have expanded and revised Landes' influential argument about a restrictive public sphere by analyzing the complex roles women played in the French Revolution, roles which may not fit into the seamless confinement of women to the domestic space.[1] Current work on gender and the public sphere has made the line between the public and private in the late-eighteenth century more difficult to determine.[2] Historians and critics have begun to ask, was there really a line between the public and the private that women like Smith needed to cross? Are discussions of gender distinctions between the public and private spheres in the eighteenth century misdirected and misinformed? Lawrence E. Klein, for example, in his polemical article, "Gender and the Public/Private Distinction in the Eighteenth Century," argues against readings of history which take for granted the "domestic thesis," a thesis which begins from the presupposition of the historical existence of separate spheres. Klein argues that the relation of public to private is ambivalent and multivalent and that it was not a fixed and comprehensible opposition within the eighteenth century.[3] Through a reading of Smith's novel, this essay suggests that while the public and private spheres were not firmly differentiated as gendered spaces that could be simply transgressed or conceded to, the ways conceptions of public and private were both distinguished and merged, separated and integrated, are meaningful markers of gender and national difference in the Revolutionary decade. It is not a question of fixed difference or stable sameness between the public and private spheres but a question of the political and ideological effects of how these differences and similarities were put into play in the sphere of political representation. In Smith's novel, her very integrations of the private and the public, the sentimental and the polemical, and the domestic and the political, paradoxically produce fixed boundaries through the particular way her novel revolutionizes family politics. We may need to revise Landes' clear separation of the public from the private sphere, but unlike recent critical revisions which refute that there is a public/private split in the first place, this essay argues that the moments in which the two are merged and the lines crossed also enabled the restrictive political effects of their divide. I hope to analyze the way Smith sketched and stretched her lines between the space of domesticity and the space of the French Revolution in order to show that the boundaries presupposed by her merging are what allowed her to bring the French Revolution into the domestic sphere in England.

The lines drawn in Smith's novel do not allow us to chart a clear and straight course from the private into the public; rather, the lines themselves are split and fragmented by their encounters with numerous other divisions. Where we locate the divide between the political and the domestic in *Desmond* depends upon where Smith draws the line between the sentimental tale and factual history, England and France, feeling and reason, or femininity and masculinity. The connections between these different terms do not operate solely within an oppositional logic. A clear alignment of all the terms on one side of the dualism (i.e., domestic, private, family, sentimental tale, England, feeling, femininity) and a placement of those terms in opposition to the other side (political, public, state, factual history, France, reason, masculinity) is not possible in the novel. An example of the lack of symmetry between the textual function of the individual dualisms is contained in the notion of Republican motherhood. On one level, Smith's claim that her politics are an extension of her proper feminine domestic life contains an oppositional rhetoric: politics and domestic life are placed in a relation of difference in order to show their similarity. The claim then presupposes a prior distinction between the public and the private and women's proper role as maternal subject. Yet, on another level, Smith's feminine political subject position is produced metonymically, as an extension of her maternal subjectivity. The doubled rhetorical movement contained in the argument of Republican Motherhood mirrors the way meaning is frequently produced in *Desmond*.[4] The boundaries between the domestic and the political are not produced oppositionally (i.e., one recognizes the domestic as that which is not political) nor are they positively created (i.e., one recognizes the domestic for a self-contained positive identity) but they are drawn, paradoxically, through their very integration. It is not just that the domestic is always already political and the political always already domestic (although that is also the case) but that the very way Smith merges the two fields produces their initial identities. Smith frequently represents the relation between the political and the domestic as analogous (for example, a revolution in the family is like the revolution in the state). But, it is through these representations of similarity that their differences come into being (it becomes clear how a revolution in the family is *not* like it is in the state). Jacobin women writers write themselves as political subjects through taking advantage of the unstable boundaries between public and private at the moment of the French Revolution.[5] Yet, these are also the textual moments when the boundaries are made visible.

Perhaps surprisingly to historians who assume the wholesale silencing of political women at the turn of the nineteenth century, Smith's excursion into politics met with the general approval of her reading public. Most reviews applauded her novel precisely for its political content. The *Monthly Review* even praised Smith's political discussion for educating women on non-domestic subjects and assumed women's right to citizenship: "Being very justly of opinion, that the great events which are passing in the world are no less interesting to women than to men, and that in her solicitude to discharge the domestic duties, a woman ought not to forget that, in common with her father and husband, her brothers and sons, she is a citizen" (ix, Sept. 1792: 406). The *European Magazine* went as far as to suggest that Smith's prefatory apology for writing on politics was unnecessary: "She has thought proper, however, to apologise for the introduction of political matter in a work professedly of another kind. To those who think an apology necessary, this will be sufficient" (xxii, July 1792: 22). Even the conservative *Critical Review*, while disagreeing with her political opinions, praised her discussion of politics because it helped to educate women: "We have often had occasion to observe, that the opportunities of modern fine ladies for information are so few, that every means of their obtaining it, incidentally, should be approved of" (vi, Sept. 1792: 100). Why was Smith's excursion into the world of politics praised and not censored?[6] What was it about the way Smith represented the relation of the political to the domestic that did not provoke wide condemnation?

Smith's text was a sentimental novel, directed at a female readership, and issued from England. Her text did not, like her acquaintance Helen Maria Williams's *Letters From France*, cross the channel from France into England. For this reason, Smith's novel and the reviews supporting it, adeptly move from women's domestic space out into the world of politics. But Smith's effective, inclusive drawing of the line depended upon her maintenance of strict national and gender boundaries. The domestic is revolutionized in Smith's novel but her political argument presupposes a secure divide between France and England and between her male and female characters. Apart from a short digression by the central heroine, Geraldine, the political content of the novel, including lengthy discussions of the French Revolution, originates from the narrative voices of Desmond and Bethel. The integration of public and private—the novel's refusal of boundaries (both generic and spatial)—depends upon other divisions and exclusions. Current critical scepticism toward the separate spheres thesis must take into account how instability on one discursive level can presuppose or be productive of other exclusionary stabilities. Because of the way Smith exploits these boundaries, this essay argues, the line she draws between the public and private, transforms the private by putting an undomesticated public firmly in place.

The central plot of *Desmond* involves a sentimental love story in which Desmond, an "English Werther," is in love with Geraldine, a virtuous and chaste but married, maternal heroine.[7] Geraldine's husband, Verney, is a tyrant, an evil aristocrat who is both a despot in his marriage (attempting to sell his wife to a French nobleman in order to pay off a gambling debt) and a supporter of the political despotism of the *ancien régime*—the two, Smith repeatedly implies, are not unrelated. In order to distance himself from his unfortunate situation with Geraldine, Desmond travels to France; he writes "I hope to find, in the present political tumult in France, what may interest and divert my attention" (I: 11). Desmond's correspondent, Bethel, is a liberal man of reason who functions in the text as the moderate counter-point to Desmond's radical enthusiasm. Bethel's is the voice of caution, registering prudence *vis-a-vis* Desmond's love for a married woman and scepticism regarding the unmitigated success of the Revolution. Desmond's sojourn in France provides the grounds for Smith's introduction of political events, including passages critiquing Burke, a discussion of the corruption of the Clergy, unfair property laws, titles and past aristocratic atrocities. Desmond also transcribes his political discussions with his friend and traveling companion, Montfleuri, a French democrat. Montfleuri introduces Desmond to his sister, Josephine, who, like Geraldine, is unhappily married; Josephine and Desmond have a brief tryst which produces an illegitimate child. The climax of the novel comes when the ever dutiful Geraldine follows Verney to France where he has gone to aid the monarchists. Verney is mortally wounded in battle and on his deathbed he acknowledges his mistakes and gives Desmond his blessing to marry his wife. The novel concludes when Desmond and Geraldine return to England with Desmond's illegitimate child and establish an ideal domestic space in the English countryside.

The use of the epistolary novel with multiple correspondences eases Smith's correlation and integration of the public and private themes. Diana Bowstead argues that Smith's choice of the epistolary form for *Desmond* (her only epistolary novel of the ten she wrote between 1788 and 1798) "has to do with the largely political and didactic import of the novel" (238). By using multiple correspondents Smith was able to present a range of liberal views (from the radical Desmond, to the more tempered Bethel) without seeming to endorse any particular position herself. The spontaneity of the letter form also provided Smith with the structural flexibility required to move between the different themes. The text constantly marks the shift between discussions of the public affairs of France and the private affairs of Desmond through the insertion of connecting sentences: Bethel writes, "So much, dear Desmond, for private news from England; as for public news, you probably receive it from those who are better qualified than I am to speak upon it" (i: 196); or elsewhere, "Enough of politics—Now, again, to domestic concerns" (iii: 103). The conventional struggle between reason and passion is portrayed in the novel through Desmond's personal conflict between France and England or between revolutionary politics and a desire for domesticity. For example, Desmond laments, "Were my heart less deeply interested for my friends in England, I should be quite absorbed in French politics" (i: 137–8). After he hears news of Geraldine's fiscal distress in England, Desmond finds it impossible to concentrate on French politics: "Montfleuri talks to me of politics . . . I can no longer enter with eagerness" into these political discussions (ii: 24).

While the divide between the registers of politics and domestic life is frequently marked in the letters, the constant intermingling of the two poles forces the reader to observe the parallels and overlaps. Smith's mixing of plots and subplots, facts and romance, fiction and personal autobiography effects a complex thematic interplay in *Desmond*.[8] She uses the technique of character-ization to merge the public and the private: characters who hold offensively conservative and tyrannical political positions also exhibit repulsive personal and sexual behaviour. For example, Stamford, a "petty tyrant," whose authori-tarian politics are evident when he viciously punishes tenants for eating any fish and game from his estate, reveals his private corruption when he serves extravagant dinners to gluttonous, unscrupulous, politicians (I: 192). Scarsdale, "a sort of modern Lovelace," combines monarchist politics with his attempt to bed Verney's wife (II: 214). In addition to characterization, the structure of *Desmond* reflects Smith's integration of the domestic and political themes. Vol-ume I contains only letters between Bethel and Desmond and concentrates on the political events in France. Volume II introduces letters between Geraldine and her sister, Fanny, and primarily recounts the domestic plot taking place in England. The last volume blends the two together when Geraldine travels to France and the domestic plot reaches its climax alongside the Revolution.

Smith's radical and feminist political agenda certainly involved revolution-izing the domestic space through the interweaving of the two themes. Nicola Watson summarizes this agenda when she writes, "*Desmond* pointedly juxta-poses politics and the sentimental plot, binding its analysis of the tyranny of the *ancien régime* and its supposedly on-the-spot reportage in Paris to a demonstra-tion of domestic tyranny which is clearly identified as an analogous system" (36). In order to revolutionize the domestic, Smith had to combine the two spheres. But, she wished the combination to operate in only one direction. That is to say, while she wanted to revolutionize the domestic, she did not wish to domesticate the Revolution. The king is to the public sphere what the husband is to the private, but the opposite is not also the case. Her feminist re-visioning of the domestic space demanded some introduction of politics; the impetus for change in the domestic space needed to come from somewhere. But where? Through whom? Smith contained the analogy of political and domestic tyr-anny within a singular direction (so that the domestic was analogous to the political but the political was not comparable to the domestic) by mediating the analogy through the opposition of England and France. National difference comes to the aid of Smith's project by way of the doubled female heroine—the English Geraldine and the French Josephine. By splitting the female subject,

Smith can allow the French Josephine to be contaminated by the public sphere (she becomes a 'public woman' in the sexualized sense of the term) while the English Geraldine remains a paragon of maternal domesticity.

If Helen Maria Williams as the heroine of *Letters From France* was accused by critics of having become "Frenchified" (a term designating the domestic British female subject becoming a French, political, public—and therefore sexual—woman)[9], Geraldine, the heroine of *Desmond*, remains steadfastly Anglicized. Her stable national identification is only one instance of her unchanging character for she does not develop over the course of the three-volume text. She never deviates from her position as ideal wife and mother and even stays on her straight and narrow path when she travels to France. Critic after critic has remarked upon the rigid, Griselda-like, perfection of Geraldine. The *Critical Review* called her "patience on a monument" who "forgets not, in any instance, that she is a wife and a mother" (vi, Sept. 1792: 99). The majority of recent feminist critics have addressed the issue of Geraldine's nauseating submission, trying to comprehend why Smith made her heroine so static and perfect.[10] Geraldine's complete passivity originates in the strict national boundary that Smith establishes between the domestic and political subjects. The domestic space is firmly ensconced in England while the space for politics is located in France. Alison Conway provides a similar reading of Geraldine's national character and the textual effect of her doubling with Josephine. Conway argues that Geraldine's power originates in the novel's production of her as an iconographic symbol rather than a dynamic character. She describes Geraldine as:

> the ultimate mother, acting out her domestic role to the point of over determining the word "duty." In fact, Smith's construction of Geraldine's performance as a wife and mother seems aimed at transforming her heroine into a symbolic figure, as opposed to a mimetic one. The birth of Geraldine's third child, who spends the rest of the novel at or near his mother's breast, establishes early in the narrative a basis for an iconography of the maternal body, *madonna con bambino* (398).

Smith invokes the symbol of Geraldine-as-maternal-icon in the repeated tableaus she draws of Geraldine's domestic scenes. Indeed, the maternal ideal so completely overdetermines Geraldine's character that her every action is inscribed, instantaneously, on her breast. Each incident of domestic tyranny has a direct effect on Geraldine's ability to breastfeed her child, thereby explicitly connecting Verney's tyrannical actions with the endangerment of his innocent child's life. Bethel writes of Geraldine: "She spoke, however, with extreme anxiety, about her youngest child, whose constitution is, she fears, quite ruined by the uneasiness that has been preying upon her own, while she has been nursing him" (III: 34). Geraldine writes of Verney's threat to her maternal breast after recovering from an episode. In true Griselda fashion, she reproaches herself: "I have, perhaps done wrong to continue nourishing at my breasts, especially as I think he [the baby] has never recovered the first shock he received, when, at his birth, I first knew so much, and so suddenly, of the disarranged state of Mr. Verney's circumstances" (II: 196). Verney's gambling debts have a direct effect on Geraldine's maternal role and, echoing Wollstonecraft's *A Vindication of the Rights of Woman*, Smith suggests that women cannot fulfil their true domestic duty until men cease to be libertines. The domestic role for women depends upon the reform of male manners.

Geraldine does venture into the world of politics in one brief passage. Shortly after her arrival in France, she writes about the Revolution to her sister. Geraldine's narrative begins by asserting that the condition of France is nothing like the anarchy and misery that is being reported in the English papers. She admits that some disorder exists but only in minor instances and she notes that the Revolution has not achieved its final goals:

> We know, from daily experience, that even in a private family, a change in its economy or its domestics, disturbs the tranquillity of its members for some time— It must surely then happen, to a much greater degree, in a great nation, whose government is suddenly dissolved by the resolution of the people (III: 124).

Significantly, Geraldine's excursion into politics includes this explicit analogy between the family and the state.[11] Geraldine's analogy presupposes the division, and not the convergence, of the state and the family. A private family is analogous to a great nation but the parallel lines she draws never cross over or intersect. In case the reader is surprised at her discussion of French politics, Geraldine affixes an explanation. In her justification, she foregrounds the fact that her political excursion happened within the confines of an appropriately private letter to her sister, Fanny, and she outlines her own democratic politics in terms of her domestic subjectivity:

> It is to my sister, to my second self I write, and from her do not fear such a remark as was made on some French woman of fashion, (who I cannot now recollect) who, being separated from her husband, changed her religion to that (whatever it was) which he did not profess—'She has done it,' said a wit, 'that she might never meet her husband either in this world or the next'—Thus it might, perhaps, be said, that I determine never to think on any article (even on these, whereon my age and sex might exempt me from thinking at all) like Mr. Verney; and therefore, as he is, he knows not why a very furious aristocrat, that I, with no better reason, become democrat (III: 131–32).

The distance between the assertion of a democratic political theory and Geraldine's own stated position in the above passage is vast. The wits' satire of a French woman of fashion could—"perhaps"—be applied to her but only if the addressee is not her "second self" and only if her age and sex do not exempt her. The endless qualifiers make it difficult to trace Geraldine's stated political intent. In addition, there is a certain amount of truth in Geraldine's negation, for what she seemingly refutes (that her politics are similar to the French woman's religion) appears to be wholly applicable. Smith's revolutionized domestic argument ultimately rests on the belief that Geraldine, in fact, needs no better reason to be a democrat than because Verney is an aristocrat.

Geraldine's absolute obedience to her husband (whom she refers to in one uncharacteristic moment as "the unfortunate man whose property I am" [III: 148]) and her status as maternal icon demand that Smith find another soldier for her domestic Revolution. Geraldine cannot transform the domestic from the inside; the revolutionary impetus must come from an external source. Since the maternal icon is repeatedly set against the background of the English countryside, the revolution, Smith implies, cannot be fought on English soil. Thus, we move to France and to Josephine.[12]

Nicola Watson is correct when she states that *"Desmond* is remarkable...for its canny handling of the erring heroine, who is explicitly associated with the 'Frenchness' of the Revolution" (36). Smith does not punish Josephine for her sexual improprieties nor does she hold Desmond accountable for his sexual relations with a married woman. Unlike Clarissa and her numerous fictional sisters, Josephine is allowed to live with the promise of a future marriage to a past suitor. Why does the disruptive plot of Josephine's active sexuality not undermine the plot of Geraldine's domestic maternal passivity? How can Desmond's fall not contaminate his future marriage? Given the fact that the two women are constantly associated with each other—in looks, circumstances and sensibility—it seems surprising that Smith did not perceive errant female sexuality as a threat to domestic felicity. Certainly surprising is the fact that reviewers were not particularly offended by the extra-marital sex. While regarding the affair as improper, most reviewers only refer to the Josephine plot in a brief aside and excuse it as a structural and not a moral problem in the novel.[13] Josephine does not offend because Smith does not present deviant female sexuality as a threat to England. The maintenance of national boundaries provides Smith with the freedom to generalize—and thereby politicize—her domestic tyranny argument without the risk of domesticating the public sphere.

Josephine's "ill-assorted marriage, which has put her into the power of a man altogether unworthy of her," directly introduces the parallel between her and Geraldine (1: 164). Like Geraldine's husband, M. de Boisbelle is a monarchist and an aristocrat who participates in the same counter-revolutionary activities which Verney joins in France. M. de Boisbelle is unaccounted for at the conclusion of the novel and the hope is that he will meet the same fate as Geraldine's husband. Josephine's and Geraldine's domestic situations are identical with the notable and necessary exception that Josephine has no children, her non-maternal status being a requirement of her sexual subjectivity. Desmond's attraction to Josephine derives from her association with Geraldine: "I have once or twice, as Madame de Boisbelle has been walking with me, tried to fancy her Geraldine, and particularly when she has been in her plaintive moods. I have caught sounds that have, for a moment, aided my desire to be deceived" (1: 187). Desmond's enchantment with the "bewitching Josephine," his fantasy of her as Geraldine, is demystified only by national difference:

"But, . . . some trait, in the character of her country, has suddenly dissolved the charm, and awakened me to a full sense of the folly I was guilty of" (1: 187). Alison Conway rightly points out that, ultimately, the only difference between Josephine and Geraldine is one of national identity: "The narrative never spells out the differences between the two women, but rather reduces them to the fact of Josephine's Frenchness" (403). Josephine's national character introduces an uncrossable barrier and she can never be perceived as a potential domestic subject and wife: "Yet all she does has so much of national character in it, that it would become only a French woman, and I think I should not admire one of my own countrywomen, who possessed exactly the person, talents, and manners of my friend's sister" (1: 165–6).[14] The parallel between Josephine and Geraldine allows Smith to make a general feminist argument about domestic tyranny (Geraldine's plight is not unique but linked to the legal and social position of women in marriage), but the interjection of national boundaries ensures that the revolution in the domestic takes place in France.

In her attempt to revolutionise the domestic, Smith exploits the conventional association of sexual license with Frenchness to further her feminist aims. While Montfleuri shares Desmond's political sentiments and both are Enlightened democrats, their sexual sensibilities are nations apart. Desmond's love for Geraldine repeatedly is designated as platonic whereas Montfleuri is presented as a quasi-libertine. Montfleuri acts as a pander between his sister and his friend; he encourages and, indeed, arouses Desmond's interest in his sister. Montfleuri teases Desmond about his sister's attraction ("Desmond, do tell me how you manage to bewitch the women in this manner?" [1: 226]) and Desmond initially takes offence but forgives his friend out of cultural sensitivity: "He has besides, from education, habit, and principles, much freer notions than I have about women" (1: 226).

Smith exploits the national difference in sexual morals when she finally recounts the affair. Desmond's affair with Josephine (which took place in Volume I) remains unspoken and unarticulated until the final pages of the novel. Previously, the affair had only been referred to cryptically; at one point Desmond marks his guilt but does not explain it: "While I find her [Geraldine] rise every moment in *my esteem, I know* that I am becoming—alas! am already become unworthy [of] hers" (II: 22). It is not until the penultimate letter of the novel that the affair is acknowledged and described. Significantly, the admittance does not come from Desmond, himself, but appears in a letter from Montfleuri to Bethel. Montfleuri describes the reason for Desmond's silence and his own speech: "though Desmond owned it was necessary you should know, he could not prevail on himself to relate to you" (iii: 341). Not only does the articulation of the affair come from Montfleuri, but he also accepts complete responsibility for the couple's sexual impropriety: "I was so indiscreet and thoughtless as to encourage, in the gay and unguarded heart of my sister de Boisbelle, an affection for Desmond" (iii: 338). Smith does not even hide behind the plea of seduction in order to legitimate an erring heroine, for Montfleuri makes a point of conveying to Bethel that Desmond did not use deception to seduce Josephine: "She told me . . . that he used no art to betray her" (iii: 340). Desmond remains untainted by the affair. Smith is able to portray sympathetically a fallen heroine and merge the revolutionary political potential of France with a private domestic relation only because she strictly enforces national boundaries.

How does Smith overcome these national boundaries in order to allow the revolutionary domesticity of France to return to England? The thick black line of sexuality that she has drawn between the female national representatives threatens to undermine the political/familial analogy she wishes her readers to make. Smith brings the revolutionary domesticity home to England in the first instance on the level of plot. Geraldine travels to France at the same time as Josephine journeys to England to deliver her child in anonymity.[15] Their temporary exchange of nations (but never national identities) allows for the final narrative climax of Geraldine's and Desmond's gothic journey to Verney's deathbed. But, more importantly than this plot exchange, Smith was able to negotiate national borders and merge the political into the domestic through her use of another boundary—that of gender. Smith maintains the analogy between domestic and political tyranny through her use of the masculine spectator. We shall see that Desmond, not Geraldine or Josephine, brings home the souvenir from France.

Smith's use of multiple correspondents allows her to embody the powerful political 'I' of the text in a masculine subject. Like Montfleuri in the sexual plot of Josephine, Desmond is the pander in the national plot, uniting England and France and, by extension, the Revolutionary public sphere and the private

English domestic scene. It is Desmond who travels between the domestic world of England (Geraldine) and the revolutionary political world of France (Josephine). The flexibility of Desmond's national identity permits the cross-over between his status as both political and domestic subject. In fact, Desmond's national identity is an empty signifier throughout the novel, only determined by his interaction with women. Like Helen Maria Williams, he is "Frenchified" by his sexual impropriety but, unlike Williams, Desmond has no problem moving back across the border to England. He is only in France, we must remember, because of Geraldine and the desire to place a distance between himself and the married woman he loves. For Desmond, England equals Geraldine and if he cannot have Geraldine, then, he insists, he cannot be English. In a letter to Bethel informing him of his impending return to France, Desmond states, "for England is not my country, when I can hear only, in whatever company I go into, of Geraldine's unhappiness" (ii: 242). Desmond threatens to leave England forever. He writes that his presence is required in France at the beginning of July. While Desmond does not give the reason, the reader finds out later that he must go to France in order to escort Josephine back to England, at which time he "perhaps, shall take leave of England *for ever*" (iii: 15). For Desmond, geographic boundaries are strictly a matter of his love for Geraldine. He quotes St. Preux ("there are . . . but two divisions in the world, that where Julie is, and that where she is not") and adds: "*To me* the world is divided into only two parts; or rather, to me, it is all a blank where Geraldine is not" (ii: 240).

A world empty of Geraldine may be a blank space, but it is the male spectator who determines political and domestic meaning. Throughout his physical and psychological travels, Desmond never relinquishes his masculine privilege to name the world. The sentimental trajectory of the love story is presented in terms of a quest for the power to name as the obstacle to the romantic closure is a woman's married name. In his personal references, Desmond tries to change Geraldine's name to Mrs. Verney in order to "break myself of calling her Geraldine (because I always long to add *my* to that beloved name)" (i: 158). Their ultimate union and the final revolutionized domestic scene are caused by Desmond's success at naming. He writes in the letter that ends the novel:

Heavens! dare I trust myself with the rapturous hope, that on the return of this month, in the next year, Geraldine will bear *my* name—will be the directress of *my* family—will be my friend—my mistress—my wife!—I set before me these scenes—I imagine these days of happiness to come—I see the beloved group assembled at Sedgewood (emphasis in text; III: 347).

The repeated possessive pronoun leaves us with little doubt about who is the king of the Sedgewood domestic castle.

Ultimately, Smith's hope for a new revolutionary domestic space depends upon the good will of a man. As Diana Bowstead points out with regard to the promise of a non-tyrannical domesticity which closes the novel, "the security of Geraldine's position in the household Desmond governs depends on his honest intention to translate his ideological opposition to political autocracy into reasonably democratic domestic policies" (261). Smith's hope for revolutionary domesticity rests on a benevolent dictator as gender boundaries in the family remain fixed and stable. The only transgression in this reconstituted domestic scene comes in the form of Josephine's illegitimate baby—the souvenir—whom Geraldine accepts into the family ("she bestows [the tender solicitude of a mother] equally on her own children and on my little girl" [III: 345]).

Perhaps a less rigid vision of a revolutionized domestic space lies in the marriage of Montfleuri and Fanny—the union of England and France which was never a possibility between Desmond and Josephine. Geraldine's younger sister is the "wild girl," a woman who possesses a "natural impetuosity" (III: 50, 108). Fanny is the subversive soldier in her English family for it is she and not Geraldine who stages a rebellion against their cruel, hypocritical mother (the mother's cruelty stems from the system of primogeniture which makes her dote on her son, Waverly, to the neglect of Geraldine). Fanny rebels against her mother's censoring of her reading material and Fanny demands the right to decide for herself what books she will read. Through this revolt, Fanny aligns herself with an unencumbered masculine access to knowledge (II: 145–64). Unlike Geraldine, Fanny's character matures and develops; Bethel had thought her too masculine and harsh when she was young but now, he notices, "she is not . . . destitute of that feminine tenderness" (II: 48–9). This observation suggests to Bethel that Desmond should switch his affections from Geraldine to Fanny, an exchange that the reader realizes is impossible for Desmond to make. With this announcement of Fanny's potential as a wife, the reader is not surprised when Montfleuri chooses to end his philandering days through a marital union with Fanny. Oddly, it is Fanny's "Englishness" that attracts Montfleuri: "I have vowed," he exclaims, "never to marry, but this beautiful little English-woman who can resist?" (III: 236). He repeatedly calls her his "sweet little English woman" (III: 236, 237). The union of the French, democratic libertine with the wild, outspoken Fanny seems appropriate yet, given the national boundaries accepted by the novel, it also registers as transgressive. The marriage presents a completely different domestic trajectory, one demarcated as sexual and cross-national (it remains unclear whether the couple will settle at Montfleuri's estate in France or be a part of the Sedgewood community). Fanny's revolutionized domestic space may have appeared too transgressive for Smith as she undercuts their future happiness by introducing the possibility of the marriage's failure. Desmond registers the caution: "Montfleuri is too volatile; he loves his wife passionately, but my adoration for her sister he cannot comprehend" (III: 345). The volatility of this Frenchified domestic space is countered by the absolute tranquillity of the rural utopia that Desmond will rule over and it is this scene which ends the novel: "I go over in my imagination our studies, our amusements, our rural improvements; a series of domestic and social happiness, for which only life is worth having" (III: 348).

The domestic scene, which closes *Desmond*, is a marked improvement on the tyrannical private sphere, which began the novel. Smith introduced the democratic politics of the Revolution into her sentimental tableau in order to make the home a more hospitable place for women. But by bringing politics into the home and not traveling into the public sphere, the text produces a female subject that is simultaneously separate from, yet determined by, the world of politics. In critical ways, a domestic female subject restricted to the private sphere came into being in the late-eighteenth century precisely because the public invaded, and did not retreat from, the home. While it may be true that a more rigid surface division between the private and the public emerged at the conclusion of the French Revolution,[16] that division functioned through the intensification and not the abandonment of the public's interest in the home.

Mary Favret argues that "[t]he most profound political questions of the revolution, were, in fact, questions about the private life: home, family, affective discourse" (287). Far from being separated in the late-eighteenth century, the
political invasion of the home integrated the private and the public to produce
a new ideal of English domesticity. But we can not conclude from this integration that meaningful distinction between public and private life did not exist
and that we should abandon historical analysis of gender grounded in the pub-
lic/private split. We see in Smith's case that while her integration of the public
and the private revolutionized the domestic sphere, she did not implicate the
private in the public in any radical way. Indeed, national and sexual divisions
are reinforced in *Desmond* to underscore Smith's specific articulation of a public and private divide. It is easy to celebrate moments of instability between the
public and private as liberatory and assume that the blurring of public and private or women's participation in the public are positive feminist moments. But
this may not always be the case. We need to look at precisely how that instability is produced and what are the effects of both divisions and boundary trans-
gressions in order to draw our own lines and conclusions.

Notes

1. See, for example, Susan Conner, "Public Virtue and Public Women: Prostitution in Revolutionary Paris," *Eighteenth-Century Studies* 23, no. 2 (1994): 221–40; Roddey Reid, *Families in Jeopardy: Regulating the Social Body in France, 1750–1910* (Stanford, Calif.: Stanford
   University Press, 1993); Robert B. Shoemaker, *Gender in English Society, 1650-1850: The
   emergence of separate spheres?* (London and New York: Longman, 1998); and Amanda
   Vickery, "Golden Age to Separate Spheres? A Review of the Categories and Chronology
   of English Women's History," *The Historical Journal* 36, no. 2 (1993): 383–414.

2. See Lenard R. Berlanstein, "Women and Power in Eighteenth-Century France: Actresses
   at the Comédie-Française," *Feminist Studies* 20, no. 3 (1994): 475–505; and Mary Favret,
   "Spectatrice as Spectacle: Helen Maria Williams at Home in the Revolution," *Studies in
   Romanticism* 32 (1993): 273–95. Favret's excellent article provides the background for
   much of my discussion of Charlotte Smith. Favret's revisioning of the public/private split
   is exemplified in her departure from Landes' reading of Jacques-Louis David's *The Oath
   of the Horatii* and *Lictors Returning to Brutus the Bodies of his Sons*. Landes argues that

David's paintings visually exemplify the absolute division of the public from the private. Favret argues, on the other hand, that the paintings display a certain ambiguity towards the domestic interiors, an ambiguity which suggests "the rhetoric of public activity may be violently inconsistent with and nevertheless endorsed by the rhetoric of home and family."

3. Lawrence Klein writes "my principal target in this essay is the tendency to overestimate or rely uncritically on the binary opposition either as a feature of people's mental equipment in the past or as an analytic device for those of us who write histories. . . . [T]he hegemonic role often assigned to binary oppositions [i.e., public/private] in the discursive worlds of past people is less solid and total than it is sometimes made out to be," Lawrence E. Klein, "Gender and the Public/Private Distinction in the Eighteenth-Century: Some Questions about Evidence and Analytic Procedure," *Eighteenth-Century Studies* 29, no. 1 (1995): 98.

4. Julie Ellison, "Redoubled Feeling: Politics, Sentiment, and the Sublime in Williams and Wollstonecraft," *Studies in Eighteenth-Century Culture* 20 (1990): 197–215, notes a similar double movement between the sentiment and the sublime in Mary Wollstonecraft's "*A Vindication of the Rights of Woman*," and Helen Maria Williams's *Letters From France*.

5. In "The Unstable Boundaries of the French Revolution," Lynn Hunt makes a particular claim for the French Revolution in the history of private life; she states that "[d]uring the French Revolution the boundaries between public and private life were very unstable" and that the eventual outcome of the Revolution was to stabilize "a more sharply differentiated private space" than had previously existed (13). Lynn Hunt, "The Unstable Boundaries of the French Revolution," in Phillippe Aries and Georges Duby, eds., *The History of Private Life,* vol. 4, trans. Arthur Goldhammer, (Cambridge, Mass.: Belknap Press, 1990), 13–45.

6. Florence Hilbish, Smith's 1941 biographer, disagrees with the claim that *Desmond* did not provoke censure. She writes regarding the novel, "The political views of Mrs. Smith shocked and offended her aristocratic friends. . . . The novel became greatly condemned both because it favoured the Revolution and because of its moral tendency" (149), Florence May Anna Hilbish, *Charlotte Smith, Poet and Novelist (1749–1806)* (Philadelphia: University of Pennsylvania, 1941). I can find no evidence of this great condemnation. Of all the radical 1790s women, Smith was the least censored and most often praised. Even Polwhele, while including Smith as an "Unsex'd Female," favorably compared her with Fanny Burney and Ann Radcliffe and wondered why such a feminine writer would "suffer

her mind to be infected with the Gallic mania" (18), Richard Polwhele, *The Unsex'd Females: A Poem* (London: Cadell and Davies, 1798).

7. There are numerous parallels between *Desmond* (1792) and Wollstonecraft's *The Wrongs of Woman* (1798) and Wollstonecraft had certainly read *Desmond*, as she reviewed it for the *Analytical Review*. Both novels are atypical in their introduction of a married heroine. Pat Elliot states regarding Geraldine: "The position of Geraldine Verney, a married woman, as the heroine is a major departure from convention. There is no precedent in traditional women's fiction for using a mature married woman as a heroine" (107), Pat Elliot, "Charlotte Smith's Feminism: A Study of *Emmeline* and *Desmond*," in Dale Spender, ed., *Living by the Pen: Early British Women Writers* (New York and London: Teachers College Press [The Athene Series], 1992), 91–112. Patricia Howell Michaelson, "*The Wrongs of Woman* as a Feminist Amelia," *Journal of Narrative Technique* 21, no. 3 (1991): 250–61, argues that Amelia is the precursor to *The Wrongs of Woman*. I think it more accurate to look to *Desmond* instead of Amelia as the main influence on Wollstonecraft's text. Both radical women's novels include the plot of a tyrant husband attempting to sell his wife to pay off gambling debts; the scenario lent itself well to the feminist argument Smith and Wollstonecraft present. While Wollstonecraft did not acknowledge her debt to Smith in the preface to *The Wrongs of Woman* (perhaps she would have had she lived to complete it), interestingly, Smith preempts any charge of her own plagiarism of *The Wrongs of Woman* in her preface to *The Young Philosopher* (1798): "the incident of the confinement in a mad house of one of my characters was designed before I saw the fragment of *The Wrongs of Woman,* by a Writer whose talents I greatly honoured, and whose untimely death I deeply regret; from her I should not blush to borrow, and if I had done so I would have acknowledged it" (v). Charlotte Smith, *The Young Philosopher* (New York: Garland Reprint, 1975 [1798]).

8. Mary Anne Schofield, "The Witchery of Fiction: Charlotte Smith, Novelist," in Dale Spender, ed., *Living by the Pen: Early British Women Writers* (New York and London: Teachers College Press [The Athene Series], 1992), 177–87, describes Smith's fictional style of intermingling plots—her "witchery"—through the metaphor of weaving. The metaphor works well to designate the effect of the thematic interplay in the novel.

9. For example, William Beloe, in his conservative satire, *The Sexagarian; Or, The Recollections of a Literary Life,* vol. 1 (London: F. C. and J. Rivington, 1817), describes Williams as completely "Frenchified." The derogatory term was widely applied to English Jacobin women.

10. Nicola Watson, *Revolution and the Form of the British Novel, 1790–1825* (Oxford: Clarendon Press, 1994), suggests that Geraldine is the "good" Julie of the second volume of *La Nouvelle Héloise,* while Josephine is the "bad" one (38). Katharine M. Rogers, "Romantic Aspirations, Restricted Possibilities: The Novels of Charlotte Smith," in Carol Shiner Wilson and Joel Haefner, eds., *Re-Visioning Romanticism: British Women Writers, 1776–1837* (Philadelphia: University of Pennsylvania Press, 1994), argues that Smith is trying "to hint that there is something unhealthy and mechanical in Geraldine's rigid obedience" (78–79).

11. In his refutation of Burke, *Desmond* employs a similar direct analogy when he quotes the famous passage from Locke comparing parental power to the government of states (II: 66).

12. Conway makes a similar argument in relation to the transgressive female body. "In both Mary Wollstonecraft's and Charlotte Smith's works," she writes, "it becomes imperative to displace, to relocate the eroticized and sexualized female body in a sphere unassociated with the English middle-class. . . . And yet, for Jacobin feminist discourse, the transgressive body, like revolution, generates a narrative of change" necessary to revolutionize the domestic sphere (396). Thus, the textual transformative function of Josephine's French body. Alison Conway, "Nationalism, Revolution, and the Female Body: Charlotte Smith's *Desmond,*" *Women Studies: An Interdisciplinary Journal* 24, no. 1 (1995): 395–409.

13. Reviewers seem to present the sexual plot as an unfortunate formal mistake in the text. *The Critical Review* wrote "The connection of *Desmond* with madame Boisbelle is unnecessarily introduced; for the only purpose it answers, viz. to increase the perplexity previous to the catastrophe, is scarcely perceived among the more affecting circumstances of the other events," *The Critical Review* 6 (Sept. 1792): 99. *The European Magazine* saw the plot as contradicting the unity of *Desmond's* character for no good reason: "our Authoress may say, she did not intend to make him perfect. Perhaps not, we are not advocates for perfect monsters, but where faults answer little good purpose, they may as well be avoided," *The European Magazine* 22 (July 1792): 23.

14. Smith directly raises the question of whether or not a French woman could be an appropriate wife shortly after this passage by way of Geraldine's brother, Waverly. Waverly seems attracted to Josephine's sister, Julie, and Desmond questions how he should handle the situation. He wondered if Geraldine "would approve of his [Waverly's] chusing a woman of another country, and another religion from his own." He leaves the question unanswered and decides not to encourage Waverly's attraction "till I knew her [Geraldine's] sentiments" (I: 167).

15. Alison Conway writes, "For a brief but critical narrative moment Josephine takes on a maternal function, switching places with Geraldine symbolically and literally." Significantly, Josephine gives birth on English soil. Conway, "Nationalism, Revolution, and the Female Body," 405.

16. See Hunt, note 5.

Works Cited

Berlanstein, Lenard R. "Women and Power in Eighteenth-century France: Actresses at the Comédie-Française." *Feminist Studies* 20, no. 3 (Fall 1994): 475–505.

Bowstead, Diana. "Charlotte Smith's *Desmond:* The Epistolary Novel as Ideological Argument." *Fetter'd or Free? British Women Novelists, 1670–1815.* Ed. Mary Anne Schofield and Cecilia Macheski. Athens, Ohio: Ohio University Press, 1986. 237–63.

Conner, Susan P. "Public Virtue and Public Women: Prostitution in Revolutionary Paris, 1793–1794." *Eighteenth-Century Studies* 23, no. 2 (Winter 1994–95): 221–40.

Conway, Alison. "Nationalism, Revolution, and the Female Body: Charlotte Smith's *Desmond*." *Women Studies: An Interdisciplinary Journal*. 25, no. 1 (1995): 395–409.

Elliot, Pat. "Charlotte Smith's Feminism: A Study of *Emmeline* and *Desmond*." *Living by the Pen: Early British Women Writers*. Ed. Dale Spender. New York and London: Teachers College Press (The Athene Series), 1992. 91–112.

Ellison, Julie. "Redoubled Feeling: Politics, Sentiment, and the Sublime in Williams and Wollstonecraft." *Studies in Eighteenth-Century Culture*. Vol. 20. 197–215.

Favret, Mary. "Spectatrice as Spectacle: Helen Maria Williams at Home in the Revolution." *Studies in Romanticism* 32 (Summer 1993): 273–95.

Hilbish, Florence May Anna. *Charlotte Smith, Poet and Novelist (1749–1806)*. Philadelphia: University of Pennsylvania, 1941.

Hunt, Lynn. "The Unstable Boundaries of the French Revolution." *From the Fires of the Revolution to the Great War.* Ed. Michelle Perot. Volume 4 of *A History of Private Life.* General ed. Phillippe Aries and Georges Duby. Trans. Arthur Goldhammer. Cambridge, Mass.: Belknap Press, 1990. 13–45.

Klein, Lawrence E. "Gender and the Public/Private Distinction in the Eighteenth Century: Some Questions about Evidence and Analytic Procedure." *Eighteenth-Century Studies*. 29, no. 1 (Fall 1995): 97–109.

Landes, Joan B. *Women and the Public Sphere in the Age of the Revolution.* Ithaca: Cornell University Press, 1988.

Michaelson, Patricia Howell. *"The Wrongs of Woman* as a Feminist *Amelia." Journal of Narrative Technique* 21, no. 3 (Fall 1991): 250–61.

Polwhele, Richard. *The Unsex'd Females: A Poem.* London, 1798.

Reid, Roddey. *Families in Jeopardy: Regulating the Social Body in France, 1750–1910.* Stanford: Stanford University Press, 1993.

Rogers, Katharine M. "Romantic Aspirations, Restricted Possibilities: The Novels of Charlotte Smith." *Re-Visioning Romanticism: British Women Writers, 1776–1837.* Ed. Carol Shiner Wilson and Joel Haefner. Philadelphia: University of Pennsylvania Press, 1994. 72–88.

Schofield, Mary Anne. "The Witchery of Fiction: Charlotte Smith, Novelist." *Living by the Pen: Early British Women Writers.* Ed. Dale Spender. New York & London: Teachers College Press (The Athene Series), 1992. 177–87.

Shoemaker, Robert B. *Gender in English Society, 1650–1850: The emergence of separate spheres?* London and New York: Longman, 1998.

Smith, Charlotte. 1792. *Desmond; A Novel.* New York: Garland Reprint, 1975.

———. 1798. *The Young Philosopher.* New York: Garland Reprint, 1975.

Vickery, Amanda. "Golden Age to Separate Spheres? A Review of the Categories and Chronology of English Women's History," *The Historical Journal* 36, no. 2 (1993): 383–414.

Watson, Nicola. *Revolution and the Form of the British Novel, 1790–1825.* Oxford: Clarendon Press, 1994.

Williams, Helen Maria. *Letters From France.* Ed. with an introduction by Janet Todd. 8 volumes in 2. Delmar, N.Y.: Scholars' Facsimiles and Reprints, 1975.

Wollstonecraft, Mary. *A Vindication of the Rights of Woman.* In Vol. 5. *The Works of Mary Wollstonecraft.* Ed. by M. Butler and J. Todd. London: William Pickering, 1989. 79–266.

The Crowd and the Public
in Godwin's Caleb Williams

Carl Fisher

Nothing is more notorious than the ease with which the conviviality of a crowded feast may degenerate into the depredations of a riot. While the sympathy of opinion catches from man to man, especially among persons whose passions have been little used to the curb of judgment, actions may be determined on which the solitary reflection of all would have rejected. There is nothing more barbarous, blood-thirsty and unfeeling than the triumph of the mob.

—*Enquiry Concerning Political Justice*[1]

Few novels engage their historical moment as cogently as *Caleb Williams*. The way in which the novel depicts individual psychology, or critiques the state, has often been documented.[2]

Personal obsession and private oppression are undoubtedly foregrounded, but always against a background of the community. The novel incorporates and involves the general populace, a public which responds to the actions of prominent individuals and reacts to violations of social norms; Godwin presents a social cross-section that strives to match the audience he defines in the preface as "persons whom books of philosophy and science are never likely to reach."[3] Identifying how Godwin integrates the public into *Caleb Williams*

—47—

underscores the essential interaction of the individual and the collective in the polarized political world of the 1790s.

Godwin envisioned *Caleb Williams* as part of the French Revolution debate, an extension of his *Enquiry Concerning Political Justice* and a fictional rejoinder to Burke's *Reflections*, anti-Jacobin propaganda, and governmental repression. Throughout Caleb's "adventures," Godwin critiques the collusion of the population with power as it operates "not merely through political institutions and the law, but through prejudice, prepossession and habit."[4] Essentially, Godwin probes the "moral economy" which defines eighteenth-century social relations, the supposed benevolence and heavy-handed paternalism of the gentry; he identifies this relationship as far from moral, and recognizes that it is based on and supported by processes of irrational and fierce identification.[5] At the same time, he critiques the passions of the people, as in the epigraph about "the depredations of a riot," with an Enlightenment-oriented fear of the mob.

The people's role, Godwin suggests, has taught them to be dominated and yet to imagine themselves free; they function with this logic, not irrationally, but conventionally within the prevailing discourse. Hence the public become accomplices and agents for the status quo, unaware of either the need for or the possibility of change. Riot, although it has revolutionary potential, is a critical factor in the eighteenth-century moral economy. In fact, popular disorder is considered a "right" by participants, and a necessary safety valve by those "above." But, the five years prior to the publication of *Caleb Williams* were unprecedented both for the level and tenor of popular activity, and for the public concern it generated among the literate and the elevated. Burke's commentary on the "swinish multitude" in *Reflections,* or on the Revolutionary mob that torments the iconic Marie Antoinette, had sensitized a culture already growing uneasy with popular disorder.

Popular disorder frightens Godwin as well; he prefers debate and rational discourse. For example, while he appreciates the rebellious impulse of the French Revolution, he also notes: "I was far from approving all that I saw even in the commencement of the revolution. . . . I never for a moment ceased to disapprove of mob government and violence, and the impulses which men collected together in multitudes produce on each other."[6] Further, in *Political Justice* Godwin often equates "mob government" and "democracy."

Godwin's fiction reflects this concern. Riot, while not a direct feature of *Caleb Williams*, appears in *St. Leon* (1799), where Godwin dramatizes the 1791 Birmingham Riots. The "confused murmurs and turbulence of the populace" leads to a riot which destroys science equipment with "shouts of infernal joy." A bystander laments,

> There was a principle in the human mind destined to be eternally at war with improvement and science. No sooner did a man devote himself to the pursuit of discoveries which, if ascertained, would prove the highest benefit to his species, than his whole species became armed against him. . . . He saw, in the transactions of that night, a pledge of the eternal triumph of ignorance over wisdom.[7]

A letter by Joseph Priestley, one of the principal targets of the Birmingham rioters, to the *Birmingham Gazette* about ten days after the riots, addresses the townspeople similarly:

> By hearing the Dissenters . . . continually railed at as enemies of the present Government, you have been led to consider any injury done to us as meritorious. When the object was right you thought the means could not be wrong. By the discourses of your teachers, and the exclamations of your superiors, your bigotry has been excited to the highest pitch. You were prepared for every species of outrage, thinking that whatever you could do was for the support of Government and especially the Church.[8]

Though Burke had raised fears of the revolutionary mob, Godwin (along with Priestley and other radicals) recognized in the Birmingham riots something much more frightening—a tendency toward regressive conservatism.[9] As Robert Bage wrote to a friend who had been a target in Birmingham, "Since the riots, in every company I have had the misfortune to go into, my ears have been insulted with the bigotry of 50 years back—with, damn the presbyterians—with church and king huzza—and with true passive obedience and nonresistence."[10] Riot, as an extreme expression of popular culture, undoubtedly fell short of the rule of reason; it seemed as likely to be reactionary as revolutionary, and certainly unlikely to lead to "political justice." By the 1790s, the temporary equality of riot and the subsequent return to order, a carnivalesque moment in the larger social equation, had been replaced, imaginatively and practically, with the uneasy aftermath of destruction and distrust.

Just as the view from above ultimately saw riot as a blow against order and subordination, intellectual radicals understood riot as a blow against progress. After all, one of the shouts of the Birmingham rioters, as they destroyed Priestley's library and scientific equipment, was "No Philosophers." Godwin, an advocate of rational dissent, imagined the people "armed against him," at times literally and always intellectually. In this situation, he and his contemporaries felt caught between suppression by the powerful and persecution by the popular.

These realms collude, as Godwin often points out, and he protests not just legal and authoritarian oppression, but the fomented loyalist hysteria that supports it. Of the Paine trial, in which the author of *The Rights of Man* was convicted in absentia, he wrote,

> We all know by what means a verdict was procured: by repeated proclamations, by all the force, and all the fears of the kingdom being artfully turned against one man. As I came out of court, I saw hand-bills, in the most vulgar and illiberal style distributed, entitled, *The Confessions of Thomas Paine*. I had not walked three streets, before I was encountered by ballad singers, roaring in cadence rude, a miserable set of scurrilous stanzas upon his private life.[11]

Any reader of *Caleb Williams* will recognize the closeness of this scene to the reception of the criminal biography which Gines produces under Falkland's authority. The inset criminal narrative is one way Godwin uses the novel to delineate a sense of the "public" as unavoidable, ubiquitous to both civic and personal life. The criminal biography denotes a world of commodification and exploitation, in which personal stories are for sale, although Godwin would want to impress on a reader that they are often fabrications. Caleb, at first, doesn't understand this, and repeatedly expresses surprise at public participation in his own story, first with the reward broadsheet which the criminals possess, then when at the public house on the road to London, and again after a close brush with Gines when he moves on to work with Mr. Spurrel, the watchmaker. When he hears a hawker tell his story exactly—except, of course, lacking the details of Falkland's guilt—he is caught in "utter astonishment and confusion."

The criminal narrative ends with a reward promise, and then "All for the price of one halfpenny." The way the broadsheet presents information, ending with the reward, creates the text as a kind of lottery ticket; a person could spend a little in hope of a larger reward, either morally, financially, or both. Like an eighteenth-century version of *America's Most Wanted*, "the public was warned to be upon their watch against a person of an uncouth and extraordinary appearance, and who lived in a recluse and solitary manner" (269). Far from rebellious, popular culture here is complicitous with patrician culture, and Caleb imagines:

> A numerous class of individuals, through every department, almost every house of the metropolis, would be induced to look with a suspicious eye upon every stranger, especially every solitary stranger, that fell under their observation. The prize of one hundred guineas was held out to excite their avarice, and sharpen their penetration. It was no longer Bow-Street, it was a million of men, in arms against me (270).

The People, who do not recognize their own exploitation, betray the individual. Godwin idealizes rational consensus but apprehends coerced opinion, created and exploited from above, accepted and desired from below.

At best, the audience for Caleb's story lacks information to make informed judgments; at worst, they fall prey to propagandistic lies and collude with the culture machine meant to keep them in place. Hence, Godwin faces a dilemma. He wants to rehabilitate the participants of popular culture, to move them from the realm of prejudice and misinformation to the presumably more free and open air of the public sphere. In fact, he sets this transition as a critical alternative to the transgressive patrician culture in *Caleb Williams* which he imagines withering away (along with government) in a progressive future. However, the conceptual entities of the public sphere and popular culture in reality associate uncomfortably, and are not easily melded.

The eighteenth-century public sphere, as defined by Jurgen Habermas, consisted of a "broad strata of the population" which, while originally integrating people in "their daily existence as consumers," becomes highly politicized by the 1790s. Habermas notes the development of "public opinion" as a key element of the British scene, "formed in the conflict of arguments concerning a substantive issue, not uncritically based on common sense in the either naive or plebiscitarily manipulated assent to or vote about persons."[12] Habermas quotes a 1791 Parliamentary speech by Fox, who argues that in determining governmental action "one thing is most clear, that I ought to give the public the means of forming an opinion." The public sphere theoretically provides a nexus of informed communication. In *Political Justice* Godwin defines what he considers a public sphere along Habermas's lines: "conversation accustoms us to hear a variety of sentiments, obliges us to exercise patience and attention, and gives freedom and elasticity to our disquisitions" (1, 295). Godwin desires this silhouette for the popular audience, to develop their individual and private senses of judgment and enhance their rational communicative capability.

The Falkland/Caleb dynamic dramatizes Godwin's sense of an information-based social economy, as Falkland "doesn't believe that facts should be freely disseminated according to public will but only deployed according to private interest.... Falkland doesn't see truth as a condition of life but as a strategy of politics."[13] When Caleb agrees originally to Falkland's bargain, he "discounts the interest of humanity-at-large by working against a system of free and unimpeded social communication.... By agreeing to protect Falkland's reputation, Caleb agrees to protect the system of his own persecution. By betraying humankind's interests, he must, like Falkland, abandon the society of free-speaking individuals."[14]

In essence, Godwin idealizes the public sphere as a world of exchanged ideas, gentrified behavior, enlightened rationalism; by contrast, popular culture embodies retrogressive belief systems, unenlightened identification, and violent potential. Crowd behavior is one aspect of this culture, as is the presumed "vulgarity" of popular entertainment (like criminal biography). If the public sphere is the coffeehouse, popular culture is the alehouse. The line between the public and the popular, in Godwin's view, must be bridged by rational discourse. The gentry, in demanding allegiance and acceptance, create a class of governed who are not able to rationally and individually consider truth; popular culture is created in relation to this demand, both from above and below, and popular opinion becomes an orgy of firmly held untruths.

For example, when Caleb travels after one of his escapes, he stops at a "public house" on the London road, and eavesdrops on the "gentry of a village alehouse" (235). Here he hears them discuss "the notorious housebreaker, Kit Williams," an authoritarian narrative passed as rumor in a market town. One of the speakers comments, "Some folks must be hanged to keep the wheel of our state folks a-going." This is not meant ironically, for the speaker has no misgivings about capital punishment. General opinion holds that Williams's real crime was not theft, but betraying Falkland's trust. Godwin highlights the hyperbole of popular narrative by those Caleb ironically styles "historians and commentators." Caleb supposedly escaped prison "no less than five times," and "made his way through stone walls, as if they were so many cobwebs" (236–7). He is given almost superhuman qualities, yet the hyperbolic narrative is spoken as truth. The innkeeper, conversely, identifies with Caleb's plight and hopes he will escape, not knowing she is talking to him. These juxtaposed views point out the contradictory nature of popular culture: the reaction of either adoration or execration is predicated on inappropriate premises. At first Caleb is alarmed: "I could almost have imagined that I was the sole subject of general attention, and that the whole world was in arms to exterminate me." He soon warms to the situation—"by degrees I began to be amused at the absurdity of their tales, and the variety of falsehoods I heard asserted all around me"—but the momentary safety evaporates quickly. Far from being harmless, popular opinion is a form of social control, and public control of his story abridges Caleb's options.

In this scene and others, Godwin clearly critiques the inconsistent and essentially unstable practices and ideology of popular culture. Each character within the novel, regardless of station, must negotiate the problem of public opinion. Not surprisingly, characters respond to the public based on their class position. Tyrrel, for example, while "tyrannical to his inferiors," enjoyed being the "grand master of the *coterie*" at the market. When he spoke, "he was always sure of an audience. His neighbors crowded round, and joined in the ready laugh, partly from obsequiousness, and partly from unfeigned admiration" (18). However, "when his subjects, encouraged by his familiarity, had discarded their precaution," he would choose a target to persecute. In critiquing Tyrrel, Godwin comments on the identification process; people feel comfortable and identify with the powerful, who can turn vicious in a moment.

Godwin presents the psychology of oppression as well as an allegory of crowd psychology. Despite his lofty position, Tyrrel still fears public humiliation. When he ruins Emily Melville, he utilizes power but is still "sensible the world would see the matter in a different light" (80). Caleb comments that tyranny, when revealed, will "level all distinctions, and reduce their perpetrator to an equality with the most indigent and squalid of his species." Ultimately Tyrrel is reviled; as Mrs. Hammond says to him on reporting Emily's death: "All the world will abhor and curse you. Were you such a fool as to think, because men pay respect to wealth and rank, this would extend to such a deed? They will laugh at so barefaced a cheat. The meanest beggar will spurn and spit at you" (91). Tyrrel transgresses against traditional polite/popular relations, which protect the gentry except in extreme and public cases. Accustomed to obedience,

> Now he looked round and saw sullen detestation in every face, which with difficulty restrained itself, and upon the slightest provocation broke forth with an impetuous tide, and swept away all mounds of subordination and fear. His large estate could not now purchase civility from the gentry, the peasantry, scarcely from his own servants. . . . It seemed as if the sense of public resentment had long been gathering strength unperceived, and now burst forth in unsuppressible violence (93).

When Tyrrel decides to attend a "rural assembly" and "meet the whole tide of public opinion," the popular and the public merge, and "The general voice was eager to abash him. As his confusion became more visible, the outcry increased. It swelled gradually to hootings, tumult, and the deafening noise of indignation" (95). Tyrrel is already an outcast when murdered.

In contrast, Falkland's ability to control and abuse the legal process makes him a strong foe, but his ability to harness public opinion indemnifies him. When Caleb first publicly accuses Falkland, "I no sooner said this, than I was again interrupted by an involuntary exclamation from every one present. They looked at me with furious glances, as if they could have torn me to pieces"

(171). Caleb's crime is insubordination; spectators, whether social equals or subordinates, identify with Falkland. The dynamic may be different—the gentry understand that taking Caleb seriously would undermine the entire social system, while the middle and lower orders depend on Falkland symbolically— but the result is the same.

If Tyrrel holds his power over the people through intimidation and physical threat, Falkland does so through a benevolent exterior. He is venerated by the people for his humanity and compassion; as in his beloved chivalric readings, the people are lieges, unquestioning in their allegiance but protected by their lord. Falkland acts in favor of the less powerful repeatedly, whether in heroically putting out a fire—where "the inhabitants were in the utmost consternation . . . [and] stood wringing their hands and contemplating the ravages of the fire in an agony of powerless despair" (43)—or saving a damsel in distress, as when Grimes tries to rape Emily.

Falkland recognizes the theatricality of his patrician position. He fears public humiliation because it would lower him from his pedestal in the eyes of the public. An early episode presages this theme, during Falkland's continental sojourn, when he reconciles with Count Malvesi after a misunderstanding, commenting that "if the challenge had been public" he would have been "obliged to be your murderer" (15). Indignity may be personally painful, but it is tolerable as long as it is private. When Tyrrel knocks him down in a public assembly, he burns with "public disgrace" (99). Later, in his confession to Caleb, he gives as the motive for murder that he had been "insulted, disgraced, polluted in the face of hundreds." He claims that he did not seek immediate revenge on Tyrrel because it would have been a selfish act, while he intends only to promote "the general good" (99).

Caleb's later conflict, not just with power but with the popular will that supports it, is anticipated by Falkland's acquittal, when the "general sentiment . . . was a sort of sympathetic feeling that took hold upon all ranks and degrees. The multitude received him with huzzas, they took his horses from his carriage, dragged him along in triumph, and attended him many miles on his return to his own habitation" (103). The carnival process represents a celebration of things as they are, a moment of seeming freedom which in fact reaffirms the status quo. In replacing one form of constraint (Tyrrel) with another (Falkland)—in fact, Caleb earlier describes a scene in which the mere presence of Falkland leads the people to desire "revolt" against Tyrrel (19)—the local population merely maintains custom. Godwin warns in a discussion of governance in *Political Justice* that the people should "beware of reverence," because custom allows the gentry to maintain a hold on a private world of privilege and information, and consequently influences all aspects of public life.

Popular culture tacitly and complicitly maintains the patrician/plebeian equation, which by Godwin's terms impedes progress. There is intended irony in Caleb's claim that "the world was made for men of sense to do what they will with it. Its affairs cannot be better than in the direction of the genuine heroes; and, as in the end they will be found the truest friends of the whole, so the multitude have nothing to do, but to look on, be fashioned and admire" (117). The popular culture which buoys Falkland will victimize Caleb; the novel dramatizes the difficulty of the individual caught between inhuman authority which will go to any extreme to maintain control, and the unruly mob, created and credulous, which cheers for all the wrong reasons.

One of Caleb's central recognitions, late in the novel, is that "Mr. Falkland, wise as he is and pregnant in resources, acts by human and not by supernatural means. . . . he cannot produce a great and notorious effect without some visible agency" (296). The agency is most directly Gines and the legal system, but includes the manipulation of public opinion, which Falkland depends on when he persecutes Caleb. Godwin reflects a public which repeatedly accepts disinformation and misinformation, labors under prejudice and misapprehension, and does not know its own interest.

The presentation of public opinion as critical to the action, a constant background and occasional foreground, provides a bridge to recognizing Godwin's desire for a world which transcends popular culture and develops a more humanized public sphere—not a commercial or political sphere, but Godwin's vision of a rational future of communication and openness.

The popular culture/public opinion nexus finds repeated representation in Caleb's narrative. Godwin sets these terms with Caleb's birth to "humble parents . . . peasants" (3). Even as a child, Caleb notes, "I had considerable aversion to the boisterous gaiety of the village gallants. . . . village anecdotes and scandal had no charms for me" (4). Caleb imagines himself apart from the rural popular culture, although he accepts "the laws of decorum" (114)—by which he means the rules of subordination and social hierarchy. Later, Caleb's persecuted state should ally him with the lower orders, for he has to struggle with the "joint considerations . . . of security and subsistence" (266). Still, he has a hard time internalizing popular concerns. When he hears his own story made public, he resents the audience, the "hawkers and ballad-mongers . . . footmen and chambermaids" (274).

The disguises Caleb uses to avoid capture—beggar, Irishman, Jew, itinerant artisan, hack writer—establish him as on the margins, a part of the crowd, yet he despises its members. He "incurs contempt with the dregs of mankind" (234), yet expresses little sympathy for the lower orders. He knows they "incur contempt" but still calls them "the dregs of mankind." This is vocabulary from above, except as used ironically in radical writings.[15] Classifying and name-calling, of course, offer tremendous power. Tyrrel and Falkland both claim they will crush enemies like "insects." When Falkland calls Caleb an "insolent domestic," Caleb feels muted, forced to passivity—the conversation no longer resembles a dialogue, and much remains unspoken. Other phrases of elite opprobrium occur throughout the novel: "vulgar classes," "scum of the earth," "dregs of mankind," "a rabble of visitors."

Caleb willingly rubs elbows with the crowd, but fashions himself above with a curious individualism not uncharacteristic, perhaps, of Godwin's own political view. Caleb's discussion with Falkland about Alexander the Great sheds interesting light on this point. Caleb questions, "How many thousands of lives did he sacrifice in his career? What must I think of his cruelties?" Falkland tells him that this is wrong thinking, that "the death of a hundred thousand such men is at first sight very shocking; but what in reality are a hundred thousand such men than a hundred thousand sheep?" Caleb suggests that this may not be an ideal way to govern, and expresses Paineite ideas about the "cheated multitude" and "the whole machine of state." Finally, he argues that "the pike and the battle axe are not the right instruments for making men wise. . . . it seems to me as if murder and massacre were but a very left-handed way of producing civilization and love" (110–11).

This passage exemplifies the dilemma of the novel. Marilyn Butler calls Caleb a "plebeian everyman" and says of the Alexander passage that "Caleb oscillates between maddening Falkland with lower-class cynicism about Alexander's nobility, and buttering him up by pretending to despise the commonality."[16] As shown above, Caleb does always have a conflicted relationship with the "commonality," and the "lower-class cynicism" is probably intended as the kind of insight Godwin might hope of a reader, who can recognize that heroes and leaders of state are far from selfless. Godwin wants to minimize the assumed distance between the upper and the lower orders. As Caleb says of his own perspective, "Mr. Falkland had always been to my imagination an object of wonder, and that which excites our wonder we scarcely suppose ourselves competent to analyse" (297). This is exactly the impression intended by the grandeur and mystery and punishment of the law, and presents the view that the lower orders have of the elite.

The only ones who seem capable of class analysis are the thieves, or at least their leader, Mr. Raymond, who argues, "Our profession is the profession of justice. [It is thus that the prejudices of men universally teach them to colour the most desperate cause, to which they have determined to adhere.] We, who are thieves without license, are at open war with another set of men, who are thieves according to law" (216). Caleb is uneasy in their company, however, and his parenthetical insight separates him from their rebellion. In fact, his sensibility becomes manifest when he sees the thieves once he is brought to shelter; he says they enter "tumultuously," and "all had a feature of boldness, inquietude and disorder, extremely unlike any thing I had before observed in such a groupe" (215). This is language resonant of the time: tumult, disorder, inquietude. He appreciates Raymond's theory of thievery—after Caleb tells his story, Raymond comments: "Who that saw the situation in its true light would wait till their oppressors thought fit to decree their destruction, and not take arms in their defence while it was yet in their power? Which was most meritorious, the unresisting and dastardly submission of a slave, or the enterprise and gallantry of the man who dared to assert his claims?" (220)—and the Alexander parallel resounds. But Caleb ultimately sees the thieves within the fearsome context of collective action, consonant with the real 1790s fear of "levellers" and the "swinish multitude," for although the government creates some "atrociously exaggerated precautions" about property, these men "commit an alarming hostility against the whole" (226) and their attention "was in the highest degree misapplied, unassisted by liberal and enlightened views" (219).

Only when in total extremity does Caleb claim kinship with the lower orders. He is hurried "from one species of anxiety and distress to another, too rapidly to suffer any one of them to sink deeply into my mind" (249). The harshness of circumstances makes him more sentient than rational—precisely the critique Godwin makes about popular disorder. Forced into "vile subjugation," he "seemed to be in a state in which reason had no power" (154). In thinking of the inequity of society, he claims: "I was astonished at the folly of my species, that did not rise up as one man, and shake off chains so ignominious and misery so insupportable" (156). Caleb's emotional and intellectual processes mimic the state of riot, even to where he claims, "I am incited to the penning of these memoirs" (3).[17]

If Caleb becomes a "monster," as he is called by several figures within the novel, Godwin makes it clear that he has been created that way, both compelled into radical rebellion and invented in the minds of the public. So too is popular disorder a creation within society and a projection of the imagination. Toward the end of the narrative, Caleb reflects, "My sensations at certain periods amounted to insanity" (306). Insanity, Godwin demonstrates, is an induced state. In much the same way the public, which had once been a tractable mass, a friendly face, a community spirit, becomes something menacing in the 1790s. Perhaps Caleb acts as alter ego for the popular voice: forced into "servile submission," his "whole soul revolted against the treatment I endured, and yet I could not utter a word. . . . it was inexperience, and not want of strength, that awed me" (144).[18] Unsure what to do, he falls back on custom. He claims that before Falkland's service he had been independent, but he is now accustomed to the will of another. His mind is often in "tumult" or "chaos" or "whirlwind"— the internalized state of external popular forces—and he feels governed by terror. Unable to make appropriate choices or have appropriate identifications, he is a miasma of received ideas. When Forester's servant finds him, after his first escape, and tries to convince him to return, Caleb argues, "I am an Englishman; and it is the privilege of an Englishman to be sole judge and master of his actions" (159). The "Free Born Englishman" ideal, both perpetual and naive, caricatures Caleb's early innocence, and Caleb himself mocks it later in jail.

If Caleb is a surrogate for the potentially revolutionary crowd—like Frankenstein's creature—he is also a strong critic of the popular will: "I saw my whole species as ready, in one mode or another, to be made instruments of the tyrant" (277). He critiques both paternalistic social relations and reifying instrumental reason. He tells Falkland that, through totalizing persecution, "You are wearing out the springs of terror" (283–4). Total desperation is more likely to foment revolution than to ameliorate it, and this is one of the claims Godwin made about the repressive measures of the government. Caleb, in many ways a creation of Falkland and of genteel culture, is as despised and feared as Frankenstein's creature becomes, and equally as dangerous. His story, like the creature's, provides a cogent social critique. Caleb upsets the status quo—like popular disorder—but things return close to their normal course by the novel's conclusion.

What does it mean that in his moment of triumph Caleb finds his will dissipated? His triumph does not change the social system; it merely provides a temporary release. Additionally, "Caleb does recognize his complicity, but in exactly the wrong way, in a way that permits ideology to continue to function invisibly behind a facade of personal psychological agency."[19] Godwin notes in *Political Justice* that "the characters of men originate in their external circumstances" (24). It is easy to imagine that he means both individual and mass character, and that his evocation of popular behavior tries to create an understanding of crowd psychology without the vocabulary. It would take the social sciences and psychology of the nineteenth century to see the crowd as something historically produced—or to find new ways to subjugate it—but Godwin's popular representation situates cultural anxieties and tells us much about the cultural contradictions of the time. *Caleb Williams* may not emphasize riot, but the fear of it provides an impetus for Godwin's critique of popular culture.

Falkland has produced passion through his oppressiveness, and according to Godwin, "Revolutions are the produce of passion, not of sober and tranquil reason" (*PJ*, 1, 244). Yet when Caleb reaches the height of his passion, he maintains, "I will use no daggers! I will unfold a tale—! I will show thee for what thou art, and all the men that live shall confess my truth!—Didst thou imagine that I was altogether passive, a mere worm, organised to feel sensations of pain, but no emotion of resentment?" (314). Resentment should lead to discourse, to narrative, to the open expression of ideas, not to "daggers" and physical violence. The ultimate arbiter becomes public opinion: "These papers shall preserve the truth: they shall one day be published, and then the world will do justice on us both. . . . they will one day find their way to the public!" (315). Godwin insists on a rational public because he recognizes a world in which revolution is possible, and not just the limited disturbances of the Gordon riots, or the Priestley riots, but a larger overthrow of society. This potential world of feeling and irrationality, this radical spirit, would be anathema to his own principles of gradual change and rational exchange. He needs to create a readership that will neither accept "things as they are" undigested nor be so outraged as to throw off their "chains" in a revolutionary action. From this perspective, the character of popular culture embodies numerous tangible problems: sheer numbers, violent potential, intense conservatism, incorrect identifications, and facile credulity. Through the alternations of Caleb's social consciousness, Godwin tries to create a reader who will not be violently transgressive, but who can develop a new sensibility of social relations.

The experiences of 1791–94 had given Godwin a great deal to think about in terms of the popular consumption of texts, from the widespread outrage over Paine to the contentious reception of *Enquiry Concerning Political Justice*.[20] But *Political Justice*, while often associated with political anarchism, was not a *revolutionary* text. It does not advocate popular uprisings or popular participation—it insists on individual reason and responsibility as opposed to collective action. For the same reasons *Caleb Williams* may be a radical social critique, but it is not a revolutionary novel. Godwin, even in the revolutionary period, disliked the "general voice." He says of democracy, "truth cannot be made more true by the number of its votaries" (*PJ*, 1, 220). Democracy, in Godwin's mind, comes to be associated with the passions, not with the rationality he so cherishes. In fact, Butler and Philp argue that "only a year after the publication of *Political Justice*, with its long vistas of progress, or perfectibility, Godwin devastatingly acknowledged the power of a prevailing ideology, through the tendency of the weak and the disadvantaged to submit to its values."[21]

Still, at some level Godwin hoped to reform the "people" through examples and principles of reasoning. The novel form would be ideal for this duty. Reading a novel is an individual act and allows for reflection. Godwin imagines a cumulative effect to the reading process. He claims in *Political Justice*, "Truth dwells with contemplation. We can seldom make much progress in the business of disentangling error and delusion, but in sequestered privacy" (1, 290). If enough individuals were influenced, it would change collective behavior from violent reaction to rational, cooperative—but not complicit—behavior.[22] It also might reach those to whom "books of philosophy and science are never likely to reach." He can hope for a wide distribution of his ideas:

> By the easy multiplication of copies, and the cheapness of books, everyone has access to them. The extreme inequality of information among different members of the same community, which existed in ancient times is diminished. . . . vast multitudes who, though condemned to labour for the perpetual acquisition of the means of subsistence, have yet a superficial knowledge of most of the discoveries and topics which are investigated by the learned (1, 283).

Godwin hopes to bridge the critical "inequality of information" which defines history.

Reading is progressive, Godwin suggests, and likely to lead to positive social change; yet he also insinuates that "knowledge is something to be selectively communicated to the lower classes, not produced by them. . . . his conception of texts and the audiences they engender is more in line with Addison and Steele than with *Hog's Wash* or *Pig's Meat*."[23] Godwin expresses a consistent anxiety, as well as a fearful fascination, with the lower orders, the same expressed in gothic novels and in much of the intellectual culture of the 1790s as well. Godwin imagines tremendous benefit, perhaps the only hope to build a future, in enjoining the transition of potential rioters to thoughtful readers.

A central paradox of *Caleb Williams* is Godwin's attitude toward the public, and particularly toward popular action. He suggests to readers they must discard previously held assumptions and be suspicious of authority, but they should not act in concert. Thompson denotes this same "ideological contradiction" in *Political Justice*:

It is as if Godwin is able to recognize the objectification of social relations under market capitalism, with its reification and alienation, and the consequent loss of the sense of community, and finally its replacement with a legalistic notion of society. Nevertheless, for all of this, Godwin is still unable to envision an alternative community, other than the vaguest notion of universal benevolence and brotherhood. . . . [he] is caught exactly betwixt and between . . . despising the false bourgeois solutions to alienation—romantic love, marriage, and the sacrosanct family, but at the same time, his vision is at the origin of the most extreme bourgeois vision of hyper-privatization and withdrawal.[24]

Rather than collectivity, Godwin insists on individuality, in part because he perceives the public as an amorphous and fickle entity, ill defined, always in flux. This attitude relegates Godwin to the status of historical oddity, neither full-blown revolutionary nor wholly enlightened ideologue.

Ironically Godwin, despite his reputation as a radical, is as fearful as Burke of the mob. He hoped, however, that he was not throwing pearls before swine. Godwin wants to educate the reader to throw off habitual prejudices and inherited constructions. The episodes of the novel would create a world the readers knew—even if only through other narrative—one they perhaps never knew to critique due to the misprision of everyday life. Hence, Godwin does not merely show "things" as they are, but the people as they are. In this sense, "the inbuilt unreliability of the first-person account throws the burden of interpretation and decision on the reader, soliciting his or her active participation."[25] This follows Godwin's belief in private judgment, and allows individuals to know what to do when confronted with public situations and extreme events. The crowd may not be subject to reform—unless enlightened one member at a time.

Godwin imagines the key to transforming potential rioters to careful readers is in controlling narrative, providing not the screed of conservative propaganda and the mass culture machine but alternative views, not stories of chivalry but those that will enact social communication and inspire civic responsibility. Novels, no less than other texts, confront a highly performative world in which it is difficult to judge real allegiances. In mass terms, this can be seen in the similar gestures of popular radicalism and popular loyalism; the fact of spectacle might have been as important as any cause, and opportunity seemed as important as political preference in whether people participated in a Paine burning or a reform meeting.[26] Godwin's novels try to cross class boundaries and create an enlightened readership.

Despite this ideal, different readers take different things from texts, as Mary Shelley noted about *Caleb Williams*: "those in the lower orders saw their cause espoused and their oppressors forcefully and eloquently delineated—while those of higher rank acknowledged and felt the nobleness, sensibility and errors of Falkland with deepest sympathy."[27] Falkland himself, after all, is not portrayed as innately evil; he is equally a prisoner of ideology and received ideas. Before his transition to villain, he says of the lower orders: "Poor wretches! they are pressed almost beyond all bearing as it is; and, if we unfeelingly give another turn to the machine, they will be crushed into atoms" (77). Falkland shows sensibility and social conscience, certainly ironic considering his later persecution of Caleb. Interestingly, his sense of the lower orders as a collective subject crushed as individual atoms marks a typical patrician refusal to acknowledge the possibility of collectivity.

The entire history of popular activity in the eighteenth century, capped by the disorder and exacerbated loyalism/radicalism of the 1790s, suggests that Godwin's ideal was not for the people to become proactive, or mass agents, but individuals who can shrug off the chains of intellectual paralysis and ingrained belief in system, hierarchy and paternal authority. He does this not by showing an ideal society, but the errors of popular culture. Popular agency is seen as either unthinking reaction or unenlightened complicity. In Caleb's final concern over the interpretation of his story, one critic sees a moment which frightens Godwin terribly; not just the perpetuation of falsehood through popular texts, but the continuing misreadings by a public "so debauched by falsehood it cannot recognize the truth when presented with it."[28]

Godwin contends with the dilemma of continued misunderstanding and passivity on one hand, and potential riot on the other. There are many public clusters in the novel—rural assemblies, anonymous city crowds, fire spectators, jury members—and many potential audiences for the novel. As Godwin points out in *Political Justice*, a "multitude of men" can only be intellectually united by "equal capacity and identical perception." Similarly, this multitude should not be emotionally moved to reactive violence by inequality; the riotous mob doesn't fulfill the requisites of the public sphere. Godwin hopes to construct this public with his novel of "things as they are," to move the culture through debate from acquiescence to progressivity, positing an idealized, alternative, utopian (but ultimately impossible) public sphere in which private individuals would employ judicious reason for the public good.

Notes

1. References in the text and notes will refer to the 1798 third edition of Godwin's *Political Justice* (1793), published in facsimile by the University of Toronto Press, 1947. This reference is to v. I, 295.

2. Critical works helpful in contextualizing the novel in the 1790s include Marilyn Butler, "Godwin, Burke, and *Caleb Williams*," *Essays in Criticism* 32, no. 3 (July 1982): 237–56, and Gary Kelly, *The English Jacobin Novel: 1780–1805* (Oxford: Clarendon Press, 1976).

3. References in the text and notes will be to David McCracken, ed., *Caleb Williams* (New York: W. W. Norton and Company, 1977).

4. Butler, "Godwin, Burke, and *Caleb Williams*," 243.

5. E. P. Thompson looks at the "traditional" nature of social relations, including popular protest, with riot legitimized by custom and only enacted when paternal protection of the lower orders failed, as in hunger riots. See Thompson, "The Moral Economy of the English Crowd in the Eighteenth Century," *Past and Present* 50 (February 1971): 76–136.

6. Quoted in Charles Kegan Paul, *William Godwin: His Friends and Contemporaries* (London: H.S. King and Co., 1876), I, 59.

7. William Godwin, *St. Leon* (Oxford University Press, 1994), 289–90.

8. Quoted in Vivian Bird, *The Priestley Riots, 1791, and the Lunar Society* (Birmingham: Birmingham and Midland Institute, 1992), 56.

9. George Rudè denotes many British examples of the conservative tendency of popular disorder in *The Crowd in History: A Study of Popular Disturbances in France and England, 1730–1848* (London: Lawrence and Wishart, 1981), including chapters on "Church and King" riots and the "Motives and Beliefs" of the pre-industrial crowd.

10. See Kelly, 6.

11. Quoted in Butler, "Godwin, Burke, and Caleb Williams," 238. In *Political Justice* Godwin points out the irony of public identification with and participation in the justice system; a criminal commits "an offence against the community at large" but because "the pursuit

commenced against the supposed offender is the *posse comitatus*, the armed force of the whole . . . when seven millions of men have got one poor, unassisted individual in their power, they are then at leisure to torture or kill him, and to make his agonies a spectacle to glut their ferocity" (335–6).

12. Jurgen Habermas, *The Structural Transformation of the Public Sphere: An Inquiry into a Category of Bourgeois Society,* trans. Thomas Burger (Cambridge, Mass.: MIT Press, 1991), 66. Tellingly in *Caleb Williams*, the entire plot is predicated on the fact that Mr. Underwood attempts to manipulate Hawkins' vote in county elections, which begins the concatenation of events.

13. Scott Bradfield, *Dreaming Revolution: Transgression in the Development of American Romance* (Iowa City: University of Iowa Press, 1993), 7.

14. Ibid., 8.

15. For example, popular journals such as Eaton's *Hog's Wash, or a Salmagundy for Swine* and Thomas Spence's *Pig's Meat; Lessons for the Swinish Multitude* self-consciously used Burke's terminology and "adopted the personae of pigs to define the character of the audience and to present radical thought as the opinion of humble swine." See Olivia Smith, *The Politics of Language, 1791–1819* (New York: Oxford University Press, 1984), 79–89.

16. Marilyn Butler, ed., *Burke, Paine, Godwin, and the Revolution Controversy* (Cambridge: Cambridge University Press, 1984), 151; Butler, "Godwin, Burke, and Caleb Williams," 247.

17. When Caleb escapes the second time, he exclaims his ecstasy at his freedom with a rhetoric similar to riot: He experiences a "sacred and indescribable moment" as he revels in "new found liberty" and "regains his rights." Along with this personal carnivalesque, he exults in his escape from "the gore-dripping robes of authority!" and hopes to further avoid "the cold blooded prudence of monopolists and kings!" (210).

18. Butler in her introduction to the 1818 *Frankenstein* (Oxford: Oxford University Press, 1994) points out the stylistic and ideological debts to *Caleb Williams*, and also notes that several critics have "developed the argument that his dark Other, the Creature, represents the newly politicized masses," (xiv) and that in the nineteenth century, particularly in political caricature, the "so-called monster" appeared "as the personification of popular, violent radicalism," (xlvi).

19. Gary Handwerk, "Of Caleb's Guilt and Godwin's Truth: Ideology and Ethics in Caleb Williams," *English Literary History* 60, no. 4 (Winter 1993).

20. *Political Justice* was read aloud in hundreds of public meetings, and excerpts were pub-

lished in Eaton's *Politics for the People* and Spence's *Hog's Wash* (See Mark Philp, "Thompson, Godwin, and the French Revolution," *History Workshop Journal* 39 (Spring 1995): 94. Pitt felt the work was harmless because it had a relatively high price and would be unaffordable for more potential readers.

21. Marilyn Butler and Mark Philp, eds., *William Godwin, Collected Novels and Memoirs* (London: William Pickering, 1992), v. I, 29.

22. Godwin, commenting on the value of Shakespeare and Milton in *The Enquirer* (1798), elaborates a theory of reading which helps explain his sense of the efficacy of literary production: "The poorest peasant in the remotest corner of England, is probably a different man from what he would have been but for these authors. Every man who is changed from what he was by the perusal of their works, communicates a portion of the inspiration all around him. It passes from man to man, till it influences the whole mass."

23. Garrett Sullivan, "'A Story To Be Hastily Gobbled Up:' Caleb Williams and Print Culture," *Studies in Romanticism* 32, no. 3 (Fall 1993): 332.

24. E. P. Thompson, "Eighteenth-Century English Society: Class Struggle Without Class?" *Social History* 3, no. 2 (May 1978): 189.

25. Clemit, *Godwinian Novel*, 6.

26. See Mark Philp, "Thompson, Godwin, and the French Revolution," 97.

27. Quoted in Clemit, *Godwinian Novel*, 42.

28. Sullivan, 335.

Injustice in the Works of
Godwin and Wollstonecraft

Glynis Ridley

Throughout the 1790s the British political establishment sought to deny the usefulness of debate on a range of constitutional matters by the simple expedient of faulting the basic form of expression employed by its detractors. Petitions to parliament and radical pamphlets were equally liable to dismissal on the grounds that their language did not permit the discussion of abstract concepts, contained an abundance of metaphors, and that they were altogether overly emotive. Radical writers of the 1790s thus faced a linguistic challenge before they could mount a political one. Was it possible to fashion "an intellectual vernacular": a prose style capable of discussing legal and constitutional precedents (drawn up by men with a classical rhetorical training) in a language accessible to all literate men and women?[1] Whilst these issues have previously been explored in relation to state trials from 1790–1820, the present paper takes as its focus the search for an intellectual vernacular in fictional trials of the same period. Out of all the fictional productions of English prose writers in the 1790s, two texts stand out for their overt exploration of linguistic norms demanded by legal precedent: *Caleb Williams* and *The Wrongs of Woman; or, Maria*. The paper will consider, firstly, the process by which fiction writers attempted to create sympathetic, radical characters who were required to be proficient in both the intellectual vernacular and the legal language of their social and political opponents; and secondly, the paper will consider whether male and female novelists of the 1790s addressed the issue of radical language in different ways. And whilst the form of the novel cannot necessarily be taken as implying that it appealed to a different reading community to radical political pamphlets or longer treatises, the paper will ultimately seek to conclude whether there is, inherent in the language of these novels, a tacit admission by their writers of the difficulty of expounding politically and socially radical agendas through fictional prose.

As the aftermath of revolutions as diverse as the French, the Russian, and the Chinese Cultural Revolution show us, those who seek to overturn a society's existing structures often ensure that the overthrow of the ruling elite is underpinned, and to some extent achieved, by the discrediting of their language: political hegemony is made possible only through linguistic hegemony, as Orwell's Ministry of Truth knew only too well. If the state can delimit the linguistic parameters of any radical debate, it can perhaps control the impact of radical thought. In the last decades of the eighteenth century, the British government sought to counter political dissent by objecting to its linguistic expression. Before moving to the problems this creates for a fiction writer with a reformist social agenda, it will be useful to illustrate briefly the attempts of successive governments to maintain political through linguistic hegemony with reference to the main linguistic faults that were supposedly the hallmarks of radical discourse.

During Paine's prosecution for the second part of *The Rights of Man*, the Crown drew attention to what was seen as the absurdity of Paine's denial that any country had a constitution before 1776, the Attorney-General insisting that England's constitution did not date merely to the Norman Conquest "but from time almost eternal, impossible to trace."[2] At once the constitution becomes an eternal verity and, as such, is placed beyond the reach of man to tamper with or even discuss (a convenient doctrine for representatives of a state accused of having no constitution). Discussion of all abstract concepts (for example "justice" and "law") was similarly proscribed by the State and the attempt of radical writers to initiate debate on such matters was cited as indicative of their ignorance. If the inability of radical discourse to discuss abstractions was the charge most frequently made by representatives of the state, the second most common complaint against radical writing was its vulgarity in containing an abundance of metaphor. This was remarked upon by Paine himself as he pointed out the dangers of being seduced by an image and, in the process, losing sight of the reality. Writing of Burke's style in his *Reflections*, Paine observes that "he is not affected by the reality of distress touching his heart, but by the showy resemblance of it striking his imagination. He pities the plumage, but forgets the dying bird."[3] The problems imposed upon radical writers of avoiding anything that might be construed as emotive language (a third fault laid to the radicals' charge) are of a rather different nature, for "emotive" frequently seems to correlate with "critical" in the eyes of government. Throughout the period 1780–1820, repeated government refusals to consider a range of petitions on different subjects from a wide social range of petitioners led Sir Francis Burdett to urge ministers to "come to some decision, in order that the people might know in what language the House would be inclined to lend their ears to grievances."[4] To the formulation of such guidelines it was objected that "it would only give these persons an opportunity of choosing words by which any such rule might be evaded, and then they would come to the House with language as offensive, or more so."[5]

Outside government, those who sought to discuss political and social reform were thus placed in the position of competitors suffered to join a game, the rules of which were not explained to them. Their starting point (disenfranchisement or social concern) was clear, as was their common goal (the empowerment of a wider range of the nation's population), but those who controlled the game seemed anxious to retain knowledge of how it might best be played to themselves. For the purposes of political debate, the ruling elite and those whom they ruled over spoke two different languages. Against this background, the engagement of radical novelists was not simply with a reformist agenda, but first and foremost with an exploration of the very means of its expression. How could one create a fictional radical protagonist capable of moving between the language of the rulers and the ruled without alienating either? In a decade of Treason Trials and social and political unrest centered on the issue of judicial and constitutional reform, verisimilitude demanded that a fictional protagonist whose role involved a challenge to the law of the land would sooner or later stand before the majesty of that law and be required to offer a defense of actions undertaken. What could fiction make of the legal process?

The courtroom drama, whether fictional or non-fictional, is a staple ingredient of the late twentieth-century entertainment industry. From dramatizations of the latest John Grisham novel to the O. J. Simpson trial, television viewers absorb a diet of courtroom procedure and legal language. Given the disputed legality of radical challenges to the political system in the 1790s, it is appropriate that our modern vogue for courtroom drama should start there and with *Caleb Williams*: a novel which turns on its protagonists' ability to utilize the law to their own ends.[6] The novel contains four trial scenes, the last being heavily revised by Godwin. Examination of each of these scenes in turn will show how their content is determined both by Godwin's desire to challenge existing politico-linguistic structures but also by his need to develop a language which cannot fall foul of received hegemonic ideas about radical language.

The first trial scene in the novel is the only one in which Williams himself is not the plaintiff. Yet in enabling him to act as a third-person narrator of events not of direct concern to him, I suggest that Godwin has two distinct though related purposes. Firstly, it is vital to what follows in the novel that Williams is revealed as a credible and just observer of the actions of others. Secondly, it is equally vital to Godwin's purposes (a reformatory social agenda) that his first account of the workings of the legal system does not alienate those whom it might hope to influence: Godwin's description of legal process must evince due linguistic propriety in late eighteenth-century terms. Thus, as Falkland presides as justice of the peace, Williams scans the courtroom for the reader, distancing himself from the "rabble of visitors" who clamor to see the vengeance of a dead man's brother have its due.[7] His language is remarkable for its earnest insistence only upon what all can see (crying, changes of complexion) or upon the briefest of suppositions; judgements which are no sooner articulated than their subjective nature is acknowledged: "Mr. Falkland assumed a look of determined constancy, and even seemed to increase in self-possession . . ."; "the accidental spectators . . . seemed to take little notice" (cw 115).

The peasant whose trial Williams reports is no less adroit at avoiding vulgar language (vulgar in terms both of its content and form): to eighteenth-century ears his language is a model of linguistic propriety (if Williams can be assumed to report without detracting or elaborating upon the accused's testimony). He lapses into use of metaphor and emotive conceits only in the closing stages of his defense: "he had loved the poor maiden who had been the innocent occasion of this with all his heart, but from this time he should never support the sight of her. The sight would bring a tribe of fiends in its rear. One unlucky minute had poisoned all his hopes and made life a burden to him" (cw 116). Even eighteenth-century readers with a strict notion of linguistic propriety can allow this since the accused then trembles with despair before the magnitude of his crime and the legal process: linguistic breakdown signals mental anguish (and not for the last time in the novel). Prior to this, the accused peasant has shown all due deference to his superiors in their role as enforcers of the law: "the accused added that he did not care what became of him. He had been anxious to go through the world in an inoffensive manner, and now he had the guilt of blood upon him. He did not know but it would be a kindness in them to hand him out of the way, for his conscience would reproach him as long as he lived" (cw 116). Contemporary readers with a vested interest in maintaining the political and judicial *status quo* can here bask in a refulgent glow as they contemplate the inherent rightness of "things as they are," for has not the peasant had impressed upon him the capital nature of his crime, and is he not ready to submit himself willingly to the judgement of his social superior? When the accused is discharged by Falkland and subsequently re-arraigned by "a magistrate more scrupulous or more despotic" (cw 117), Godwin's novel no longer threatens to undermine the existing hierarchy. In the second courtroom scene in the novel however, Godwin places not only Williams on trial, but the system which prosecutes him: intimating in terms that contemporary readers could not have failed to understand that satisfaction at the hands of the law depends upon one's ability to manipulate language.

At no stage in *Caleb Williams* does Godwin allow his protagonist, who loves Falkland's library and reading above all things, to indicate the scope of any of his contemporary reading matter. And yet Williams's language prior to and during his first trial must have signaled for contemporary readers that the narrative was nothing less than a fictional exploration of the feasibility of turning Paine's theories into practice. In *The Rights of Man*, as has already been indicated, Paine denies abstraction and immutability to such concepts as "constitution" and "hereditary crown;" these, he insists, are not "production[s] of Nature" but man-made concepts and as such should serve all men rather than privilege an isolated few.[8] (For the judiciary and parliamentarians, this merely provided confirmation that political agitators were unable, rather than unwilling, to discuss abstract concepts.) To assert that *Caleb Williams* is a novel about justice in the abstract is therefore to ally oneself unwittingly with Paine's opponents. Caleb momentarily sees that justice is not a Platonic ideal to be striven for in the abstract, but a Painean particular that he must confront in its specific local manifestation, and where is more fitting for this contemplation of ideality and actuality than Falkland's library: "I was conducted to the library where I had passed so many happy and so many contemplative hours, and found there Mr. Forester and three of four of the servants. . . . Every thing was calculated to suggest to me that I must trust only in the justice of the parties concerned, and had nothing to hope from their indulgence" (cw 146). "Justice" is, as Paine suggests, far from an abstract concept when its particular manifestation places an accused man on trial under the roof of his economically and socially more powerful accuser, who calls as witnesses those financially dependent upon him. For Caleb to obtain justice in this situation he must attend to its specific circumstances and not rely upon appeals to abstract principles which alone cannot save him. But the circumstances of the trial are designed precisely to throw Caleb into a mood of hopeless despondency in which resolutions regarding self-presentation are abandoned to the type of emotive hyperbole which was seen as the hallmark of radical language.

Charged with indignation at his powerlessness, Caleb rails, "I am innocent. It is in vain that circumstances are accumulated against me: there is not a person upon earth less capable than I of the things of which I am accused. I appeal to my heart; I appeal to my looks; I appeal to every sentiment my tongue ever uttered" (cw 150). The speech is shrewdly calculated by Godwin to open up the contemporary gulf between the receipt of such emotional declarations from servant and master. Caleb's language is taken as evasive, deceitful and (against an implicit Painean background), radical. When Falkland opens his verbal assault with a similar, fervent declaration of unsubstantiatable beliefs ("It has been the principle of my life never to inflict a willful injury upon any thing that lives" [cw 147]) he is told that he should not be afraid to "speak to the point" and should not apologize for himself. At the end of the trial, though it is declared that Falkland speaks "the language . . . of romance, and not of reason" (cw 155), the magistrate, Forester, insists that he "cannot but be struck with the contrast exhibited before me of the magnanimity of virtue and the obstinate, impenetrable injustice of guilt" (cw 155). As a member of the ruling aristocracy, Falkland may wander from the point with impunity: his emotional appeals are regarded as indicative of the sensibilities of a gentleman; Caleb's passion is regarded as unseemly and indicative of the sort of unfocused, uneducated mind that would overlook making appropriate arrangements for the disposal of stolen goods.

Forester's final condemnation of Williams makes explicit Godwin's construction of Williams as a representative of all those whose articulate challenge to the existing hegemony of aristocracy and judiciary would be dismissed as the wily insinuations of a social malcontent: "I see in you a new instance of that abuse which is so generally made of talents the admiration of an undiscerning public. I regard you with horror" (cw 154). In Forester's glib assertion that the swinish multitude can be easily duped but that those who rule over that multitude will save them from emotive radical oratory, Godwin perhaps maneuvers the reader into questioning what might happen if men like Caleb could master the language of their social and legal opponents. If Caleb can learn to moderate his declamatory style, might he not be able to meet representatives of the judiciary on their own terms? The answer to this question is provided in Caleb's second examination before a magistrate in which Godwin shows social class to be the main determinant affecting linguistic acceptability. A servant may learn to use the language his masters deem appropriate at any given point only to encounter the charge that such usage is a social abomination.

When the imprisoned Caleb is to be transferred from one county to another, he seizes the administrative procedure as an opportunity to present his case before a magistrate, though on this occasion he has learnt that he must moderate his language and pay close attention to the exigencies of the legal process. Accordingly, he claims that he is able to reveal a hitherto undetected murderer and that this is a specific charge the magistrates cannot overlook: "I presume, gentlemen, that you do consider it as your business to take this declaration" (cw 242). Caleb has here learnt linguistic compliance with the law: to be credible, he must demonstrate a due regard for legal process. His accompanying condemnation of Falkland is a model of clarity and betrays none of the hyperbolic flaws of his earlier rhetoric. For the first time in his account of events, Williams pares them down to a logically impeccable train of reasoning: "I now declare more than [the guilt of my accuser], that this man is a murderer, that I detected his criminality, and that for that reason he is determined to deprive me of life" (cw 242). In his only reference to abstract emotions in the speech, Williams is at pains to avoid the charge that passion has got the better of him: "all patience and submission have their limits." He has re-fashioned himself from radical to rational man and expects a concomitant improvement in his treatment.

The magistrate needs only to establish Williams's hireling status in Falkland's household to make Williams's new-found form of expression a perversion of established class structures: "A fine time of it indeed it would be, if, when gentlemen of six thousand a year take up their servants for robbing them, those servants could trump up such allegations as these, and could get any magistrate or court of justice to listen to them!" (cw 243). The last clause is telling: Williams's allegation is dangerous because it is now couched in a language previously the preserve of his oppressors. If the magistrate in this scene, like his real parliamentary counterparts, can no longer dismiss petitioners on the grounds that their language violates accepted linguistic codes, then the apparatuses of state control are open to scrutiny, and criticism. The magistrate seeks to repress Caleb's challenge to existing legal and linguistic hegemonies by maintaining that that power nexus is all that prevents the state from collapsing into anarchy: "there would be a speedy end to all order and good government, if fellows that trample upon ranks and distinctions in this atrocious sort, were upon any consideration suffered to get off" (cw 243). The "distinctions" that Caleb has "trampled" upon are not only of rank, but the linguistic registers thought to define different ranks of society. Established government, as represented both physically and verbally by the magistrate is unquestionably "good," whilst the "order" that he sees about him is one in which the social gradations of the body politic have their most literal expression in a linguistic hierarchy: for Caleb to meet the magistrate linguistically on his own terms is a violation of both linguistic and social norms.

Desperately seeking to re-iterate his understanding of what is and is not possible under the law, Caleb asks the fulminating magistrate "do you refuse, sir, to attend to the particulars of the charge I allege?" (cw 243). At this point the magistrate illustrates his ability to change the rules of the game at a stroke.

Affirming his refusal to initiate legal investigation on the words of a "servant," he yet offers Caleb the chance to produce witnesses who can testify to the truth of his allegations. Williams is dumbfounded. Though he has learnt an appropriate linguistic presentation of his own case, he cannot yet marry this with enough confidence to challenge the language of another, though the magistrate's question is clearly flawed. Any witnesses to the murder could only be other servants, liable, like Williams, to charges of malevolence: had Williams an aristocratic witness to the events he describes, he would not be before the magistrate in the first place. Williams's second direct experience of the law's intransigence in the face of linguistic assault is thus quite distinct from his first trial: there Williams's language is designed to be as emotionally charged and hyperbolic as radical language was alleged to be. In his second trial Williams has learned to dispense with emotional appeals and has replaced them with an appropriation of his oppressors' linguistic norms. He lacks the experience and the confidence, however, to direct the overall movement of a courtroom, an ability that Godwin would reserve putting to the test until the novel's concluding trial. Finding an explanation for Williams's more finely honed rhetorical skills in his third and final trial, Godwin toyed with the idea of making explicit a link between Williams's prison reading and that of the decade's most persistent agitant for linguistic and legal reform, as an examination of a passage cancelled in the first edition of *Caleb Williams* will show.

As Williams recuperates from his persecution in an "obscure market-town in Wales" (cw 254), he recounts how he fills his leisure hours. In all editions following the first, Godwin elaborates upon Williams's reading matter at this time. The resultant passage is worth quoting at length for the striking similarity that can be observed between this and the declared reading habits of the veteran of 1790s treason trials, Horne Tooke. Williams tells us that, feeling the desire for an "additional and vigorous pursuit,"

> I met by accident, in a neglected corner of the house of one of my neighbours, with a general dictionary of four of the northern languages. This incident gave a direction to my thoughts. In my youth I had not been inattentive to languages. I determined to attempt, at least for my own use, an etymological analysis of the English language. I easily perceived that this pursuit had one advantage to

a person in my situation. . . . I procured other dictionaries. In my incidental reading, I noted the manner in which words were used, and applied these remarks to the illustration of my general enquiry (cw 328 n.281).

An "etymological analysis of the English language" is a new departure for Williams who has never evinced such interests before, yet it is appropriate that this becomes a focus of Williams's studies in all editions after the first of 1794, in which year John Horne Tooke went on trial for high treason; dedicating the second volume of the *Diversions of Purley* (1805) to his trial jury of 1794, and centering the text upon an imaginary dialogue between himself and Sir Francis Burdett, a radical member of Parliament whose unsuccessful attempts to receive clear guidelines for the linguistic formulation of parliamentary petitions have already been mentioned. Tooke's belief "that intellectual confusion and political oppression were efficiently interwoven" led him to devote much of his time as a student to studying the etymology of the English language.[9] It was a study that he had already attempted to turn into the basis of a legal defense, when put on trial in 1777, on the charge that he had claimed the King's troops had committed murder in an advertisement soliciting subscriptions for the widows and orphans of those soldiers killed at the Battle of Lexington. Upon his conviction and in his subsequent appeal summarized in *A Letter to J. Dunning* (1778), Horne Tooke disputes the accepted status of many parts of speech, questioning "with jealous watchfulness, the meaning of words to prevent being entrapped by them."[10] The importance of his method to radical political debate in the 1790s can be clearly illustrated with reference to Horne Tooke's exploration, in the *Diversions of Purley,* of the word "rights."

Just as mention of the word "culture" made Goering wish to reach for his gun, so Canning is credited with claiming that on hearing the word "rights" he was prepared for "some desolating doctrine. It seems to me to be productive of some wide spreading ruin, of some wasting desolation."[11] In the *Diversions* Horne Tooke insists that the etymological origins of "rights" lie in the Latin verb "regere" and that, as this translates as "ordered" or "directed," use of the term "rights" is symptomatic of man's natural propensity to develop rational systems. Where Canning associates use of the term with radicalism and therefore chaos, Horne Tooke claims it to be the quintessential expression of man's rational faculties.

Hence etymologies may be cited in support of radical political argument. In the second volume of the *Diversions*, the fictive conversational exchange between the author and Sir Francis Burdett includes elaborate discussion of etymologies. In devoting his time to "an etymological analysis of the English language," Caleb Williams is therefore linked with political agitants during the 1790s, for whom "justice" was not only far from an abstract ideal, but a word, like any other, with a particular history; a history that was part of its contemporary meaning. The importance of Caleb's linguistic study is the power that it gives him in his final confrontation with Falkland. After the first edition of *Caleb Williams* in 1794, Godwin's explicit account of Caleb's etymological studies is reflective of an author who had sat beside Holcroft in the 1794 Treason Trials, and who knew that judicial and linguistic hegemony were inexorably intertwined.

To explore Williams's final encounter with the law in both Godwin's original ending and that very different conclusion which was ultimately published is, I would suggest, to trace Godwin's rapidly developing ideas about the importance of a mastery of legal language and precedent during 1794. Godwin's diary indicates that his first completed draft of the novel was finished on 30 April but, being dissatisfied with the ending, Godwin produced a revised version of this from 4–8 May. Four days later, on 12 May 1794, Horne Tooke, Holcroft and ten others were arrested and charged with high treason: a government ploy to attempt to prevent the holding of a radical convention organized jointly by the London Corresponding Society and the Society for Constitutional Information. Given the politically charged atmosphere in late April-early May, Godwin's revised ending is arguably a statement of faith not only in the eventual triumph of reformist politics, but in the validity of the linguistic war the radicals continued to wage. And in what looks remarkably like a case of life imitating art, the October trials would see Horne Tooke share the stand with the counsel for the defense, Erskine, reportedly reducing the Attorney General to tears, just as Godwin's final published version of *Caleb Williams* sees Williams have an emotional and legal impact upon the magistrate's proceedings.

In the build-up to both his cancelled ending (hereafter referred to as ending 1) and his final published ending of the novel (ending 2), Godwin prepares us from the outset for a very different approach from Williams to the judicial system. Instead of making general appeals to the magistrate's abstract sense of justice, as he had previously done, Williams now grounds his case in the specific detail of legal requirement. The relevant passage is worth quoting in its entirety in order that Williams's newfound acquaintance with legal precedent might be appreciated:

> Upon what pretence did he refuse my deposition? I was in every respect a competent witness. I was of age to understand the nature of an oath; I was in my perfect senses; I was untarnished by the verdict of any jury, or the sentence of any judge. His private opinion of my character could not alter the law of the land. I demanded to be confronted with Mr. Falkland, and I was well assured I should substantiate the charge to the satisfaction of the whole world. If he did not think it proper to apprehend him upon my single testimony, I should be satisfied if he only sent him notice of the charge and summoned him to appear (cw 269–70).

Williams's language is, for the first time in his encounter with a magistrate, focused purely upon the technical features of his case. He now offers a "deposition" and to "substantiate charges" rather than making vague, unsubstantiatable claims against his former employer and, through him, society's hierarchical structure generally. Furthermore, Williams demonstrates his newfound realization that the pursuit of justice is not the prerogative of the magistrate: he is merely a servant of the law and his private likes and dislikes cannot alter Williams's legal entitlements. In the final sentence, Williams shows a keen grasp of a nice legal distinction: he may initiate a summons even if the magistrate is unwilling to apprehend Falkland directly. Significantly, he then refuses the magistrate's ruse of drawing him into discussion of Falkland's health: "to all these representations my answer was short" (cw 270). After direct experience of two trials and indirect experience of a third, Williams is finally able to meet representatives of the law upon their own legal, that is to say, linguistic, terms.

The most significant difference between endings 1 and 2 is that, having made such a focused opening of his case before the magistrate, Williams then forgets himself in ending 1 and reverts to type: making impassioned pleas that are not focused upon any particular charge, nor suggestive of a course that the law might take: "I said, I stood there for justice. I observed that it was of consequence, in a degree beyond any thing they could suspect, that justice should be done. I intreated them by every thing that was honourable, I conjured them by every thing that was tremendous, to deal impartially and truly" (cw 336–7). This is not a specific charge to which the magistrate can make Falkland answerable and, worse still for Williams's case, in his specific request that he be dealt with "impartially and truly" he implies that the law is sometimes the opposite: partisan and a smokescreen for deceit. He himself acknowledges the "rapidity, perturbation and vehemence that were absolutely alarming to my hearers" (cw 337). There is therefore little to be wondered at when the magistrate demands silence and insists that Williams has been heard "too long. Never was the dignity of administrative justice in any instance insulted with so bare faced and impudent a forgery!" (cw 337). The dignity of the law is of course compromised if trials can become places where unsubstantiated charges and general declarations of principle are aired by a ranting plaintiff. The law must deal with specific events, and in this regard the magistrate has no option but to consider Williams a "forgery" since, as Williams originally represented himself, he demonstrated a highly specific knowledge of appropriate legal behavior, and gave every indication that this would be followed through in a court of law. Appropriately, after Williams's indecorous outburst, ending 1 closes with a total breakdown in his ability to communicate clearly to the reader. Whilst indicative of his extreme mental anguish, the tortured syntax and cryptic meaning are also, at this point, fitting symbols of Williams's ultimate failure to control his own language and influence that of others throughout the book. In ending 2, Godwin gives Williams the degree of linguistic control necessary to influence his auditors' emotional reaction and the impromptu court's legal proceeding.

Whereas Williams in ending 1 is unnerved enough by the sight of Falkland to launch into unsuitable rhetoric, that same sight of Falkland in ending 2 leads Williams to a moment of self-discovery: "now or never was the time for me to redeem my future life from endless woe" (cw 272). Williams recalls that he is called upon "immediately to act" and, crucially, this realization comes as part of a reminder to himself that he is in front of a magistrate where Falkland is "to answer a charge of murder." Williams thus never loses sight of the specificity of legal procedure in ending 2: he is in front of a magistrate not to indict the corrupt hegemony of landed interest and legal power of which Falkland is the living embodiment, but to place verifiable charges leveled against one individual before those able to act upon them. In his own words, he tells a "plain and unadulterated tale" (cw 275) that makes continuous reference to Falkland's noble nature, and in a final *volte face,* he confesses himself bowed by the realization that he has acted irrationally in raising the spectre of his relationship with Falkland once more, when this could have been forgotten: "I came to accuse, but am compelled to applaud . . . am myself the basest and most odious of mankind . . . Do with me as you please! I ask no favour. Death would be a kindness, compared to what I feel!" (cw 275). Whilst this expresses genuine remorse, it is also an expression of superb oratorical skill, for Williams is not on trial for his life and knows that Falkland cannot level a capital charge against him. Williams bows to the power of the court whilst his language triumphantly announces the law's inability, as an institution, to further what is now his dearest wish: a re-run of the last four days. Like Horne Tooke, Williams's language finally announces to the establishment that here is a radical who has learnt to play the establishment game, to the extent that he can now challenge the limits of the law to punish and contain him.

Significantly, ending 2 closes with a declaration of the importance of finding the "right" words in order that "the world may at least not hear and repeat a half-told and mangled tale" (cw 277). Williams has gained the *desiderata* of those radicals who, in May 1794, moved towards a similarly climatic confrontation with the legal system: he has mounted a successful legal defense because he has mounted a radical linguistic offensive against the vested interests of the court. Yet are there limits to empowerment? Could all reformers ultimately achieve justice before the law? In *The Wrongs of Woman: or, Maria* (1798), long before twentieth-century feminist linguistic theory canvassed the idea that women are disadvantaged by being forced to use alien (that is, male) linguistic structures, Wollstonecraft explores precisely this dilemma.

The politico-linguistic challenge to the established hierarchy articulated by Paine in *Rights of Man* had direct bearing upon the formulation of Wollstonecraft's radicalism, not in the obvious sense that *A Vindication of the Rights of Woman* asks Paine to consider the gendered implications of his text, but rather in the way in which Paine's questioning of the use of terms such as "constitution" and "hereditary crown" crystallized for Wollstonecraft both a class-based and gender-based inequality in language. An examination of her criticism of accepted usage of the term "rights" and "divine right" will demonstrate her basic frustrations with received linguistic practice, and as the etymology of "rights" was something that particularly concerned Horne Tooke (above), Wollstonecraft's response to the term is not only illustrative of her problematic encounters with male radical language, but is germane to further consideration of Maria's presentation of herself before the law.

In *A Vindication*, Wollstonecraft urges that women be freed from "all restraint by allowing them to participate in the inherent rights of mankind."[12] Like Horne Tooke, Wollstonecraft sees "rights" as simply an established rational order and she implies that it cannot be reasonable to deny a large part of the populace participation in the life of the state. Universal participation in the governing mechanisms of society may however have to "wait, perhaps, till kings and nobles, enlightened by reason, and, preferring the real dignity of man to childish state, throw off their gaudy hereditary trappings" (VRW 22). The hegemonic order which oppresses women is coterminous with that which subjugates the majority of the people. Paine also focuses on hereditary interests: "Mr. Burke talks about what he calls an hereditary crown, as if it were some production of Nature; or as if, like Time, it had a power to operate, not only independently, but in spite of man; or as if it were a thing or a subject universally consented to. Alas! it has none of those properties, but is the reverse of them all. It is a thing in imagination."[13] He reminds his audience that the potency of such terms lies in the awe in which they are held and is not dependent upon some immutable quality in the institution of an hereditary crown itself. Treating all titles of church and state in the same way (pointing to man-made origins designed to meet the exigencies of particular circumstances) Paine, like Wollstonecraft, rejects all idea of the established social hierarchy as a precious finely-balanced instrument brought to the peak of perfection, which one recalibrates at one's peril.

Unlike Paine however, Wollstonecraft sees all hereditary systems as enshrining not only social but sexual injustice and links discussion of inheritance to that of divine right, attacking "tyrants of every denomination, from the weak king to the weak father of a family;" suggesting parallels between the "divine right of husbands" to the "divine right of kings" (vrw 5, 41, 157). Whereas Paine, Horne Tooke and Godwin focus primarily on the social injustice they see enshrined in such terms as "hereditary crown" and "divine right," Wollstonecraft's power-based comparison of husbands and kings protests that even the weakest male member of the proletariat enjoys a status in law that is denied to women of all classes. Recognizing this, the last completed chapter of *The Wrongs of Woman* focuses on its protagonist's attempt to make legal language and precedent her ally rather than an instrument of her oppression in virtue of both her class and gender.

Wollstonecraft's construction of this chapter is a structural embodiment of society's failure to give women a voice. The first sentence's reference to the "dogs of law" not only turns Maria into a pursued hind, but echoes a perverse satisfaction at the thought of battle: "Cry 'Havoc, and let slip the dogs of war."[14] The conclusion of either metaphorical train of thought is that the parties to the struggle are grossly unevenly matched: those who unleash the dogs generally do so from an easy conviction that they will win. A counsel for Venables opens the courtroom proceedings, and they are closed with the judge's pronouncement on Maria's case: she is thus doubly oppressed by linguistic conventions; having to present her case in a language acceptable to the court whilst being physically constrained by the dominance of male speakers who are part of the legal system she fights against. At the root of Venables's attack is a charge that could only be leveled at a woman: "after the birth of her child, her conduct was so strange, and a melancholy malady having afflicted one of the family, which delicacy forbade dwelling on, it was necessary to confine her" (ww 178). The same word, "confinement" ironically describes physical limitations placed upon Maria in virtue of both her pregnancy and her imprisonment in a private mental asylum. In a male-dominated society, Wollstonecraft implies that the perceived effects of the first confinement are used to sanction the latter: pregnancy thus becomes a malady as far as those sitting in judgement on Maria are concerned. Against this background, Maria's declaration is read to the court. So hostile does Wollstonecraft view the legal system as being towards women, that even Maria chooses to marginalize her own language. Indeed, in contrast with Caleb Williams's three separate defenses of himself, it is not incredible to suggest that Maria's one courtroom appearance, in which she feels compelled to deny her own voice, is Wollstonecraft's indication of the marginality of women to legal proceedings. *Caleb Williams* may have initiated a vogue for courtroom dramas across Europe, but Wollstonecraft saw little applicability for this model to discussion of the plight of a woman seeking divorce.

Asked to predict the lexical content of Maria's declaration, a reader might reasonably suppose to find the word "rights" at some point, but it is strikingly absent from Wollstonecraft's frame of reference in the text. The reason for its absence is to be found at the conclusion of Chapter One where Maria vents the thought: "Was not the world a vast prison, and women born slaves?" The text is surely a conscious echo of Rousseau's famous assertion that "Man is born free, but everywhere is in chains." In rejecting Rousseau's fundamental belief in the freedom man might enjoy under a differently constituted political system, Wollstonecraft insists that, under any reformist system currently envisaged, women will always be second-class citizens. If one is born a slave in an inescapable prison, there is little point in talking of "rights." Maria's courtroom battle is thus as revealing in its lexical omissions as its inclusions, for Maria cannot even use a term like "rights" despite the fact that it had been given concrete definition by Horne Tooke.

Such attention to the linguistic detail of Wollstonecraft's text leads to a proliferation of puzzling questions about her representation of women before the law. Whereas *Caleb Williams* draws attention to its protagonist's efforts to reconcile his own integrity with the forging of a language acceptable to his social and legal superiors, *The Wrongs of Woman* seems to insist that any such accommodation is a betrayal of the individual concerned. Accepting that Wollstonecraft's text articulates a very real discrepancy in eighteenth-century English law's treatment of men and women, why is her protagonist less capable than Godwin's of learning to manipulate the law to her own ends? In refusing Maria the ability to articulate the injustice she has suffered in terms the legal establishment must respond to (as Williams's charge finally demands a response), is there not a danger that Wollstonecraft may be taken to indicate not only that male and female radicals inhabit different linguistic spheres, but that women are incapable of learning to move beyond the limitations society imposes upon them?

If *Caleb Williams* shows how radical writers and their fictional creations could develop a rhetoric more acceptable to the ruling hierarchy they challenged, *The Wrongs of Woman* initially seems to offer that politico-legal hierarchy conclusive evidence of radical intransigence. With its description of heightened emotion, its blurring of dreams and actualities, and a heavy dose of Gothic atmosphere, the novel's opening page embraces all of the flaws with which radical writing was charged. These are still very much in evidence when, in Maria's closing testimony, an appeal is made to the "justice and humanity of the jury" whose "private judgment must be allowed to modify laws" (ww 181). Extraordinarily, Maria's testimony here invites her jury to replace accepted judicial norms with her own unmodified radical agenda. Yet the last paragraph of the novel that Wollstonecraft completed shows her to be perfectly aware that emotive, metaphor-laden language invited instant dismissal from the political and legal establishments.

Having heard Maria's case, the judge alludes to "the fallacy of letting women plead their feelings" (ww 181). In denying Maria any way of articulating the injustice she has suffered other than a passionate outpouring of feeling, Wollstonecraft's message is surely a more complex one than the simple observation that the law marginalizes women and therefore silences them. Throughout the text, the intrusion of settings and characters from the world of the Gothic novel compel the reader to the realization that true horror lies not in a recoil from the supernatural, but in the conditions of the oppressed in England in the 1790s. How is Maria's first-person narration able to articulate this crucial difference when behavioral norms are presented to her through the literature of sensibility? Where Caleb Williams prepares to meet his oppressors by understanding the language they use, Maria is merely confirmed in her emotive linguistic usage by reading matter such as Rousseau's *Heloïse* (ww 95). That Wollstonecraft considered such texts to be partially responsible for women's arrested intellectual and emotional development is apparent in *A Vindication* where she rails against "books of instruction" written for women by men which "have had the same tendency as more frivolous productions." Assuming the latter to be novels, they are among the productions that lead Wollstonecraft to her "profound conviction that the neglected education of my fellow-creatures is the grand source of the misery I deplore." Viewed against this background, Maria's experience in court emerges not just as a symbol of the silencing or marginalization of radical women but as a powerful indictment of the linguistic precedents through which such women learn to articulate their grievances. The language of sensibility through which Maria's counsel pleads for justice is as fatal to her case as the emotive outbursts of Caleb Williams in all trials bar Godwin's last revision. And surely the irony of the situation is not lost on Wollstonecraft: aware of the radicals' struggle to find an appropriate form of expression for their political and social grievances, she must deny Maria the ability to articulate injustice that she herself possesses. Maria's situation can thus be presented to the reader as a particularly ugly manifestation of a norm in respect of which Wollstonecraft's own circumstances will always be an exception.

The circumscription of Maria's language in virtue of her gender thus acts as a fitting symbol for the incongruity of assuming she can be treated as equal to a man in a court of law. A male counsel will read her words for her, denying quite literally that women have a right to be heard. The emotive pleading Maria forces him to articulate on her behalf demonstrates that contemporary linguistic conventions are doubly oppressive to women seeking to challenge the status quo. Their habitual silencing ensures that, when they do find a voice, their articulation of the injustices which they suffer will be reliant upon linguistic registers entirely alien to the law. The net result is a questioning of the status of radical male and female agitants before the law. Clearly all radicals are unequal (to their political masters) but some are more unequal than others. Godwin's revised conclusion to *Caleb Williams* affirms his faith that society's oppressed could learn to speak the language of their oppressors. Implicit in Wollstonecraft's text is a realization that, if women radicals are to be heard, they must learn a language more acceptable in both its intellectual and emotional content. But readers of Godwin's and Wollstonecraft's texts surely also intuit something more from the differing forms of the two works. Both *Caleb Williams* and *The Wrongs of Woman* are first-person narratives regarding a search for justice, but there a similarity of form ends. Godwin's text is an innovative psychological thriller; a story of detection and pursuit; and as the paper has shown, a courtroom drama. Wollstonecraft expresses impatience with women's reading matter in *A Vindication* yet she cannot entirely escape the mechanisms of Gothic fiction (a form popularly produced and consumed by women) in her own fictional work. Both authors highlight not only the difficulty of forging an "intellectual vernacular" but, in their contrasting approaches to the problem, they vividly demonstrate the greater difficulties faced by radical women writers.

Notes

1. Olivia Smith, *The Politics of Language 1791–1819* (Clarendon: Oxford, 1984), x. Hereafter referred to simply as Smith.

2. *A Complete Collection of State Trials* compiled by William Cobbett and later by T. B. Howells, 34 vols., xxii, 384.

3. Maurice D. Conway ed., *The Writings of Thomas Paine* 4 vols., (1894–6), ii. 288.

4. Hansard's *Parliamentary Debates*, xxxv. 993.

5. Ibid., xxxv. 994.

6. Henry Crabb Robinson comments in his diary for 1830 that a Neapolitan drama recently seen "is bad enough certainly, but it is worthy remark how this adoption of legal incidents as the source of romantic and dramatic interest, which began with Godwin, has thus run from one end of Europe to the other." Cited in *Caleb Williams: The World's Classics* ed. David McCracken (Oxford University Press, 1982), xiv.

7. William Godwin, *Caleb Williams* ed. Pamela Clemit in *The Collected Novels and Memoirs of William Godwin,* General Editor Mark Philp (Pickering: London, 1992) 8 vols.: vol. 3, 114. All subsequent references to *Caleb Williams* are to the Pickering edition and will be cited in the text by *CW* and page number.

8. Maurice D. Conway ed., *The Writings of Thomas Paine* 4 vols., (1894–6), ii. 363.

9. Smith, 111.

10. Ibid., 112.

11. Ibid., 114–5.

12. Mary Wollstonecraft, *A Vindication of the Rights of Woman*, ed. Carol H. Poston, 2nd ed. (Norton: New York, 1988), 175. All subsequent page references to the *Vindication* are to this edition and will be cited in the text by *VRW* and page number.

13. Maurice D. Conway ed., *The Writings of Thomas Paine* 4 vols., (1894–6), ii. 363.

14. Mary Wollstonecraft, *The Wrongs of Woman; or, Maria* ed. Emma Rees-Mogg in *The Works of Mary Wollstonecraft*, General Editors Janet Todd and Marilyn Butler (Pickering: London, 1989) 7 vols.: vol. 1, 178. All subsequent references to *The Wrongs of Woman* are to the Pickering edition and will be cited in the text by *WW* and page number. "Cry 'Havoc'" is part of Mark Anthony's soliloquy at the close of Shakespeare's *Julius Caesar* III.i.

Radcliffe, Godwin, and Self-Possession in the 1790s

Barbara M. Benedict

In 1794, William Godwin was reading Ann Radcliffe's *The Mysteries of Udolpho* while writing *Caleb Williams*.[1] From Radcliffe, Godwin borrowed not only the archetypal struggle between youth and authority, and the Gothic mood of brooding oppression, but also Radcliffe's central trope: curiosity. Both books are plotted around the consequences of unregulated inquiry, and notwithstanding their enlightened philosophies, both portray curiosity as a cultural ambition that dangerously sexualizes identity and threatens the very integrity of the self.

Curiosity has long produced contrary responses in Western culture. Deplored by religious conservatives as a sacrilegious usurpation of God's prerogative, it has also been represented as man's noblest trait, the impulse driving him to exploration, discovery, science, and improvement.[2] In the Christian tradition, curiosity impels Eve to eat the forbidden fruit, stimulates the lust of the eyes, and excites the Athenian itch. Representing curiosity alternately as a threat to established institutions and as a promise of progress, traditional discourse both lauds the Aristotelian urge to know and denigrates the impertinent desire to inquire. For the writers of 1794, the familiar issue took on added significance for they were living in a period of post-empirical disillusion, when it seemed that the methods of science could not answer the problems of society.[3] Under the pressure of contemporary debates, these novels transform a traditional

—89—

exploration of the limits of curiosity into a political drama about what happens to identity in an environment rent by tyranny and oppression. The topical issue of the conflict between interpretations of mankind's nature as nobly free or as perilously wild is thus dramatized through reworking a traditional discourse testing the limits, consequences, and rewards of curiosity. Curiosity expresses the struggle to define the self for oneself, and the correlative fear of disintegration of identity in a post-revolutionary period.[4]

Since, in the years following the French Revolution, as Ronald Paulson has explained, all Gothic fictions assumed an ideological dimension, these two novels share political attitudes.[5] They both dramatize the great conflict for English liberals between the ideal of all humans' intrinsic freedom and the nightmare of unrestrained passion.[6] Despite obvious differences, notably Radcliffe's apparent conservatism and Godwin's notorious radicalism, the two novels alike uphold the Jacobin tenets of detestation of patriarchal tyranny, advocacy of sexual egalitarianism, and reverence for reason over passion or unreason—be this superstition as in *Udolpho* or prejudice as in *Caleb Williams*.[7] Godwin even names his heroic sentimental symbol Emily as Radcliffe does. While condemning despotism in the climate of horrified reaction to the Terror, Radcliffe and Godwin also reprove sentimental excess, "ill-governed sensibility," by depicting the dangers to virtue, sanity, and control offered by sentimental feeling.[8] "Above all, my dear Emily," warns St. Aubert on his death bed, "do not indulge in the pride of fine feeling, the romantic error of amiable minds. Those, who really possess sensibility, ought early to be taught, that it is a dangerous quality" (79). Valancourt's emotionalism pollutes his virtue as Emily St. Aubert hazards her virginity in *Udolpho*, while the romantic passion Caleb and Emily Melville feel for Falkland costs both of them their self-determination.

Advocating a rationalism that resists submission to the body, both writers laud mental cultivation as the route to freedom. After her father's death, Emily escapes grief through intellectual exercise: "it was now that she understood the full value of the education she had received from St. Aubert, for in cultivating her understanding he had secured her an asylum from indolence, without recourse to dissipation, and rich and varied amusement and information, independent of society, from which her situation secluded her" (99). Emily's "self-command"—her ability to restrain her feelings and listen to her reason—

protects her from the contagion of her aunt's and Montoni's society and makes her superior to the sentimentally indulgent Valancourt (5). Like Caleb, despite imprisonment and physical debility, Emily remains mentally free, as long as she avoids conventional ideas.

Nonetheless, as I have argued elsewhere, in practice Radcliffe endorses a sentimental perception she ostensibly reproves, and recently Claudia L. Johnson has shown how sentimental responses garner applause when exhibited by men.[9] In both novels, the foremost sentimental motif is the use of sexual coercion to symbolize political despotism. In *Udolpho*, Emily's adventures center on her prohibited marriage; attempts to compel her to marry undesirable suitors highlight Montoni's political machinations. The struggle between the political world of the tyrant and the personal world of the female is emblematized by the syncopated discussion between Emily and Montoni: impatient to perform more combat, he ignores her demands for freedom over her own body (360–63). Emily's sexuality thus symbolizes liberation from slavery. In *Caleb Williams*, every catastrophe results from a dispute over the (usually female) body. It is Tyrrel's treatment of Emily Melvile that causes Falkland's reproof and the consequent murder; a fight over a woman causes the murder for which a peasant is tried before Falkland and that leads to his confession of his crime to Caleb. The female body is thus the site of oppression.

This sexualized oppression galvanizes the two novelists' most significant similarity: their ambiguous treatment of their propelling motive, curiosity.[10] Curiosity establishes fresh identity by deconstructing conventional roles. These two heroes' inquiry enacts their liberation from repressive custom and opens their way to social equality. By questioning Montoni's behavior and motives, Emily challenges his usurped authority, exposes his wickedness, and asserts her probity. Caleb's probing eventually reveals Falkland's crimes and the corresponding flaws in the social structure that supports him. This portrayal of free inquiry—the individual challenge to the status quo—marks the two books as post-revolutionary rejections of political oppression. Nonetheless, both authors also depict inquiry as compromising not only to society, but to the virtue and integrity of the heroes themselves. Although Emily and Caleb display courageous independence in interrogating Montoni and Falkland, their questions reveal morally suspect desire that mirrors that of their oppressors—the desire for power, for domination, for superiority, for property.[11] Because Montoni repeatedly ignores, attacks, or evades Emily's curiosity and she must take recourse in silence, she is restored to her integrity as submissive sufferer, but Caleb's success transforms him into his own enemy. Releasing yet imprisoning, these heroes' curiosity is at once the sign of the free-born mind and of irrational, undisciplined appetite. This paradoxical quality expresses the contemporary tension between enlightenment and traditional ideals.

This trait of intellectual ambition or pride is traditionally condemned in both myth and English literature: characters from Pandora and Eve to Marlowe's Doctor Faustus fall because of it. Associated with the temptation to taste forbidden knowledge, curiosity connotes the satanic rejection of the God-given world and the indulgence of unlicensed, sexual appetite. Like desire, it is predicated on lack, on the absence of what is desired, knowledge. Thus, in these novels, the bold confrontation of the status quo implies an impious quest for spiritual freedom in a fallen world—the Gothic quest itself. This quest rejects material reality revealed through empirical science for its negative, the world of wonder, idealism, irrationality, available to the popular imagination through folk tradition. Both novels indeed dramatize the limitations of empiricism in a world always partly inexplicable. As Terry Castle has argued, Radcliffe spectralizes her others.[12] Representing the irrepressible, irrational shadows of the mind, these spirits threaten to possess her heroine Emily; she must use empirical observation and reason to combat them. Although she triumphs, even at her wedding a ceremonial tapestry celebrating "necromantic feats" symbolizes her partial inhabitation in unseen spheres. Similarly, Godwin infuses Caleb's curiosity with a mesmerizing, anti-rational power: it is a "demon" that "possesse[s]" him at the expense of his life and sanity, rather than a tool that he can use.[13] By depicting curiosity as a trap and an escape, these novels articulate the tension between the contemporary ideal of transparency—the conviction that if everything were revealed by clear questions and honest answers, all would be reasonable and controllable—and the traditional, pessimistic conviction that what is hidden is wisely hidden, a philosophical fear growing as the century drew to a close.[14]

The double view of curiosity in these fictions reflects their mediating function as bridges between philosophical treatises and entertainment for middle-class and servant audiences, familiar with Biblical indictments against undisciplined curiosity.[15] Godwin refers explicitly to this function when he defines his novel as aimed at "persons whom books of philosophy and science are never likely to reach."[16] Indeed, he alludes to the popular tradition in his 1832 preface when he records playing with the resemblance between his idea and Bluebeard, a story that first appeared in English in 1729, but was made famous by George Colman's farce, *Blue-Beard; or Female Curiosity!* in 1798: "Caleb Williams was the wife, who in spite of warning, persisted in his attempts to discover the forbidden secret" (340). Radcliffe not only wrote for readers of her class and gender, but simultaneously published verse in periodicals bought by the same audiences.[17] The tales inserted in both novels, Radcliffe's romance of Lady Blanche De Villefort and Godwin's story of Emily Melvile, resemble in their typical characterology, self-enclosed narratives, and sentimental motifs the republished vignettes culled from Sterne, Mackenzie, Goldsmith, and other sentimental writers littering the popular market at the end of the century.[18] Moreover, just as both writers mix indictments and endorsements of sentimentalism, both move between narrative modes: Radcliffe employs poetry, meditation, description, and narrative while Godwin, less heterogeneously, merges reportage and fictional autobiography. Their medley of forms permits a medley of messages characteristic of the genre of the novel, founded on the audience's multiple desires for novelty, sensation, and revelation.[19] These novels are intended to sell: they are commodities purveying instruction through delight to an audience accustomed to buying culture. This fluidity of genre is mirrored by the instability of the Gothic heroes, moving between idealized exempla and cautionary protagonists.

Both Radcliffe and Godwin explore the way curiosity demarcates and dismantles identity on several fictional levels: plot, characterization, and metaphor. The books possess different structures. Telling her tale through a third-person narrator, Radcliffe recounts a romance ending in marriage whereas Godwin, through an autobiographical speaker, recounts a tragedy ending in death. Yet both books confuse the reliability of the narrative. Caleb, as Robert Kiely points out, deceives Falkland by manipulative questions even while asseverating to the reader his naivete, while Radcliffe's narrative viewpoint wavers between describing Emily pictorially, expressing her imperfectly informed thoughts in a version of *style indirect libre*, and satirizing her credulity.[20] In a typical passage, the point of view slides from that of the heroine to that of a spectator:

> When the dreadful hour arrived, in which the remains of St. Aubert were to be taken from her for ever, she went alone to the chamber to look upon his countenance yet once again, and La Voisin, who had waited patiently below stairs, till her despair should subside . . . forbore to interrupt the indulgence of [her grief], till surprise . . . and then apprehension overcame his delicacy, and he went to lead her from the chamber . . . and found Emily lying senseless across the foot of the bed . . . (87).

Radcliffe begins the passage from Emily's perspective—she is the one who deems the hour "dreadful"—and then shifts to that of Voisin, whose "surprise" and "apprehension" prompt the reader to similar feelings, and thus away from identification with Emily to identification with his shock at encountering her "senseless" body. By rejecting limpid empirical narrative, the fictions thus themselves unsettle their own simple polemics on how to judge the characters or the action.

As a variety of passion, the opponent of enlightened reason, curiosity is a fundamental motive in both novels. Both plots center on the discovery by a disenfranchised seeker—young woman or young servant—of a concealed past that liberates their identity. In *The Mysteries of Udolpho*, Radcliffe's heroine Emily St. Aubert, orphaned and stripped of her rightful estate, is given over to the care of a tyrannical guardian Signor Montoni, ambitious, restless, mercenary, a perpetrator both of civil wars and domestic discord. Through observation and inquiry, Emily discovers that he is a robber and a murderer, and that she herself is by birth the legal owner of his estates. After a series of sensational adventures and rational decisions, including relinquishing her claim on the property in order to preserve her life, Emily wins not only her own estate but that of her father: law conquers violence. A subplot dramatizes the alternative to her self-disciplined submission through the figure of Signora Laurentini di Udolpho, who commits murder for sexual passion and becomes insane. While Emily triumphs through her rational virtue, her superstitious curiosity torments her throughout the novel. Her trials arise as much from the transgressive probings of her mind as from the tyranny of her guardian.

Caleb Williams similarly recounts the exposure of murder, the madness murder produces, and the (belated) restoration of social justice through curiosity.[21] Caleb, observing the melancholy of his master Falkland, inquires persistently into his past finally to discover him to be a murderer thrice over; this hidden knowledge eventually frees Caleb from his dependant role and enables him to stand equal with his master. Falkland, however, is a murderer obsessed by his secret, and as Caleb himself realizes, equality with a murderer makes Caleb into a murderer himself. Caleb's curiosity liberates him from servitude and dooms him to wandering without a social identity. In the traditional characterology of seventeenth-century satire, the types of the credulous and the curious man are linked as believers in an unsubstantiated world.[22] Both Emily and Caleb suffer from this mental debility: both reject the apparent for the invisible, the accepted for the unacceptable. Such debility subjects them both to mental instability.

Indeed, it is on the level of character conveyed through the psychological texture of the narrative that the ambiguity of curiosity is dramatized. These heroes are flawed by their very virtue. Their curiosity, the same impulse that drives them to seek the truth and see justice done, marks them as discontented, possessed by irrational, antisocial urges, even superstitious: motivated by impulses antagonistic to neoclassical ideals of control and self-possession. Emily's exemplary father St. Aubert—and the plot—reprove Emily for indulging emotions that spur her imagination. Whereas Emily learns to discipline desire to control her curiosity, however, Caleb's curiosity overwhelms him. Self-cultivated, Emily resists the identities of wife, servant, lover, nun, and madwoman thrust upon her by Montoni, Count Morano, her aunt, Agnes, Dupont and others. Indulging his passionate curiosity, however, Caleb pursues information, and in the end destroys his master's mastery, and thus his own identity: Caleb's desire to own the other consumes himself. As a moral example, Emily inherits; she possesses culture where Caleb is possessed by it: "I have now no character," he admits at the end of his chronicle (326).

In *The Mysteries of Udolpho*, curiosity elides the central poles of value. Positioned between empiricism and superstition, reason and imagination, it represents the distinction between mental masculinity and femininity, and between supervisory, elite mastery and instinctive, uncontrolled subordination. In St. Aubert, Emily's father and tutor in self-command—the control of sensibility and imagination—curiosity is the disciplined examination of nature. He and M. Barreaux botanize rather than rhapsodize over nature, exercising an amateur science that replaces romantic enthusiasm and testifies to a pious, enlightened reason. Upon seeing a mysterious light in the woods, he identifies the "glow worm" where Emily sees fanciful fairies (15). His "science, rather than the eye, enable[s] him to describe" scenes beyond his vision, such as Emily can describe only through unreliable imagination. Her ignorance of such science induces her to believe that the pictorial image of death, inadequately observed, is a murdered body.

Emily's curiosity, moreover, like Eve's original curiosity, is transgressive with specifically sexual implications. Despite serving as her avenue to self-discovery and as the principle which drives the truth from the shadows, it torments her with irrational fears throughout the novel. When she peeps at St. Aubert's grieving over the miniature of his sister, she understands the scene as illicit love (26); Radcliffe enables her to reassert her innocence by burning his papers "*without examining them*," a task almost beyond her power (78; original italics). As she begins it by pulling papers and money from their secret cavity, her "excellent understanding" suffers from a "temporary failure" manifested by "superstition" in the form of visions of the ghost of her father watching her perform his command (102–3):

> Returning reason soon overcame the dreadful but pitiable attack of imagination, and she turned to the papers, though still with so little recollection, that her eyes involuntarily settled on the writing of some loose sheets, which lay open; and she was unconscious, that she was transgressing her father's strict injunction, till a sentence of dreadful import awakened her attention and her memory together. She hastily put the papers from her, but the words, which had roused equally her curiosity and terror, she could not dismiss from her thoughts. So powerfully had they affected her, that she even could not resolve to destroy the papers immediately; and the more she dwelt on the circumstance, the more it inflamed her imagination. Urged by the most forcible, and

apparently the most necessary, curiosity to enquire farther, concerning the terrible and mysterious subject, to which she had seen an allusion, she began to lament her promise to destroy the papers. (103)

But her "re-animated . . . sense of duty" brings about "the triumph of integrity over temptation" (103). In an interesting discussion of three varieties of the female sublime, Patricia Yaeger defines a "failed sublime" of balked transcendence which aptly describes Emily's reaction here: she cannot escape patriarchy, possession, and domination.[23] Emily's obedience cures her of Pandora's crime and Eve's sin; this obedience is portrayed as equivalent to "reason" and opposed to "inflaming" imagination, superstition, and curiosity.

Even while overtly reproving it, however, Radcliffe identifies this curiosity as the female sublime associated with non-genteel ignorance. Predicated on ignorance and awe, it produces the sensation of terror and humility that Burke identified as the pious apprehension of mortality. Whereas St. Aubert experiences sublimity through the scientific understanding of nature, Emily feels it through inquiry into human affairs. When she determines to examine the veiled picture "which had attracted her curiosity," she experiences "a faint degree of terror" from its "mystery" that the narrator condones: "But a terror of this nature, as it occupies and expands the mind, and elevates it to high expectation, is purely sublime, and leads us, by a kind of fascination, to seek even the object, from which we appear to shrink" (248). Later, sensing movement on the ramparts, "a thrilling curiosity" draws Emily to stay (356). Even as this curiosity reveals her own mortality to Emily and fills her with religious awe, it seeps into superstition, the enemy of reason. Like superstition, female curiosity refutes empirical fact and privileges unsubstantiated rumor and traditional mythic wisdom. Most of Emily's misobservations, including that of the veiled *memento mori*, are conditioned by her gossiping with her serving maid Annette. Indeed, Annette scoffs at Emily's decorum by declaring that the servants "'had all a little more *curiousness* than you had,'" and the narrator identifies "surprise and curiosity" as "natural to her" (279, original italics; 297). Emily's curiosity threatens her class status.

Similarly, in *Caleb Williams*, through the examples of the tyrannical Tyrrel, the chivalric Falkland, the independent yeoman Hawkins, the curious peasant

Caleb, and the peripheral exemplary characters of the soldier Brightwel and the poet Clare, Godwin scrutinizes the commodification of identity by class assumptions. In what would become the libertarian tradition, he asks who owns this commodity: the self or the state, represented by land-owning gentry or governmental institutions such as law or the military.[24] His attack on the "despotism" of social institutions in a book originally titled "Things as They Are" proclaims his polemical answer, but within this dichotomy lies another, more troubling to the post-sentimentalists (Preface, 1). Even granting that the individual possesses him/herself, what part of the self possesses what other part? Self-ownership is predicated on a radical division of the self between an owner-part and an owned-part. Both this division and the commodification of self implicated in it rend Godwin's novel, and both are represented by his ambiguous protagonist, Caleb. Simultaneously a rebel and a conformist, a new man and a collaborator, Caleb demonstrates that the very formula for freedom from tyranny is seen to contain the structures of tyranny itself.

Caleb's "ruling passion" is curiosity (118). Since it is a "principle stronger in my bosom than even the love of independence," it serves as the tyrant over his mind: it is his owner, the element of his identity that possesses the rest.[25] Thus, it is equivalent to Falkland's love of fame or reputation, the "ruling passion" that tyrannizes over his benevolence (122). Caleb admits that "Curiosity is a restless propensity" that brings on its own danger (113), that it is "infantine and unreasonable" (144), yet this is the trait that defines Caleb as socially ambitious, a threat to the established order. His curiosity lifts Caleb above his birth. Although a peasant, Caleb explains, "I had an inquisitive mind, and neglected no means of information," yet "My curiosity . . . was not entirely ignoble" in prompting him to high tales rather than low gossip (3–4). Caleb's curiosity protects him from tyranny by redeeming him from degradation in prison: asking "Have I not been employed from my infancy in gratifying an insatiable curiosity?" he employs his imagination to remain "insensible to the disorder" surrounding him (184). Moreover, Caleb's curiosity penetrates the mystification of social rituals and prejudices, bringing reason and logic to replace superstition. Although "Mr. Falkland had always been to my imagination an object of wonder, and that which excites our wonder we scarcely suppose ourselves competent to analyze," Caleb penetrates this "marvel" to find the murderer (297). After his initial wonder at Collins's recital of Falkland's history, he "turn[s]" the tale "a thousand ways" to extract its mystery, explaining that "To do what is forbidden always has its charms, because we have an indistinct apprehension of something arbitrary and tyrannical in the prohibition" (107). In his account of the composition of the novel, Godwin writes that his vision of a Gothic pursuit tale "could best be effected by a secret murder, to the investigation of which the innocent victim should be impelled by an unconquerable spirit of curiosity."[26] Curiosity thus designates the individual quest to defeat despotism.

Caleb's curiosity, however, transgresses the limits of reason and becomes tyrannical: he no longer possesses curiosity; it, as an irrational impulse, possesses him. He blames his curiosity for his fate, asserting that, "My offence had merely been a mistaken thirst of knowledge . . . ungoverned curiosity" (133). While this certainly suggests irony on Godwin's part, it also points to the pollution in curiosity itself. If this trait permits Caleb to excel, it also drives his downfall. This ambiguity arises from the double nature of curiosity as an intellectual appetite, the product of reason turned into passion. Godwin blatantly locates his narrator-hero within a Christian tradition that records the history of the chosen people after the Fall.[27] As Robert Kiely notes, Caleb's curiosity leads to the loss of innocence, a Biblical parallel to the contemporary political condition of surveillance.[28] He confesses his adventurousness in "the gratification of an infantine and unreasonable curiosity" (143, 144). It drives him to open Falkland's "trunk," releasing like Pandora all evils and leaving only Hope.

In this regard, Caleb's Eve-like curiosity resembles sexual passion, bringing to the fore the ominously erotic quality of his relationship with the sentimentally feminine Falkland. Despite his use of the fictional convention of coerced marriage, Godwin condemns the sentimental sanctification of the body not only because it detracts from rationality, but also because it sexualizes identity and underscores sexual difference. Falkland's feminine qualities of sensitivity, compassion, and gentleness prove him superior to the brutal Tyrrel, yet also produce a dangerously irrational self-regard that leads, like the lust of Signora Laurentini, to murder. In fact, his original crime, the destruction of another's body, results from the injury to his pride manifested on his body when Tyrrel beats him. His belief in the sacredness of his own body expresses a sentimental self-regard parallel to the fetishized female body. After Falkland's thrashing, Mr. Collins explains,

> He was too deeply pervaded with the idle and groundless romances of chivalry ever to forget the situation, humiliating and dishonorable according to his ideas, in which he had been placed upon this occasion. There is a mysterious sort of divinity annexed to the person of a true knight, that makes any species of brute violence committed upon it indelible and immortal. (97)

Falkland's self-deification endows his body with the same aura of mystified chastity as virginity. When he is raped by Tyrrel, as Tyrrel seeks to have his tool Grimes rape Emily, his virtue is lost. By rating the physical over the mental, he loses control of himself.

This sexualized sense of self compromises identity by making it vulnerable and anti-rational. Caleb and Falkland love each other because, in the post-lapsarian world, they create each other. Falkland's crime creates Caleb's identity—curiosity—and Falkland's crime is the result of commodifying his own identity. He is "the fool of honour and fame" (102, 135). He makes reputation, the public shadow of himself, his "idol," his "jewel" (102). It is in defending this property—this sexualized, objectified self—that he commits every one of his crimes. Like marriage partners, Caleb and Falkland are locked together in a domestic dictatorship. The sexual element in this relationship has been characterized by critics as a feminization of Caleb, a demonstration of repressed homoeroticism, or narcissism. The sexual dynamic certainly seems fluid, with Caleb acting as much as the aggressor as the recipient: "The more impenetrable Mr. Falkland was determined to be, the more uncontrollable was my curiosity," he declares (108). But if Caleb's curiosity represents the masculine desire to possess Falkland, Caleb as Falkland's social subordinate reprises the role of the sentimental heroine. Indeed, Godwin employs several of the tropes of Samuel Richardson's *Pamela* and *Clarissa* to dramatize the hothouse struggle for power between the master and the servant. Like *Pamela*, the book includes the preferment of a peasant fine beyond his (or her) birth, the mode of confessional epistolarity, peripheral characters including the reputable but timid servant

Collins, and the dramatic reconnoiters between Falkland and Caleb as one leaves one door while the other enters at another (163). From *Clarissa*, Godwin borrows the tropes of Emily's compelled marriage and elopement with the duplicitous Grimes, and Caleb's imprisonment and mad ravings from the first ending.[29] Like *Clarissa*, moreover, *Caleb Williams* severs ownership of the body from that of the soul. In virtually Clarissa's words, Emily exclaims to her cousin-guardian Tyrrel, "You may imprison my body, but you cannot conquer my mind"—words that summarize Emily St. Aubert's experience in *Udolpho* (57). Like the Harlowe family, Tyrrel claims rights over Emily's body based on "the right of possession," since she dwells in his house (57), as Montoni does over Emily (216–17), and Godwin's Emily, like Clarissa, resists to the death. Both Caleb and Falkland act as pursuer and pursued, attempting to possess rather than be possessed by the other.

This power struggle has sexual overtones that underscore the Biblical context of curiosity as forbidden knowledge, carnal knowledge, the knowledge of human origins. When he has convinced himself of Falkland's crime by watching his guilty response to a parallel case brought to him as a justice of the peace to try, Caleb rushes into the garden, ecstatic with knowledge:

> While I thus proceeded with hasty steps along the most secret paths of the garden, and from time to time gave vent to the tumult of my thoughts in involuntary exclamations, I felt as if my animal system had undergone a total revolution. My blood boiled within me. I was conscious to a kind of rapture for which I could not account. I was solemn, yet full of rapid emotion, burning with indignation and energy. In the very tempest and hurricane of the passions, I seem to enjoy the most soul-ravishing calm. I cannot better express the then state of my mind, than by saying, I was never so perfectly alive as at that moment. (129–30)

Released from the house, in the garden Caleb experiences a kind of orgasm, a sexualized penetration of Falkland's secret which sows the seeds for and eventually gives birth to an alternative, albeit negative, identity as not a servant. Immediately after this, he discovers that "it was possible to love a murderer" (130). He and Falkland are bound together: "There was a magnetical sympathy between me and my patron" (112).

In showing how sexualizing identity leads to the commodification of the self, Godwin indicts the social dependence on property. All aspects of society value property in *Caleb Williams* and thus participate in the "despotism" that defends it. In his original Preface, Godwin declares that his novel comprises "a general review of the modes of domestic and unrecorded despotism, by which man becomes the destroyer of man" (1). While such modes as legal and sublegal persecution, and customary dictatorship over voting rights and property seem evident, Godwin also exposes the "unrecorded" modes of social surveillance.[30] Through the instrument of Grimes, a thief-taker and traitor to his own principles, Falkland watches Caleb's every move; unwittingly, townspeople prejudiced against foreigners, Jews, the Irish, and the poor collaborate with Falkland. Godwin thus exposes the network of ingrown customs, habits, and traditional prejudices that collaborate to protect customary procedures and especially property, and thus work in support of Falkland's persecution. Radcliffe makes a similar point in *Udolpho* by portraying the utter dependence of Emily and her aunt, Madame Montoni, on the master of the house. Emily, indeed, cannot escape the conventional structures of family and property to marry where she wishes.

The tendency of curiosity to fragment identity, to overtake or possess the possessor, operates also through the symbolic power of possessions within the novels. In the eighteenth century, works of art or skill, or unique fragments of natural material were considered curiosities, objects used to demonstrate the aesthetic taste or scientific knowledge of connoisseurs and scientific collectors. Indeed, collecting was known as the "habit of curiosity" from at least the Renaissance. Acquisition of such objects demonstrated class: knowledge of the past, interest in national or personal heritage, sensitivity to beauty, and thus power and nobility.[31] At the same time, however, for free-thinkers during the revolutionary fervor at end of the century, such fine objects represented not merely spiritual or intellectual puissance but a problematic investment in the status quo, and thus in a heritage of oppression and tyranny. At the same time, middle-class objects for consumption, particularly books, showed the moral ambition for self-improvement.[32] Collected objects announce a public identity that might betoken an imperialistic greed for acquisition, whereas purchased intellectual culture showed moral seriousness.

Radcliffe and Godwin both exploit the way objects represent identity. As a radical reformer, Godwin regarded possessions as theft, devices that possess the spirit, that usurp freedom and turn men into slaves. In *Caleb Williams*, Falkland conceals his crime and thus his identity within a mysterious "trunk": although Caleb never succeeds in opening this, when he spies Falkland weeping over it he speculates that it contains a written confession—such a document as Radcliffe provides in the inset history of "Laurentini Di Udolpho" in her last pages.[33] This putative history remains untold in *Caleb Williams*; Falkland's secret possesses him to the end. Interestingly, Godwin revised the term "trunk" from "chest" in the second edition, possibly to dramatize the objectification of Falkland's public identity.[34] No single object really embodies Falkland; rather, his entire estate represents his public character, for he was born "to the possession of hereditary wealth" (255). It is this possession which ignites Falkland's idealized identity as a "gentleman," and controls his mind and soul.

Falkland's identity is, however, as empty as Caleb's since it rests on false reputation. Never does Godwin forget that this identity as possessor rests on the bodies of others since inherited wealth relies on the labor of enslaved and colonized peoples. Caleb, beginning as a peasant who works for a landowner, becomes like Mr. Collins a servant who waits on a master in the house. Godwin underscores the moral ambiguity of such collaboration in servitude by contrasting Caleb and Collins with the heroic independence of Hawkins who earns the hatred of another tyrannical landlord, Tyrrel, because he refuses to sell his son to him as a servant. Godwin reiterates the point through Caleb's transformations. Under the duress of Falkland's pursuit, Caleb assumes the guise of a series of disenfranchised others who substitute metonymically for the underclasses in English society. Caleb himself comments on the parallels between despised servants and distrusted colonials. When disguised as a beggarly Irishman, he observes ironically that his brogue and poverty "would be sufficient to convict me" (240). When disguised as a hack-writer Jew, he records that his printer marvels that, "he writes . . . extremely fine, and yet he is no more than a Jew" (264). As a mutable "Other," Caleb represents the vacant identity of the owned, opponent to the "Owner," Falkland.

Godwin indicts such national and racial prejudice by associating it with a colonialism that expresses the greed of the landowners. To satirize his printer's racial provincialism, Caleb adds parenthetically, "To my honest printer this [fine writings by a Jew] seemed as strange as if they had been written by a Cherokee chieftain at the falls of the Mississippi" (264). The foreign language of the other, like political opposition, evidently seldom sees print. Godwin connects this implicit censorship with Falkland's tyranny by revealing that "Mr. Falkland, in addition to the large estate he possessed in England, had a very valuable plantation in the West Indies" which had been "greatly mismanaged" (307). When Falkland sends the benign Mr. Collins to correct the problem, the voyage destroys his "constitution" (318). Falkland's possessions undermine others—and others' rights—as well as himself. Similarly, when Caleb has Falkland's "secret . . . in my possession," he is himself destroyed (321). This antagonism to possessions structures Godwin's method. Since he condemns ownership as theft, his narrative concentrates on psychological action and motive, eschewing all but the most basic physical description.[35]

This seems quite unlike Radcliffe's method and message. In contrast to Godwin's entirely interior narrative, the narrative of *The Mysteries of Udolpho* rhapsodizes over beauties of nature and curiosities of art, often sacrificing action and characterization to description. In detailing antique beauties and denigrating ostentatious fashion, Radcliffe doubtless pleased her largely middle-class, notably female audience, who were by the end of the century defined by consumption.[36] She thus echoes eighteenth-century sentimental philosophers like Shaftesbury and Hume by using taste in dress, painting, and furniture to exhibit the morality of her characters. Moreover, when Emily acquires her estates, comes into possession of her identity as the social equal of Valancourt, and liberates herself from dependence, she is inducted into the world of history and art. At the end of the novel, Radcliffe demonstrates this by unifying her with Lady Blanche as a bride and luxuriating in the lavish details of their marriage:

> The feasts were held in the great hall of the castle, which, on this occasion, was hung with superb new tapestry, representing the exploits of Charlemagne and his twelve peers; here, were seen the Saracens, with their horrible visors, advancing to battle; and there, were displayed the wild solemnities of incantation, and the necromantic feats, exhibited by the magician *Jarl* before the Emperor.

The sumptuous banners of the family of Villeroi, which had long slept in dust, were once more unfurled, to wave over the gothic points of painted casements; and music echoed, in many a lingering close, through every winding gallery and colonnade of that vast edifice. (670–71)

Even as she details curious antiquities, Radcliffe indicts the collection of fine objects in the modern style as an exhibition of rapaciousness and corrupt taste by blaming the acquisitive businessman M. Quesnel for the loss of St. Aubert's tree-lined family estate.[37] By counterpointing sublime nature with splendid possessions, Radcliffe suggests that wealth possesses the souls of superficial sophisticates like Madame Cheron, whose corrupt desires lead to her disastrous marriage.

The objectification of value further compromises identity in the novel by showing how easily individuality can be replicated. Andrea K. Henderson explains this Romantic dynamic by arguing that "early Gothic novels represent personal identity as violently polarized and are driven by a fascination with the vagaries of exchange-value identity."[38] Radcliffe exhibits this fascination throughout the plot by replicating artful representations of the body, especially miniature paintings such as those of Signora Laurentini, of the Marchioness De Villeroi over which St. Aubert mysteriously weeps, and of Emily herself, stolen from her mother's bracelet by Du Pont at the story's start. These representations suggest hidden relationships, some endorsed by the plot and some fantasized by Emily as she mistakes her aunt for her mother, a sister for a lover, a *memento mori* for a body. Eliding individuality, these art objects represent an objectified self that can be circulated and exchanged, a self improved by art. This exchange undermines the very uniqueness of heroic identity on which the plot is ostensibly predicated.

This dynamic between the possessing self and the possessed self unifies the political, philosophical, and moral issues of these books. Despite their differences, these novels both dramatize the struggle to possess the self in a world oppressed by tyranny from without and shaken by its internalized effects that threaten to dismantle identity from within. Radcliffe wavers between narrating her tale as a moral lesson and giving her heroine a voice to describe her own experience; this methodological ambiguity expresses her heroine's troubling negotiation of seeming and being. This disintegration of identity parallels the disintegration of society in both novels. Like identity itself, curiosity comprises both desire and reason, elements continually at war in society as well as the self. In *Udolpho*, Montoni promulgates chaotic civil wars that spin out ceaseless violence; in *Caleb Williams*, law and its obverse, the lawless theft of the highway gang, circulate injustices without end. Correspondingly, Godwin's Romantic hero loses narrative authority throughout the novel as his story documents the collapse of pragmatism in the face of a ruling passion. Godwin demonstrates that the regard for property structures the mental and emotional economy of even the most benevolent of men, Falkland—and even men who have no property but themselves, Caleb. Caleb's very curiosity is a symptom of his corruption as a member of the fallen world of ownership.

The ambiguity of curiosity as a definition of identity continues to characterize the Romantic hero and the Gothic heroine as they appear in narratives after the close of the eighteenth century.[39] Murder mysteries, detective stories, and crime tales dramatize the struggle between mankind's rational capacity for improvement and his immutable appetite-driven nature. Discovering the latter, however, does not necessarily prove the former: novels by Paul Auster that show how inquiry destroys personality and television series from *Inspector Morse* to *NYPD Blue* depicting the loss that knowledge brings suggest that ambivalence about inquiry marks fin-de-siècle pessimism even into our own millennium, where Gothic mysteries of supernatural possession present a self usurped by scientistic inquiries beyond the limits of reason. But while the novels of 1794 cannot be said to alone epitomize the feeling of the entire decade, they do articulate what happens to a traditional debate under the pressure of an urgent, political dilemma. They embody the commercialization of moral discourse by straddling traditional and revolutionary tropes. These novels prohibit and permit transgression, reinscribe the necessity of traditional limits and reinscribe the necessity of violating them, advocate restraint and yet license excess.[40] They are the vehicles for readers to consume curiosity while removing themselves from their own transgression.

Notes

1. Godwin also read other contemporary and older matter, including Horace Walpole's tragedy *The Mysterious Mother,* Swift's *Gulliver's Travels,* Burke's *A Philosophical Enquiry
   into . . . the Sublime,* and novels by, notably, Smollett and Richardson. See Vijay Mishra,
   The Gothic Sublime (New York: State University of New York Press, 1994), 130.

2. For a theoretical and historical account of the combat over the value of curiosity, see
   Benedict, "'The Curious Attitude' in Eighteenth-Century Britain: Observing and Owning," *Eighteenth-Century Life* 14 n.s., 3 (November 1990): 59–98. See also Steven Shapin,
   A Social History of Truth: Civility and Science in Seventeenth-Century England (Chicago
   and London: University of Chicago Press, 1994).

3. As Vijay Mishra explains at length, the historical similarity between the 1790s and the
   1980s suggests a parallel, postmodern mood; see *The Gothic Sublime* and also Jean-François
   Lyotard, *The Postmodern Condition: A Report on Knowledge,* trans. Geoff Bennington and
   Brian Massumi, foreword by Fredric Jameson (Manchester: Manchester University Press,
   1986).

4. This theme echoes the formal ambiguities of Romantic literature. For a theoretical dis-
   cussion of the connections between "sublimity and indeterminacy" and the use of inde-
   terminate irony as a structuring principle, see Lucy Newlyn, "'Questionable Shape': The
   Aesthetics of Indeterminacy," in *Questioning Romanticism,* ed. John Beer (Baltimore and
   London: Johns Hopkins University Press, 1995), 209–33. See also Gary Kelly, *The English
   Jacobin Novel, 1780–1805* (Oxford: The Clarendon Press, 1976), 189.

5. Paulson, *Representations of Revolution, 1789–1820* (New Haven and London: Yale University Press, 1983), 215–47.

6. See Chris Jones, *Radical Sensibility: Literature and Ideas in the 1790s* (London and New York:
   Routledge, 1993), 101–2; Marilyn Butler, *Jane Austen and the War of Ideas* (Oxford: The
   Clarendon Press, 1975), esp. 57–87; Pamela Clemit, *The Godwinian Novel: The Rational
   Fictions of Godwin, Brockden Brown, Mary Shelley* (Oxford: The Clarendon Press, 1993), 41.

7. Compare Marilyn Butler's argument in *Jane Austen and the War of Ideas,* 30–31, and *Romantics, Rebels, and Reactionaries: English Literature and Its Background, 1760–1830* (Oxford and New York: Oxford University Press, 1981) with Deborah D. Rogers, ed. *The
   Critical Response to Ann Radcliffe* (Westport, Connecticut and London: Greenwood Press,
   1994), xxxvii–xxxix and Claudia L. Johnson, *Equivocal Beings: Politics, Gender, and Sentimentality in the 1790s: Wollstonecraft, Radcliffe, Burney, Austen* (Chicago and London:

University of Chicago Press, 1995). While Godwin certainly advocated a more radical egalitarianism than Radcliffe, both criticize sexual inequality through their portraits of sexual violence against the heroines.

8. Radcliffe, *The Mysteries of Udolpho,* edited and with an introduction by Bonomy Dobrée (Oxford and New York: Oxford University Press, 1970), 80; all citations refer to this edition. This critique of excessive feeling as hazardous to the status quo is typical of sentimental fictions even before the French Revolution: see Benedict, *Framing Feeling: Sentiment and Style in English Prose Fiction, 1745–1800* (New York: AMS Press, 1994).

9. See Johnson, *Equivocal Beings;* also Benedict, "Pictures of Conformity: Sentiment and Structure in Ann Radcliffe's Style" *Philological Quarterly* 68, no. 3 (Summer, 1989): 363–77.

10. For discussions of this ambiguity, see Clemit, op. cit., 39 and Rogers, op. cit.

11. In *Ann Radcliffe: The Great Enchantress,* Robert Miles argues that Emily's desire makes her an active subject; see Chapter 7, "The Hermeneutics of Reading: The Mysteries of Udolpho" (Manchester and New York: Manchester University Press, 1995), 129–48.

12. Terry Castle, "The Spectralization of the Other in The Mysteries of Udolpho" in *The New Eighteenth Century: Theory, Politics, English Literature,* ed. Felicity Nussbaum and Laura Brown (New York and London: Methuen, 1987), 231–53.

13. William Godwin, *Caleb Williams,* intro. by David McCracken, ed. (New York and London: Norton, 1977), 119; all citations refer to this edition.

14. Jean Starobinski, *L'Invention et la Liberté, 1700–1789* (Geneva: Skira, 1987).

15. See Butler, *Romantics, Rebels, and Reactionaries;* James P. Carson, "Enlightenment, Popular Culture, and Gothic Fiction" in *The Cambridge Companion to the Eighteenth-Century Novel,* ed. John Richetti (Cambridge, New York: Cambridge University Press, 1996), 271.

16. Quoted from Godwin's 1831 Preface to *Caleb Williams* in Clemit, 47 (from *Caleb Williams,* i, p. v [2]/1).

17. For an account of the female audiences of the 1790s and of the influence of Radcliffe's Gothics, see Stuart Curran, "Women Readers, Women Writers" in *The Cambridge Companion to British Romanticism,* ed. Stuart Curran (Cambridge, New York: Cambridge University Press, 1993), 177–95, esp. 187–88. In *The Progress of Romance: Literary Historiography and the Gothic Novel,* David H. Richter argues that Radcliffe's novels "presume an identification between the reader and the focalizing character that goes well beyond" earlier fiction (Columbus: Ohio State University Press, 1996), 117.

18. See Benedict, "Literary Miscellanies: The Cultural Mediation of Fragmented Feeling," *ELH* 57, no. 2 (1990): 407–30.

19. M. M. Bakhtin, *The Dialogic Imagination*, ed. Michael Holquist, trans. Caryl Emerson and Michael Holquist (Austin: University of Texas Press, 1981); also J. Paul Hunter, *Before Novels: The Cultural Contexts of Eighteenth-Century Fiction* (New York and London: Norton, 1990).

20. Robert Kiely, *The Romantic Novel in England* (Cambridge, Mass: Harvard University Press, 1972), 81–97; see Jacqueline Howard's claim that Radcliffe ironizes Emily in *Reading Gothic Fiction: A Bakhtinian Approach* (Oxford; The Clarendon Press, 1994), esp. 117–39.

21. In the original ending, Caleb does go mad; Godwin claimed that he wrote this ending before completing the rest of the tale, even though he changed it before publication.

22. Walter E. Houghton, Jr., "The English Virtuoso in the Seventeenth Century," *Journal of the History of Ideas* 3 (1942): 51–73; 4 (1942): 190–219.

23. See Patricia Yaeger, "Toward a Female Sublime" in *Gender and Theory: Dialogues on Feminist Criticism*, ed. Linda Kauffman (Oxford: Basil Blackwell, 1989): 191–212.

24. The libertarian thesis is clearly articulated by G. A. Cohen: "each person enjoys, over herself and her powers, full and exclusive rights of control and use, and therefore owes no service or product to anyone else that she has not contracted to supply" (*TLS* "Letters to the Editor" November, 1996). For a contemporary debate over the question of self-ownership as a challenge to liberal policies, see G. A. Cohen's *Self-Ownership, Freedom, and Equality* (Cambridge, New York: Cambridge University Press, 1995) and Robert Nozick's *Anarchy, State, and Utopia* (New York: Basic Books, 1974).

25. Robert Kiely observes that Caleb's curiosity is "more like a physical hunger than a quality of rational intellect" in *The Romantic Novel in England*, 90.

26. *Caleb Williams*, 337. This account formed part of the Preface to Fleetwood in the Standard Novels edition of 1832, and was therefore written and published well after Mary Shelley's *Frankenstein* (1818), which similarly focuses on the evils of (scientific) curiosity.

27. Godwin himself, a Calvinist clergyman who lost his faith and left his congregation to write in London, must have been well acquainted not only with the Biblical account of Caleb, but also with the connotations of the story. For an account of *Caleb Williams* as a religious allegory, see Kelly, *The English Jacobin Novel*, 208. The "logic of internalized conscience" characteristic of Godwin's novel marks his debt to religious structures of meaning: see Victor Sage, *Horror Fiction in the Protestant Tradition* (New York: St. Martin's Press, 1988), 90.

28. Kiely, op. cit. 93; James Thomson, "Surveillance in William Godwin's *Caleb Williams,* in *Gothic Fictions: Prohibition/Transgression,* ed. Kenneth W. Graham (New York: AMS Press, 1989), 173–98.

29. Godwin clearly borrows from both Daniel Defoe's *Moll Flanders* and Henry Fielding's *Amelia* in the prison and judicial scenes.

30. Michel Foucault, *Madness and Civilization: A History of Insanity in the Age of Reason,* trans. Richard Howard (New York: Vintage, 1973); see also John Bender, *Imagining the Penitentiary: Fiction and the Architecture of Mind in Eighteenth-Century England* (Chicago and London: University of Chicago Press, 1987).

31. See Douglas and Elizabeth Rigby, *Lock, Stock and Barrel: The Origins of Museums* (Philadelphia, New York and London: Lippincott, 1944); *The Cabinet of Curiosities in Sixteenth- and Seventeenth-Century Europe,* ed. Oliver Impey and Arthur Macgregor (Oxford: The Clarendon Press, 1985); James H. Bunn "The Aesthetics of British Mercantilism," *New Literary History* 11, no. 2 (1980): 303–21.

32. See Benedict, *Making the Modern Reader: Cultural Mediation in Early Modern Literary Anthologies* (Princeton, New Jersey: Princeton University Press, 1996).

33. Jane Austen mocks this device of representing written documents within a fictional text by her Gothic laundry list in *Northanger Abbey,* originally written in 1796.

34. David McCracken, Intro. to William Godwin's *Caleb Williams,* xxv. Samuel Johnson's *Dictionary* terms "trunk" a French term while "chest" is given the primary meaning of a wooden box (London: W. Strahan, 1755).

35. Godwin articulates the philosophy that ownership is theft in the pronouncement of the lawless band of robbers; see esp. 222.

36. McKendrick, Neil, John Brewer and J. H. Plumb, *The Birth of a Consumer Society: The Commercialization of Eighteenth-Century England* (London: Hutchison, 1982).

37. Howard, *Reading Gothic Fiction,* 115–16.

38. Andrea K. Henderson, *Romantic Identities: Varieties of Subjectivity, 1774–1830* (Cambridge, New York: Cambridge University Press, 1996), 7.

39. John Beer documents Godwin's influence on the Romantics following him in *Romantic Influences: Contemporary, Victorian, Modern* (New York: St. Martin's Press, 1993), esp. 26–32.

40. In *Gothic Fictions: Prohibition/Transgression,* Kenneth W. Graham allows Gothic novels each only one of these stances (New York: AMS Press, 1989).

Lewis's The Monk and
the Matter of Reading

Clara D. McLean

Perhaps one of the fullest flowerings of
the genre of the Gothic novel, Matthew G. Lewis's *The Monk*[1] (1796) is corrupt
to the core, narratively driven and riven by a consumptive quest for knowledge. Pursuers of the tantalizing secret, curious to the point of deadliness, wind
their way through a marvelously labyrinthine architecture which the novel both
thematizes and structurally repeats. In one of the several interweaving plots, a
group of men engage in a prolonged effort to "worm out the secret" (213) of the
nun Agnes's imprisonment inside the "massy walls" (346) of her convent. Their
inquisitive "worming" consists of a series of schemes to penetrate the convent's
interior regions, never before "pervad[ed]" by "a man's profane eye" (213). They
press on to unearth the dark female secrets hiding there, in the pitch-black
passages of the convent called, ironically enough, "St. Clare." The truth they
seek is a physical one: the body of a woman, perhaps tortured, perhaps dead. To
find it they must undertake an archaeological burrowing through both the
convent's complex layers and the narrative blockages imposed by its forbidding
prioress. The men are driven, even overtaken by their quest to uncover this lost
flesh, by their need to see it, to drag it to the surface. This seemingly noble
project has a dangerous side: as the mystery deepens it becomes apparent that
the urge to pursue it is as much carnal as rational—a ravenous animal digging.
When he finally gains admission to the convent's catacombs, Agnes's brother

Lorenzo is "carried away by his eagerness to clear up this mystery . . . to penetrate into which he was impelled by a movement secret and unaccountable" (347). When the secrets of the convent are finally publicly aired, a frenzied mob pours in, "searching out" (345) the nuns, tearing apart the building in a wild drive to uncover its horrors. Their desire does not stop, moreover, at a bodily exposure of the corrupt prioress: after having "forced a passage" toward her and "dragged her from her shelter," they drive on into her body, rupturing its skin, reducing it at last to "no more than a mass of flesh, unsightly, shapeless, and disgusting" (344). The desire to know here culminates in a dismembering, ruinous need to get to the heart of the matter, its very fleshy core.

Discussions of the Gothic novel, as Eve Sedgwick has suggested, have too often emphasized the genre's concern with depth—the depths of the human psyche, the bowels of the earth, minute interior spaces—over its simultaneous and related concern with surfaces.[2] The genre's omnipresent veils, for example, can perhaps too easily be reduced to a straight-forward thematic of concealment or disguise over the secret "truths" that lie hidden. Sedgwick complicates this critical model by showing how these Gothic textural layerings can interpenetrate, how flesh and its covering refuse to remain separate, arguing persuasively that "the attributes of the veil, and of the surface generally, are contagious metonymically, by touch," and that "a related thematic strain depicts veils, like flesh, as suffused or marked with blood."[3] Such metonymic contagion of surface and depth, cover and flesh is evident throughout *The Monk*, where the layered folds of the veil become as much object of, as obstacle to, desire; and where, just as the veil can be soaked with blood, so too can the flesh of the body become covering, layers of skin to be peeled back and lifted. In *The Monk*, the revelation of flesh is never enough, for that flesh itself instantly becomes another layer begging to be rent.

In *The Monk*, Antonia, the eminently desired object, is fascinating precisely because of her veil and the complex ways it entwines with, and indeed becomes indistinguishable from, her body. She is introduced as

> a female, the delicacy and elegance of whose figure inspired the youths with the
> most lively curiosity to view the face to which it belonged. This satisfaction was
> denied them. Her features were hidden by a thick veil; but struggling through

the crowd had deranged it sufficiently to discover a neck which . . . was of the most dazzling whiteness. . . . Her figure . . . was light and airy. . . . Her bosom was carefully veiled. Her dress was white . . . (37)

The whiteness of the skin matches the white of the dress, beneath which the body's "light and airy" ephemerality belies any substantial difference it might have from the rustling clothes. Even when Antonia is naked and (she believes) unobserved, "an in-bred sense of modesty induced her to veil her charms" (269) with her hands. In a complex layering of fabric and flesh, and flesh-that-is-fabric, Antonia veils with her body a body that is already veil. The referent, the thing "hidden," continually slips and recedes. Penetrating the mystery of the veil, as in this scene, where Ambrosio the monk spies furtively on Antonia's naked flesh, only leads to more layers, and the overpowering eroticism of the scene for Ambrosio rests upon this acute frustration, this deferral.

The "worming" action of the characters and narrative of *The Monk*, I will suggest, participates at a number of levels in this rage of investigation, this drive, furious in (and at) its impossibility, to get to the bottom of things. It is precisely the conflation and contagion of layers that pushes this urge onward, through architectural passages, the shifting folds of story, levels of cloth, and finally through the thickness of skin itself. "Worming" can serve as an emblem of the probing of both body and text, a motion which seems, here, to ruin even as it comes to "know."

There is however another side to the position of the worm in this novel, and one which points to a certain recuperation of a textual and bodily limit which resists the system of ceaselessly lifting layers. For at the very bottom of the convent's subterranean vaults, whose "depth was buried in obscurity" (355), Lorenzo finally finds the emaciated and half-dead Agnes, who holds in her arms the "small bundle" which is the final secret of this story, the final secret of flesh. Agnes tells in the last pages of this narrative how the evil prioress punished her for her illegitimate pregnancy by confining her to the dungeon, where she gave birth to a child that soon died. "I rent my winding-sheet," she says, "and wrapped in it my lovely child," a child which, as the months go on, becomes "a mass of putridity" (393). Agnes, though, "vanquishes" natural repugnance, insists on holding that final veiled bundle to her breast, gazing upon it and *into* it, and even endeavoring, with that terrible investigative scrupulosity of so many of the novel's characters, to read its face, to "retrace its features through the livid corruption with which they were overspread." The moment of abject horror which stops even this desperate act of deciphering comes when, as Agnes at last recounts: "Often have I at waking found my fingers ringed with the long worms which bred in the corrupted flesh of my infant. At such times I shrieked with terror and disgust; and . . . trembled with all a woman's weakness" (396). This is truly the pit of the narrative, the moment to which all the digging and lifting of inquiry has led, when the penetrating gaze of the reader can go no further. It is as though the final veil were lifted, the final secret "wormed" out, and behind it were . . . worms. I will explore here the double function of the worm in this text, as both the movement of penetration, of investigative inquiry, and as a possible point of arrival, a kind of stop.

Each of the enfolded stories of *The Monk* is a story of tyranny, of a terrible will-to-mastery through the body. This tyrannical desire to master is composed of a strange entanglement of lust and curiosity, with the need to know playing as fatal a role as the need to gratify the flesh. This mixing—even inseparability—of the pursuits of knowledge and sex underscores the characteristic Gothic tension between, on the one hand, an apparent triumph of reason, and, on the other, an ir- or anti-rationalism that amounts, some have argued, to a perverse nostalgia.[4] The drive to investigate which is structurally and thematically built into *The Monk* is a highly scientific drive, one exhibiting a faith in rational explanation, in discovering meaning through the empirical gaze. Both characters and reader are encouraged to explore, to solve by sense and reason what would appear to be inexplicable phenomena. Thus when the strange moanings in the crypt are at first interpreted by the nuns as the voices of spirits, Lorenzo scoffs at their superstition, calling it "ridiculous in the extreme" (349). He, by contrast, decides to investigate, thereby saving the day. Lorenzo, whose "curiosity, which was ever awake, made him anxious to solve this mystery" (350), becomes the skeptical scientist-hero, exposing and mastering an elaborate series of booby-traps designed to play upon irrational fears and stave off further inquiry. He listens for clues, measures the intervals of the groans, "examine[s]" the supposedly haunted statue of St. Clare with "enquiring eyes" (353), "applie[s] his fingers" to its forbidden surface, and when it begins to move, "easily comprehend[s]" that the mystery it conceals is a trap-door, not a ghost. With the flock of nuns cowering behind him in archaic terror, Lorenzo's investigation stands as the triumph of a vigorous masculine rationalism over the childish—and feminized—fears of the past.

This apparently rationalist stance, though repeated elsewhere in the novel, is countered not only by the obviously contradictory presence of "real" ghosts in the text, but also by the disturbingly parallel investigations that are carried on elsewhere to no good or liberating end. Just a few vaults down, in fact, Ambrosio too is involved in a project of probing a hidden female body—the virginal Antonia's—which is every bit as dedicated as Lorenzo's. Just as Lorenzo employs his senses to "master" the mystery of the statue of St. Clare, so Ambrosio simultaneously explores Antonia's body with "gloating eyes" (366), roving hands, and eager lips, and "made himself master of her person, and desisted not from his prey" (368). A deliberate twinning and overlapping of the rational pursuit of knowledge and the distinctly irrational pursuit of animal lust goes on throughout *The Monk*, in ways which, as I will elaborate, carry broader implications about the possibilities and limitations of any reading of the evidence. The novel self-consciously invokes a pornographics of investigation, whereby any desire for knowledge cannot be detached from that other ravenous desire embedded within it. With equally interesting implications, the converse is also true here: sexual desire is always caught up with the desire to unveil the mystery, to know. In *The Monk*, these two pursuits go hand in hand, pressing toward some "truth" through the pleasurable deceits of clothing, bodies, language. And interestingly, both end up at the same point: at that foreign body, that other worm which is the bottom of the mystery, the ruin of desire and curiosity.

The Worm and the Rose: The Matter of Desire

The motif of the rose, that paradoxically half-opened flower and ever popular poetic emblem, figures prominently in *The Monk*. Like the rosaries which are strewn into even the most obscure corners of the novel—including Agnes's tiny cell—the rose seems to invite meditation on its mysteries. The character Rosario, a layered character if ever there was one in his disguise-upon-disguise, is the farthest realization of the elaborate, petal-like wrappings by which nearly all of the characters are cloaked. Rosario, whose very name and sexual identity are covers, suggests by the very elaborateness of his enclosure a secret opening somewhere beckoning exploration. Seeming to unfold one dark secret after another, he/she is exactly the flower necessary to lure the upright Ambrosio into sin: the rose presents the irresistible pull of concealment, of a mystery calling him in. Looking down after Rosario into the "secret, subterraneous passages," Ambrosio "longed to penetrate into this mystery" (234). In the recurring figure of the mysterious rose, lust and curiosity are once more made inseparable. One might even be tempted to say (risking a very bad pun) that the Foucauldian "will-to-power/knowledge" is emblematized in *The Monk* as a will-to-*flower*/knowledge, with the rose, at once penetrable and resistant, standing as the very structure of desire.

The actual entry of Ambrosio—and the novel—into the mysterious world of sex finally rests upon his plucking Rosario's rose—she actually "point[s] to a bush of roses" (92) and tells him to pick one—here synechdocally associated with both her "heart" (92) and her genitals. This symbolic act is soon followed by Rosario's bodily defloration, which turns out to be a problematic act: as the word implies, such deflowering of a flower eliminates, even as it penetrates, the very tantalizing mystery it yearned to know. Even the multiply-enfolded Rosario cannot escape this logic. Sexuality as structured in *The Monk* enacts an eighteenth-century libertine economy of desire—a cycle of "illusion, conquest, and disgust" recurrent in erotic texts of the period.[5] Plucking Rosario's rose leaves Ambrosio with the exposed woman Matilda, Rosario's "real" identity, a left-over excess of flesh who repels Ambrosio and leaves him "glutted with the fullness of pleasure" (236). The erotic poignancy of the rose, in this system, is its deferring layers: like the virgin Antonia, to whom Ambrosio now turns, with her "rosy" lips and ever-present rosary (39), it inflames desire because, and not in spite of, its hymeneal veils.

Turning to Antonia—upon whose body he will enact the same sexual cycle—Ambrosio plays out the "compulsion to endless repetition"[6] of the libertine, trapped in a system where desire requires a veil. The beauty of the half-opened rose is that, by its layers, it invites penetration but suggests the ideal of an indefinite deferral. It evokes the fantasized possibility of an endless act of penetration, a mystery always in the process of revealing itself, an eternal ecstasy of discovery. Since this fantasy is unrealizable upon any one body, the only direction for the desiring subject to move in his quest for the intact flower is horizontally, along a chain of replaceable objects, where a rose is a rose is a rose. Here the moment of deflowering is repeatable; here the hymen is always intact. Its endless resistance produces the fine frustration that turns libertine desire toward Sade's "lubric rage."[7]

The act of de-flowering, then, implies a vanishing: upon being probed, the object of desire evaporates. Rousseau and Porter write that Enlightenment ideology encouraged male sexual promiscuity, while at the same time enforcing the increasingly contradictory position that the ideal woman was utterly sexually closed off, "angelified,"[8] floating above the flesh. Throughout, *The Monk* is haunted by such spectral female presences. Again and again, the bodies of women are sacrificed to desire, forced to undergo an agonizing shedding of flesh. In this light, the female ghosts of this text appear not as aberrations but rather necessary effects of the machinery of this economy, where the hymeneal veil synecdochally stands for, but also displaces, the body of the woman as the object of desire. By the consistent logic of this fetishistic displacement, when the hymen disappears, the lady too must vanish. The veil, it seems, was already the most solid thing about her—the desired object itself. The rending of the metonymically "contagious" veil, then, produces a bodily disappearance that only makes explicit the female fleshlessness that the libertine economy always already requires.

In the logic of this economy, then, desire requires a bodily erasure that fuels the motion of the investigative machine. Ambrosio's overwhelming desire to penetrate the virgin space—his addiction to discovery—finds its logical culmination in the annihilation of the colonized body. Lorenzo's heroically virile investigation into the catacombs finds a chilling parallel here. In both cases the compulsion to worm out the secret is a compulsion to master, to penetrate all layers, with the spectral body of a woman at, and as, its end. The function of the worm takes on a suspiciously Freudian significance in this context, reminding us of his argument in "Medusa's Head" that the terrible "absence" of the female genitals, their frightening "castrated" state, causes the male spectator (and penis) to grow "stiff" with a horror that translates into arousal.[9] The horror of the female genitals, for Freud, is precisely their hauntedness by the spectral flesh of the penis, the organ that was-and-is-not there. The entire absent/present fe-male body in *The Monk* synecdochally repeats this ambiguous effect of stiffen-ing. First, by its mysterious, rose-like hiddenness, its original half-substantive ambiguity stiffens the spectator, inviting penetration. Second, it stiffens through horror in its spectral state: when Raymond sees the ghostly Bleeding Nun, his response bears an uncanny resemblance to Freud's theorized encounter with the Medusa. "I gazed upon the spectre," he recounts, "with horror too great to be described. My blood was frozen in my veins . . . and I remained in the same attitude inanimate as a statue" (170). When Lorenzo breaks into the tomb in which Agnes lies, "he felt a piercing chillness spread itself through his veins" (355). He sees a woman "half naked," whose "long dishevelled hair fell in dis-order over her face"—most Medusa-like—and he is "petrified with horror. He gazed upon the miserable object with disgust and pity" (355).

After a long worming search, this horror converted into "disgust and pity" parallels Freud's absent-genital horror, which, to make heterosexual intercourse possible, must be converted into a healthy "depreciation of women."[10] Lorenzo's "stiffness" can be seen as the investigator's triumph over absence, a kind of defiant proof of his possession of the tools of discovery: as Freud so bluntly puts it, "I am not afraid of you. I defy you. I have a penis."[11] In the terms of this discus-sion, it is the investigator's proof of mastery—through the wielding of the worm-like penetrating instrument—over the secret, the dark passage, the nothing-to-be-seen. The function of the worm would, from this perspective, be entirely complicit with the mastering urge of that rational/desiring quest which drives so much of this narrative. The phallic worm here furiously uncovers the "truth" of the castrated other, making the flesh confess its disappearance. The apparent distinction between the horror of the good guys in this novel—Raymond and Lorenzo—and Ambrosio's perfidious arousal, becomes as troubled now as that between their different investigations. The boundary be-tween the worming of rational inquiry and the worming of desire is further weakened by the confusion between these different forms of stiffening at the sight of the haunting, half-absent bodies of women.

A number of recent critical discussions of the histories of pornography and science may help to contextualize this evident collapse of boundaries. Foucault, to begin with, famously argues that the rise of modernity coincided with the rise of a "science of sexuality," a relentless drive to control sex through knowledge, by forcing a discursive "confession of the flesh."[12] This scientification of sexuality, according to Foucault, extended through a wide range of interests, including medicine, psychiatry, and pornography. Linda Williams's *Hard Core* uses Foucault's argument as a point of departure to show that the "frenzy of the visible" of contemporary hard-core pornography—its need to affirm and reaffirm the visual "evidence" of pleasure—is an outgrowth of the scientific scrutiny of the body behind such eighteenth-century forerunners of the pornographic genre as Diderot's *Les Bijoux Indiscrets* (1748).[13] A number of recent studies would suggest, in a similar vein, that pornographic writing, with what Lynn Hunt has called its "truth telling trope," took off as a genre in the mid to late eighteenth century, during the high period of the Enlightenment.[14] This leads to the suggestion that pornography, as Peter Michelson has argued, "is coextensive with modern life and its vexations,"[15] and that its deep links to a rising scientific concern with perversion, anomaly, and the interior of the body are what distinguishes it from the sundry erotica of earlier ages. Michelson calls the pornographic aesthetic evidenced in this newly explosive genre a "poetics of obscenity,"[16] stressing the textual over Williams's visual focus, but both pointing to a strikingly similar shift: a shift toward the scrutiny of the open and opened body into which a kind of eroticized "positivist investigation"[17] is not only possible but to some degree compulsory.

The Marquis de Sade stands as the most notable marker of this shift, a sort of logical terminus of this obscene/scientific aesthetic. Sade's heroes enact their eighteenth-century "compulsion to pursue sex as knowledge"[18] on the dangerous meeting ground between the fantasy of endless defloration—the drive from intact body to intact body—and the increasingly medicalized discursive drive to open that body, to get, in effect, to its meat. The erotic friction of Sade's texts comes from the tension between the penetrating, scientific will-to-mastery and the cloaking resistance of hymens, narratives, laws, and other deferring structures.[19] Sade's libertine butcher-heroes are scientists of a sort: Justine's Rodin is a surgeon, a medical "researcher" who takes pains to investigate his pupil's bodies.[20] Rodin's surgical skills allow Sade to exploit erotically the resistance of flesh: the libertine's pleasure here comes from the power to drive through the skin, to force it to yield up its secrets under examination. As with other, perhaps more innocuous libertines, Sade's mad libertine-scientists require a hymen: Rombeau explains in Justine that his experiments need "the hymeneal membrane; we must, of course, find a young girl for the dissection,"[21] and the narrative progress of the *120 Days* is structured around the painstakingly planned, progressive entry into the virginal bodies of its victims. What sets Sade apart from more mainstream pornography, I would argue, is that he literalizes in his works the synecdochal displacement of the body of the desired object by its hymen. Sade graphically turns the whole body into a hymen to be pierced, torn and penetrated. The wasteful libertine economy of desire is thus made both more explicit and, in a perverse sense, more efficient: the hymeneal region expands, and the whole body of the victim becomes a surface through which the pleasure of discovery can be enacted again and again.

Sade's narrative structures, too, exploit to the fullest the erotic tension between penetration and resistance. Always recognizing that the will-to-knowledge requires, and does not merely overcome, a mystery, Sade's pornographic narratives are intricately structured to defer the ultimate unfolding of their plots. In the *120 Days*, the exploits of the libertines are carefully cloaked by coy digressions and euphemisms, and an elaborate structure of stories within the story, so that they are only gradually made explicit in the narrative. The libertines themselves are never permitted to enact an "experiment" which has not first been narrated to them by another character. Just as Sade exploits the resistance of the flesh's tissues, so he exploits textual resistance, playing between the inevitable, deadly progress of the narrative and the layers of language that both incite it and slow it down.

Sade's pornographic scientists are all too aware of their need for textual mediation, and of the pleasures at stake in their investigations. They stand in ironic contrast to the ideal of the objective empirical scientist disinterestedly engaged in the hunt for truth, a figure who can perhaps be seen as the culturally legitimate brother to Sade's furiously curious libertine. Barbara Stafford in *Body Criticism* discusses a "shift toward visualization" that pervaded eighteenth-century scientific discourse and practice, a penetrating scientific gaze which marks the beginnings of modern science.[22] In its urge to get below deceptive surfaces, to establish a new order in the face of a damaged old one, eighteenth-century science rigorously pursued the new arts of dissection, microscopy, and meticulous representations of interior bodily anatomy such as those in Diderot's *Encyclopédie* (1772), wherein, as Stafford writes, "forms were flayed and divested of superfluous ornament. . . . Thus pithed and cored, they were made congruent to an undeceptive ideal nakedness, or to a profound sincerity."[23] Diderot, not insignificantly, was also a pornographer; and in his *Les Bijoux Indiscrets* women's genitals are actually compelled to confess their secrets, suggesting a related discursive drive to get below the obstructing foliage of signification, to discover a language that "yields direct access to the flesh."[24] Diderot's straddling of both discourses again underlines the disguised similarity of their aims, a similarity which no one punctuates more vehemently than Sade. Sade's texts in this light can be seen as parodying the self-professed disinterestedness of the scientific drive into the flesh, suggesting (as Stafford does) an unacknowledged excess in its self-perpetuating, and sometimes deadly, desire to know.

The emergence of the genre of the novel, with its emphasis on an exhaustive verisimilitude, from this same eighteenth-century socio-historical matrix, would suggest a link to the shift toward this pornographic/scientific aesthetic. Connections suggest themselves between the penetrating gazes of pornography and science and the early novelistic impulse to probe into private spaces, to minutely dissect human life, and to present the illusion of authorial absence, of the "facts" simply presenting themselves. In Ian Watt's well-known formulation, the rise of the novel is identified with a "dispassionate and scientific scrutiny of life"[25] achieved in part by abstinence from the superfluous flourishes of style which, as Locke objects (quoted half-ironically in Watt) "'. . . like the fair sex, involve . . . a pleasurable deceit."[26] It is more than incidental that Samuel Richardson—perhaps the "realest" of the early realists by Watt's account, takes, like the bulk of the medical and pornographic discourse of the time, the bodies of women as the preferred objects of his empirical gaze. The illusion of objectivity is coercive: the pretense of naturalness elides the implicit violence of a scopic, textual, and bodily entry. And if, as in Richardson's texts, the "fair sex," like flowery rhetoric, must be cut and opened, laid bare in the chase for the elusive "real," we cannot dismiss the Sadean implications of such a venture.

Stafford discusses Enlightenment science's "fearful disdain of mixtures,"[27] a disdain intimately linked to a horror and fascination with the muddiness of representation. The "sickly" and "extravagent"[28] genre of the Gothic novel there-fore repelled many critics of its time, with its use of a style and thematic that magnifies, rather than represses, the discrepancies in representation which Lorenzo in one of his own stories calls a "violence upon truth" (209). The Gothic novel interrogates novelistic realism in the same way that Sade's texts interro-gate science. The worming pursuit of the endlessly receding referent is thematized here as a destructive chase, although one which the novel self-con-sciously participates in as much as critiques. What *The Monk* calls into question is any inquiry that claims disinterest, any "truth" that claims non-mediation. Like Sade, it foregrounds the act of penetration and the textual/bodily resis-tance it requires: it insists upon the ravages of the worm.

Another Matter

The process of desire in *The Monk* is a digestive process: the curious worm seems to eat everything it moves through, leaving only spectral absence in its wake. The problem with this characterization, though, is what it, and the worm, leave out—the left-over flesh which is both by-product and excess of this sys-tem. This is what Stafford calls the "undigested phenomena"[29] of a system ob-sessed with making sense of the world; it is matter which somehow cannot be abstracted, dissected, known. In Stafford's usage, it characterizes the role of the grotesque and hybrid in the eighteenth century, forms unassimilable to the new scientific/aesthetic ordering systems, and fascinating to them precisely for that reason. In *The Monk*, this excess takes the form of flesh that is outside the scope of desire. There is a kind of anorexic logic at work here, a paradoxical logic by which even as the body disappears into that insubstantiality required by desire, it becomes nothing but flesh, just as tissues wasting away become waste. Ambrosio rejects Matilda out of "loathing" for her carnal excessiveness; the Bleeding Nun, too, is a reject of desire, her ghostly ephemerality itself haunted by a disturbing physicality: "icy fingers," "bloodless" lips, and lusterless "eye-balls" (170). Agnes's emaciated form in the climactic dungeon scene is actually the most concrete of her many appearances in the text—her wasted body here is described in exacting detail. These left-over bodies, though the inevitable product of the ravenous desire to know, nonetheless remain strangely outside this economy. They stop desire/knowledge in its tracks: they are its end in both senses—telos and terminus. Not only are they undesirable (although Agnes is recuperable because her flesh is not yet completely wasted), they are also *unreadable*, uninterpretable and thus effectively meaningless. The wild mob's desire to know the truth about the convent ends up turning the prioress into a "shapeless" fleshy mass, a form finally unrecognizable, stopping the progress of inquisitive rage. The Bleeding Nun too is unreadable, requiring a special interlocutor to make her needs known; and Agnes in her corpse-like state is referred to only as "the unknown" (360). The unwanted body, the body that can sustain no further inquiry, is the unknown of this system—unreadable, unclassifiable matter.

Within such excess flesh, again and again in this novel, appear worms. Agnes's dead baby, the excess flesh for which she is exiled, breeds them; they "prey[ed] upon" (385) the rows of mouldering nun's bodies in the crypt; they appear even in the book Antonia picks up to read, a book of "old Spanish ballads" which "excited her curiosity" (306). Therein, with an interesting gender-reversal from the norm in this book, the cast-off Alonzo comes back to trouble the woman who deserted him: "All turned with disgust from the scene/The worms they crept in, and the worms they crept out/ And sported his eyes and his temples about" (308). Antonia's readerly curiosity is effectively stopped: she puts down the book and "trembled so violently that she was unable to proceed" (309). In a moment that prefigures Agnes's recoiling from the project of deciphering her baby's wormy face, the worm here again appears at the limit of reading, the collapse of curiosity. If excess flesh holds an uncertain place in this world, disturbingly filling up space without fitting in, then the worm can be seen as the final confirmation of its unassimilability by the reading/desiring subject. The worm confirms that flesh's excessiveness, its horrible lack of value within this economy. Nothing can be done with flesh eaten by worms, nothing can be made of it, nothing seen. The interior worm which has somehow claimed it faces down the worming investigator. It is the inevitable end of flesh, yet somehow, in this work, it is always unexpected, an outsider-inside, irreconcilably other.

One of the most significant worms in this text is the worm that springs from the innermost layers of Rosario's rose. For even though Rosario stands as the consummate rose in this text, wrapped up and ripe for investigation, there is, we discover, already a worm at the heart of this flower. When Ambrosio reaches to pluck the rose which becomes the figure for Rosario's deflowering, there is a sudden turn of events: "He approached the bush, and stooped to pick one of the roses. Suddenly he uttered a piercing cry. . . . 'I have received my death . . . concealed among the roses—a serpent'" (92). Ambrosio's piercing by the serpent (archaic appellation: worm) seems to be a case of the rose biting back, of the deflowered—and soon to be wasted—flesh getting its revenge. It is as though the spectator's erotic triumph over the mysterious nothing-to-be-seen were suddenly reversed, his penetrating phallus confronted with another phallus, an instrument poised to open his own body. This reading of the worm would seem to be confirmed by the strange gender-reversed progress of Ambrosio's fate. For though he remains a penetrator through most of the text, the "wound" (93) which Rosario's worm has given him brings out the rose in Ambrosio. The gender-reversing motif initiated with the cross-dressed Rosario is carried through with the feminization of Ambrosio at the end of the novel. Stepping into a position reminiscent of Agnes's during her relentless interrogation by the nuns, he is "put to the question" (404) by the "Grand Inquisitor" (402), pierced and prodded by "various iron instruments," a situation which causes him to "turn pale," "tremble" and faint (402). The Inquisition worms out secrets with a vengeance, but now Ambrosio's skin is the surface under which the truth is sought in its "examination" (404). The novel closes upon the wasted remains of Ambrosio's body, "prey" (419) of Lucifer, who, it turns out, was all along the real worm inside Rosario. Ambrosio ends up like the excess flesh of women whose bodies litter the text, another matter worked through by the worm.

But does this ostensibly gender-bending worm really pose a challenge to the consumptive patriarchal economy that dominates *The Monk*, or is it just more of the same? Isn't this worm's final triumph just a turning of the tables, so that Ambrosio, the studious male reader, is feminized into the object of study, finally read (and red)? The man who had to know every seductive mystery before him is himself summarily figured out, his body dissected, exposed. This reading would seem to leave the structure of desire and knowledge intact: the worm remains on the side of the aggressive, investigating subject, always behind that ravenous urge to get under the skin of an object who, in this symbolic system, is almost always gendered female. Perhaps Matilda's worm is just a "counter pe-nis,"[30] the showdown of worms here just another phallic battle.

On the other hand, though, the worm can be seen as thoroughly outside this economy: drawing on French feminism, Matilda, her "rose" crawling with snakes, could be the image of that *other* Medusa, the one subversive because of her incomprehensibility, her position outside familiar structures of knowledge and desire. Cixous's rewriting of Freud in "The Laugh of the Medusa" takes the dismembered specter of Freud's formula and makes it a powerful Other, one whose function is not, this time, merely to facilitate the reproduction of patriarchy by "horrifying" into arousal.[31] The snakes that surround this Medusa's head, she claims, are not phallic substitutes; rather they are the visionary back-talk of excess feminine flesh, the undeniable fleshy presence of a truly *other* body with an *other* desire not predicated upon castration. If the worm that springs from inside Matilda/Rosario can be figured in this way, it is a worm which subverts, rather than merely mirroring, the dangerous investigations of the phallic worm. Its wormwork, rather than advancing the progress of phallic desire, halts it by undermining all its requisite layers, its requisite identities. It claims flesh for a system wherein gender as we know it is irrelevant, wherein the body can no longer be read as a sign. Hence the radical indeterminacy of Matilda's name, sex, and even her substantiality. The wormy baby, too, whose face Agnes strains to read, is such an "unknown" that even its gender remains unreadable in the text. And the worm at the bottom of Rosario is the one secret that Ambrosio cannot finally worm out with his questioning, the one thing that truly escapes him, making a mess of both desire and inquiry.

This other worm to which the text's investigations so often lead, I would argue, is more likely a combination of these two models. Indeed, the repeated facing off of the investigative worm, in this novel, with the worm that refuses investigation undercuts the idea of a strict opposition between them. *The Monk* points to a dual position for the worm: at once outside the mysterious body/ text, hungrily looking in, and also always already implicated within it. After Ambrosio finally achieves his goal with Antonia, penetrating her virginal body in the "friendly night of Mystery" (366), repeatedly "wounding" her in "the violence of his lustful delirium" (368), he, in turn, encounters a worm there: touching her hand, "he dropped it again as if he had touched a serpent" (371).

Ambrosio's desire is extinguished by this other worm: it "penetrates" (371) his conscience, interrogates all the evil worming he has done. In this sense it seems like a voice from outside, an elsewhere which estranges the object from a desiring system based on mysteries, veils, and lack. This worm purges the flesh of the mysteries which made it so enticing, leaving it just dumb flesh. On the other hand, this inner worm, much like the one that sprung from Matilda, could be the inevitable telos of a desiring system which renders women first absence and then excess. Does the phallic worm, after all, need this other worm, this limit to desire and comprehension, this thing that stops its probings? Is this the very limit which compels it to displace its desire onto the next, (illusively) intact object? This other worm's complicity with, or subversiveness of, *The Monk*'s desiring economy is finally left as uncertain as Matilda's identity. But its consistent and troubling presence within "investigated" bodies hints at the possibility of a "worm-hole" leading out of this economy, to an elsewhere where its careful layers literally fall apart.

The Matter of Reading

The worming investigation of the mystery is, of course, enacted at another level in *The Monk*, for the novel's own complex and self-conscious narrative layerings, its teasing "veiling" and unveiling of secrets, structurally repeat, for reader and text, the relationship of the worm and the rose. *The Monk* too, like Sadean pornography, depends upon textual embedding for its affective impact. This impact is built, in both cases, on the keen tension between inevitability and deferral which the structure works ever to amplify. The narrative and generic embeddings so notable in this work facilitate, as in Sade, the dropping of deadly clues: we are led to suspect the outcome of events in the larger narrative based on what happens in the myriad poems, epigraphs and stories appearing within it. Sometimes the hints are quite direct, as when the gypsy's song tells Antonia of her chilling fate: she ignores it; we, of course, do not. Other clues are based on echoing motifs, as when the Bleeding Nun's case thematically predicts that of the nun Agnes. Even the main narratives echo one another: the parallel descents into the catacombs of Agnes and Antonia, the "inquisitions" of Agnes and Ambrosio, and on and on. Through this conspicuous scattering of clues the reader is virtually compelled, like a true scientist, to formulate hypotheses and push on to investigate them through the resistance of text.

The novel's textual embeddings do not merely provide clues to an opening into the text's dark mysteries; they also actively obstruct our enlightenment. The interrupting tales within tales stand massively in the way of the reader who, armed with collected clues, is eager to resolve a particular narrative. Like the catacombs of St. Clare, like the structure of the pornographic text, the structure of suspense here titillates through peeks at a secret indefinitely veiled and deferred. The narrative gets in our way not just by obstruction but also by deception: just as Lorenzo must grapple with the statue of St. Clare, so must we contend with decoys deliberately placed to mislead us. In the case of Rosario, for example, hints are dropped to let us suspect the first of his unveilings: we glimpse the "beauty" (66) of his features, we hear the leading story of "Matilda" that he tells. But we later find that the matter is far from settled, and the growing evidence of deception places the reader in an adversarial relationship to the narrative as we try to wring the "truth" from this story.

In a number of ways, then, we as readers are implicated within the aggressive drive to know which *The Monk* thematizes. One might even say that its structured suspense encourages a sort of violence to the text, for we must cut across its elaborate enfoldings, cut out its misleading concealments, to get to the heart of the matter. And yet *The Monk* frustrates, even as it encourages, our mounting rage to explain. With the final, and unforeseeable, twist in Matilda's identity, the novel trips up all of our speculations, our carefully collected "facts," seeming to laugh in the face of any expectation of a real conclusion, a plausible resolution.

At the very structural center of the book is an embedded text which plays out this readerly-textual relation. Here Raymond reads with "pleasure" (205) the poem of his young page Theodore, a composition bedecked with roses, virgins, and flowery prose. Having read this, Raymond launches into a long diatribe against the critic: "An author . . . is an animal whom every body is privileged to attack. . . . A bad composition carries with it its own punishment—contempt and ridicule. A good one excites envy, and entails upon its author a thousand mortifications" (204). This literary moment seems an odd interruption to the book. Yet in the context of this wormy reading of the novel, perhaps we can somewhat account for its sudden appearance and its structural central- ity. For Raymond's theorizing makes explicit the textual aspect of the preda- tory worming thematized throughout the book. The reader here, quite graphically, becomes a parasite upon the corporeal, "animal" body of the text. By the magic of metonymic association, the word is made flesh for infestation, the critics its hungry eaters. Raymond's abhorrence of the "wounding" (204) damage of the reader is such that he cautions Theodore against ever baring his work to anyone at all. Any reading of a text, in this view, becomes corrupting: like Ambrosio's assiduous study of Antonia, to read a virginal work is to "work her ruin" (244).

As if to demonstrate the critic's destructiveness, Raymond follows up this speech with a mortifying review of the helpless poem, faulting it for its "ter- rible confusion of metaphors," its shameless intertextual "borrowing," and for lines which "consist more in words than sense" (205). The specter of Gothic fiction and its reception lurks in these ironic lines, with their accusations of hybridity of form, archaism, and flowery entanglement of prose. *The Monk* is itself a well-documented instance of multiple literary "borrowings,"[32] and its flowery layers are precisely the titillating source of its appeal. Perhaps this nar- rative moment, then, stands as an ironic defense of "bad" reading matter, of texts that do not comply with a rising novelistic aesthetic of representational transparency and naturalness. Raymond himself takes "pleasure" in the evi- dent affectations of Theodore's writing; a pleasure which his subsequent criti- cal attack denies. What these passages seem to indict, finally, is not the wormwork of reading per se but any pretense of critical objectivity, the essen- tial lie of a reading which denies that its real purpose is not a quest for a "true" evaluation, but the pleasure of the struggle with the text.

The Monk suggests that any penetration of the rose-like mysteries of bodies and narratives is implicitly or explicitly corrupting. Any appeal to a pure en- gagement with knowledge is ironized here because it denies its own pleasure, the excruciating pleasure of discovery which is the secret all those leaves of text were hiding. Yet if this appears to promote a Sadean and familiarly gendered model of reading, Lewis's worms take us beyond this, because there are already worms within the text, whose horrible presence troubles such gender divisions and formulations of the readerly ruin of the literary work. If Raymond's criticism seemed to be the worm at the center of this text, the destructive critical voice that de-composed Theodore's creation, the preface of *The Monk* points to a worm in the work beyond the invasion of the critical eye. In the introductory poem, an "Imitation of Horace" (itself, not insignificantly, an overt intertextual borrowing) Lewis imagines his own book, rejected and unread after its "novelty" has worn off:

> Soon as your novelty is o'er,
> And you are young and new no more,
> In some dark dirty corner thrown,
> Mouldy with damps, with cobwebs strown
> Your leaves shall be the book-worm's prey (33, 34)

The book here, used up and disposed of by a merciless readerly economy, becomes excess text, thrown out of the system, crawling with worms like the rejected flesh that figures so prominently in *The Monk's* narratives. The book itself is figured here in all the disturbing corporeality of these Gothic bodies. Like the old book that Antonia opens, this book breeds worms from within, worms that, like those worms, "sport about" with its left-over fleshiness. And just as the other worms in the novel stop the progress of the reader, defiant in their unintelligibility, this "book-worm" at the beginning of the text interrogates the power of the critic by suggesting that even the violence of worm-work is not his prerogative. If the text is a body bound inevitably for corruption, then the "bookworm" suggests a fundamental unreadability, an epistemological block, at the heart of any literary work: whether circulating or not, the book in Lewis's universe is always already prey.

Lewis's work forces the reader to face the presence of that other worm; to face that the matter we come up against in our textual probings is always another, an unknown something, not what we sought. *The Monk* suggests that all we can do as readers, and what I have attempted in this wormy reading, is to sportively take pleasure in the worm's undoings. Taking the worm as an emblem of this text, my reading is already ripe for infestation.

Notes

1. Matthew G. Lewis, *The Monk*. Louis F. Peck, ed. (New York: Grove Press, 1952). (1796)

2. Eve Kosofsky Sedgwick, "The Character in the Veil: Imagery of the Surface in the Gothic Novel." *PMLA* 96, no. 2 (1981): 255–70.

3. Ibid., 256.

4. See, for example, Kenneth W. Graham, ed., *Gothic Fictions: Prohibition/ Transgression* (New York: AMS Press,1989).

5. For discussions of this cycle, see James Turner, "The Culture of Priapism," *Review* 10 (1988), and "Sex and Consequence," *Review* 11 (1989) 133–65, as well as G. S. Rousseau and Roy Porter, eds., *Sexual Underworlds of the Enlightenment* (Manchester: Manchester University Press, 1987).

6. Rousseau and Porter, 3.

7. Marquis de Sade, *The 120 Days of Sodom and Other Writings*, Austryn Wainhouse and Richard Seaver, eds. and trans., (New York: Grove, 1966), 606.

8. Rousseau and Porter, 4.

9. Sigmund Freud, "Medusa's Head," in *Sexuality and the Psychology of Love* (New York: Collier, 1963), 212.

10. Sigmund Freud, "The Infantile Genital Organization of the Libido," in *Sexuality and the Psychology of Love* (New York: Collier, 1963), 174.

11. Ibid., 213.

12. Michel Foucault, *The History of Sexuality*, v. I (New York: Vintage, 1990).

13. Linda Williams, *Hard Core: Power, Pleasure, and the "Frenzy of the Visible,"* (Berkeley: University of California Press, 1989).

14. Lynn Hunt, ed., *The Invention of Pornography: Obscenity and the Origins of Modernity, 1500–1800* (New York: Zone Books, 1993), 33–37. See also Peter Michelson, *Speaking the Unspeakable: A Poetics of Obscenity* (New York: SUNY Press, 1993).

15. Michelson, 1.

16. Ibid., 4.

17. Ibid., 21.

18. Turner, "Culture," 7.

19. Luce Irigaray has written eloquently on Sade: "*What fantasy of a closed, solid, virginal body to be forced open* underlies such a representation, and such a practice, of sexuality? In this view, the body's pleasure always results from a forced entry—preferably bloody—into an

enclosure. . . . The pornographic scene is *indefinitely repetitive*. It never stops. It always has to start over. One more time. And another. The alibi of pleasure covers the need for endless reiteration." Luce Irigaray, *This Sex Which is Not One*, Catherine Porter, trans. (Ithaca: Cornell University Press, 1985), 201.

20. See Jane Gallop, *Thinking Through the Body* (New York: Columbia University Press, 1988), 51. Gallop writes, "what we have here is the Sadian version of the *coupure epistemologique* . . . which is to say research into the origin and nature of knowledge" (52).

21. Marquis de Sade, *Justine, Philosophy in the Bedroom, and Other Writings*, Austryn Wainhouse and Richard Seaver, eds. and trans. (New York: Grove, 1965), 551.

22. Barbara Maria Stafford, *Body Criticism: Imagining the Unseen in Enlightenment Art and Medicine* (Cambridge: MIT Press, 1991), 2.

23. Ibid., 18.

24. Turner, "Sex," 135.

25. Ian Watt, *The Rise of the Novel* (Berkley: University of California Press, 1957), 11.

26. John Locke, *An Essay Concerning Human Understanding*, Book III, ch. 10, sec. 34; qtd in Watt, 28.

27. Stafford, 211.

28. William Wordsworth, preface to *Lyrical Ballads*. In *Selected Poems and Prefaces,* Jack Stillinger, ed. (Boston: Houghton Mifflin, 1965), 449.

29. Stafford, 274.

30. Simone de Beauvoir on Cixous and Irigaray. From a 1984 interview qtd. in Margaret Whitford, ed., *The Irigaray Reader* (Oxford: Blackwell, 1992).

31. Helene Cixous, "The Laugh of the Medusa." In *The Signs Reader* (Chicago: University of Chicago Press, 1983).

32. See, for example, Syndy M. Conger, "Sensibility Restored: Radcliffe's Answer to Lewis's *The Monk*," for an account of some of Lewis's intertexts, openly acknowledged by him. In Kenneth Graham, *Gothic Fictions: Prohibition/Transgression* (New York: AMS, 1989).

The Imprisoned Female Body in *Mary Hays's* The Victim of Prejudice

Eleanor Ty

In her Advertisement to the Reader, Mary Hays states that what she wants to question in *The Victim of Prejudice* (1799) is the "too-great stress laid on the *reputation* for chastity in *woman*" and the "*means* ... which are used to ensure it."[1] This aim echoes that of Mary Wollstonecraft, who in *The Vindication of the Rights of Woman* (1792), had also argued that "regard for reputation" was "the grand source of female depravity" because it causes women to adopt an "artificial mode of behaviour."[2] What both writers deplored was the way the customs and society of late eighteenth-century England put more emphasis on the external sign of chastity, or reputation, than on chastity or purity itself. In their works, both Wollstonecraft and Hays sought to differentiate between outward representations of female virtue and the morality that sprang from women's understanding and strength of character. This insistence on the separation between reputation and the actual possession of virtue ultimately made Wollstonecraft, Hays, and other radical women of the 1790s the subject of much criticism and censure by the conservative thinkers of the time.[3] Their claims for moral, economic, and intellectual liberty were viewed simply as a justification for sexual freedom and licentiousness.

By the time Hays wrote *The Victim of Prejudice*, she had already suffered what she called "the cry of slander" due to her first novel, *Memoirs of Emma*

Courtney, which depicted a woman's passion and pursuit of her desire.[4] Nevertheless, she continued to resist the dominant culture's beliefs in the "proper lady" and persisted in demonstrating how the bodily experience of women differed from that of the fabular or linguistic construction of woman.[5]

In her second novel, she is concerned with the way the female subject is shaped and constructed by ideologies defined by class and gender-hierarchies. Using Edward Moore's *Fables for the Female Sex* (1744) as an intertext, she rewrites the story of the seduced woman highlighting the emotional and psychic pain, the bodily sufferings of her heroine. In Foucault's terms, one could say that *The Victim of Prejudice* demonstrates the way the "female body is transformed into a feminine one" by being disciplined and punished.[6] In his study of prisons, twentieth-century historian Michel Foucault argues that it was in the late eighteenth century that there was a shift in penal justice from one of corporeal punishment to a more subtle form which intends to "correct, reclaim, cure."[7] He notes that "the body now serves as an instrument or intermediary: if one intervenes upon it to imprison it, or to make it work, it is in order to deprive the individual of a liberty that is regarded both as a right and as property. The body, according to this penality, is caught up in a system of constraints and privations, obligations and prohibitions."[8]

It is such a system of constraints and deprivations that Hays illustrates in her novel. Her narrative reveals how systems of power and authority manipulate and operate to create a docile body out of one originally of "robust constitution, a cultivated understanding, and a vigorous intellect" (5). In her words, the "means" used to ensure that women paid attention to their "reputation" lead to "hypocrisy, not virtue" (1, 174).

My paper explores the roles that language and the cultural representations of women play in the construction of the heroine's subjectivity in *Victim of Prejudice*. It shows how the confinement of the heroine in the penitentiary is linked to eighteenth-century society's need for control and surveillance, especially of female sexuality. The heroine's lament that she has become "the victim of a barbarous prejudice" (174) is not just the story of one woman's loss, but becomes indicative of the way the culture circumscribed what it perceived to be unruly and uncontrollable in women. Through her polemical novel, Hays reveals that the violation of women's bodies and women's lives is not inevitable or natural, but is enabled by "narratives, complexes and institutions which derive their strength not from outright, immutable, unbeatable force but rather from their power to structure [women's] lives as imposing cultural scripts."[9]

From the short introduction which begins the novel, it is clear that Hays was attempting to recast one script, which Susan Staves calls the "seduced-maiden tales" in different terms.[10] Her heroine, Mary Raymond, repeatedly asserts her "innocence" in spite of her lost chastity (3). She represents herself as "a child of misfortune, a wretched outcast" from her society, someone "driven with ignominy from social intercourse" (3), rather than a sweetly pathetic fallen woman. The language, which reverberates with Jacobin polemics, is much more reminiscent of William Godwin's *Caleb Williams* or Mary Wollstonecraft's *Maria; or the Wrongs of Woman* than that of a distressed maiden. Typically, as Staves notes, the seduced-maiden tales "rely heavily on a romantic idealization of maidenly devotion to chastity, a devotion rewarded not in this life but in the purer world toward which the dying maiden so frequently turns her final glance."[11] In these literary seductions, the girl's father plays a prominent role; he is seen "both in law and in fiction" as the "chief victim."[12] While Hays's narrative follows the plots of these seduction tales to a certain extent, there are a number of important deviations worth noting. One of the crucial differences between *The Victim of Prejudice* and works such as Elizabeth Inchbald's *Nature and Art* or Amelia Opie's *The Father and Daughter,* both of which are cited by Staves, is the use of the first-person narrative. By letting her heroine tell her own tale, Hays empowers Mary Raymond's subjectivity and validates her experience rather than romanticizing her. Gary Kelly has argued that the use of the first-person or confessional mode was characteristic of Jacobin novels of the 1790s, as it was a genre that could have "political and revolutionary implications." It had the "function of showing how an individual developed from personal experience a critical consciousness about his or her own 'rights' in the face of social oppression."[13] Using this mode, Mary Raymond is able to distinguish her mental or emotional state from physical and social circumstances over which she, as a woman, has little control. Even in her last days, she judges herself by personal rather than social standards. She claims to derive "firmness from innocence, courage from despair," and, even in prison, asserts that she possesses an "unconquerable spirit, bowed but not broken" (3).

Another cultural script or narrative that Hays was revising is "The Female Seducers" by Edward Moore and Henry Brooke. This fable is part of a collection of sixteen fables published as *Fables for the Female Sex* initially in 1744 and reprinted frequently throughout the eighteenth and early nineteenth centuries. This extremely popular work from which Hays quotes in the epigraph and towards the end of the novel teaches young women about vanity, modesty, coquetry, cleanliness, and other lessons. "The Female Seducers" is one of the longer fables which does not use animals as characters and which teaches women that "honour is a woman's life."[14] In the fable, a young girl at the "crisis of fifteen" leaves her parents' care to go on a journey. Her aged parents warn her that as a woman she is "frail as fair," and that if once her foot strays from heaven's "appointed way," then "reproach, scorn, infamy, and hate" shall await her.[15] She is seduced by Sirens and by Pleasure and returns disgraced and in despair. At the end, only angels in heaven welcome the "lovely penitent" who finds no asylum elsewhere.

This fable, which is longer and contains a more developed narrative than the others in the collection, has much in common with the seduced-maiden tales. In these narratives, a woman's whole subjectivity is predicated upon her sexual chastity. Once a young girl has lost her virginity, she is no longer fit for earthly society and becomes an outcast and spends the rest of her life as a penitent. What Hays does in *The Victim of Prejudice* is to call upon these narratives and to show how they are not reflections of woman's experience, but rather are ideological representations or cultural scripts which transmit a set of assumptions or values of patriarchal society. The intention of the fables is similar to those of conduct-manuals and of some domestic or sentimental novels, notably those by writers such as Samuel Richardson or Jane West. They are designed to teach young women of marriageable age that they are to be modest, chaste, and dutiful. Although critics such as Nancy Armstrong have argued persuasively that domestic fiction helped produce the modern female individual who "understood herself in psychological terms,"[16] this subject, who could represent her desire, took over a hundred fifty years to develop and she did not emerge without conflict. For the most part, domestic novels, like conduct-books, helped, in Vivien Jones's words, to "regulate social and sexual behaviour, teaching women to discipline themselves into acceptable forms of femininity in order to achieve and maintain respectability."[17] Hays, like Mary Wollstonecraft, struggled with these socially and culturally established notions of what a woman ought to be and for what qualities she should be most valued. Unlike the author of "The Female Seducers," she did not believe that "honour" in a woman's life was necessarily equated with virginity. Though her heroine, like the young girl in the fable, eventually has nothing but death to look forward to, she is unwilling to follow the script of the fable or to be defined in terms of virginity, frail beauty, seduction, or penitence. The fact that she is nevertheless forcibly cast into these roles by others demonstrates the pervasiveness of these ideologies about women, and the violence used on her to enforce them reveals the arbitrariness and unnaturalness of these positions for women.

Although the plot of *The Victim of Prejudice* substantially follows that of the fable, one of the ways in which Hays renders her text polemical is by accentuating the bodily experience of the woman. In Moore's fable, the body of the young girl is curiously absent from the narrative. For the most part, the fable describes the unnamed maiden in idealized and ethereal terms which fit with the universalizing and moralizing tendency of the fabulist. She is the daughter "too divinely fair," the "brightest beauty," who is betrayed (273, 280). When she is seduced, she is the "nymph" with "her treasure flown" (285). She becomes the "lonely Trembler" and the "lovely penitent" after her transgression (286, 288). Such epithets distance readers from identifying too closely with the actual emotional or physical state of the girl. She remains an unreal example of lost virtue and innocence. In contrast to this deliberate effect of remoteness in the fable, Hays's novel, which uses techniques we associate with realistic fiction, focuses on details and the woman's life experiences. Hays shows how various texts, language, and the ways in which women were represented in the late eighteenth century have a detrimental effect on the lives of actual women of the time.

The Victim of Prejudice is a novel whose author and heroine react to texts and textuality. Aside from Moore's *Fables*, Hays was also rewriting Richardson's *Clarissa*, as I have argued elsewhere.[18] In fact, the *Anti-Jacobin Review* condemned the novel because it was so unlike the tone and moral nature of *Clarissa:*

> In the *dishonour* . . . of 'Mary,' there is something like an imitation of Clarissa; but how unlike to the original!—In conformity to the general spirit of this

authoress, and her party . . . religion is utterly, and with zealous care, excluded from her writings. The pious addresses of Clarissa to her Creator, affect the heart of the reader with the most delightful and grateful sensations; while the furious declamation of 'Mary' to the God of nature, and the God of reason, excite no sentiment but disgust.[19]

The *Anti-Jacobin* reviewers saw the comparison Hays intended, but what they found so objectionable was the "furious declamation of Mary." This declamation was Hays's repetitive critique of social practices, institutions, the legal system, and the power of the aristocracy. Unlike Clarissa who after her seduction accepts her fate with resignation and equanimity, the heroine Mary Raymond rages against her oppressors, those who defeat what she calls her "right to exist" (141). She is unwilling to accept the notion that a woman who has lost her virginity must necessarily be socially banished and must look towards heaven for redemption. Mary's attitude to life is contrary to that shown by the maiden in the fable or Richardson's heroine:

> My bosom swelled with honest indignant pride: I determined to live; I determined that the devices of my persecutors should not overwhelm me: my spirit roused itself to defeat their malice and baffle their barbarous schemes. (141)

This spirited stance is not in keeping with the passive and submissive demeanor required of the feminine subject in traditional conduct-books. It is not surprising that Hays aroused the ire of conservative thinkers of the time.

Another text which affects the heroine adversely is her mother's memoirs which Mr. Raymond presents to her. This intradiegetic text occupies a central position in Mary's life and is symbolically situated in the middle of the two-volume novel. It is the last narrative of a woman, but framed by the discourse of a man, albeit a progressive and liberal one. Mary does not have direct access to her dead mother, or to her maternal body, and her access to the body of text left by her mother is problematic. The packet containing the pages written by Mary's mother is enclosed within letters to Mary written by Mr. Raymond. He, in effect, has the task not only of introducing and ending the story, but also of directing the response of the reader. While as a former suitor of Mary's mother, he is sympathetic to her plight, his language reveals that he is very much a product of patriarchal culture and of his age. When he describes her mother to Mary, it is in romantic and idealized terms, much like the language in Moore's fable. He remembers her as "a young woman, amiable and accomplished," as "lovely Mary, whom Nature had formed in her most perfect mould" (58). The mother is presented as an object of male desire at first, and then, after her seduction, she becomes a madwoman and whore. When Mr. Raymond sees her five years later she is "a woman, with a wan and haggard countenance, her clothes rent and her hair dishevelled" (59). He perceives "the remains of uncommon beauty," but she is "stained with blood, disordered by recent inebriation, disfigured by vice, and worn by disease" (60). His representations of Mary's mother are polar opposites, showing that he can conceive of his former lover only in terms of the angel or the whore.

Mary's introduction to her mother, and to the text left by her mother then, is influenced by these representations of woman as either lovely angel or contaminated whore. Her reading of her mother's legacy is mediated by these textual depictions. As well as gathering information, Mary and we, as readers, have to learn to decipher and read the text written by the mother. The mother's narrative is that of the seduced maiden, and though in prose, has reverberations reminiscent of the paternalistic and judgmental tone of Moore's fable. The memoirs reveal that, following the codes of society, the mother's standards of right and wrong behaviour are based, not surprisingly, on sexual purity. Once she has lost her "innocence," she feels that she has also lost all dignity, self-respect, and self-worth. This disintegration affects her physically, emotionally, socially, and economically. Significantly, she increasingly speaks of herself as a victim, as someone without control over her destiny, and someone lacking in agency and subjectivity. The language she uses reflects her sense of powerlessness. She changes from active to passive voice as she writes of her fall from grace. For example, she says that at eighteen, she "rejected" an honorable man, and instead, "yielded" to a man of fortune and rank (63). After months of "varied pleasure" however, she writes: "I found myself suddenly deserted . . . thrown friendless and destitute upon the world, branded from infamy, and a wretched outcast from social life" (63). Here, she describes herself as a being to whom things are done rather than one who does things. The danger of this kind of thinking and representation is that it reinforces the notion that a seduced woman is necessarily passive and helpless, and can no longer fend for herself.

What the narrative teaches young Mary is that there is no social space open to seduced women. The seduced woman simply becomes a site of abuse or a site of pleasure for men. When she asks for her parents' help, she "was treated as an abandoned wretch, whom it would be criminal to relieve and hopeless to attempt to reclaim" (64). Other men see her as an easy target for their sexual pleasure, partly because of her low self-esteem, partly because of her poverty. Her helplessness becomes a reason and a justification for further sexual liaisons:

> Unable to labour, ashamed to solicit charity, helpless, pennyless, feeble, delicate, thrown out with reproach from society, borne down with a consciousness of irretrievable error, exposed to insult, to want, to contumely, to every species of aggravated distress, in a situation requiring sympathy, tenderness, assistance,—From whence was I to draw fortitude to combat these accumulated evils? (64–65).

This account of the mother's life inevitably scripts the woman as victim, as passive and helpless being, and prey. When she describes her life with the libertines, it is still either in the passive voice or narrated as if she had no control over her actions: "I found myself betrayed," "I was compelled," and "The injuries and insults to which my odious profession exposed me eradicated from my heart every remaining human feeling" (66–67). In addition, she has internalized the image of the sexual woman as a monstrous sickness: "I became a monster, cruel, relentless, ferocious; and contaminated alike, with a deadly poison, the health and the principles of those unfortunate victims whom, with practised allurements, I entangled in my snares" (67). These representations of women, as victim, as prey, as monster, are part of the damaging images with which the heroine has to contend when she is later placed in a similar situation. She has to learn to read herself and her body differently from her mother.

Besides texts—real, fabular, or fictional ones—another way in which the ideology of the "proper lady" is transmitted is through the disciplining, controlling, and shaping of female habits and their desire. Early on in the novel, Hays reveals how education and the prejudices of society can create and channel a woman's aspirations. As a young girl who is brought up in idyllic Wales, Mary is brought up to exercise and develop her mind and body. This system of education follows the recommendation of Mary Wollstonecraft, who encouraged women to "endeavour to acquire strength . . . of mind and body" rather than to become soft and weak creatures.[20] Mary says that she was "early inured to habits of hardiness; . . . to endure fatigue and occasional labour; to exercise [her] ingenuity and exert [her] faculties, arrange [her] thoughts and discipline [her] imagination" (5). Hays demonstrates how girls can be as physically active and dexterous as boys when given the opportunity. Her heroine narrates:

> At ten years of age, I could ride the forest horses without bridle or saddle; could leap a fence or surmount a gate with admirable dexterity; could climb the highest trees, wrestle with the children of the village, or mingle in the dance with grace and activity. (5)

While these claims may sound like idle boasting, Hays was making an important point here about the relation between women's abilities and their education. Given a liberal education where she is taught languages, geometry, algebra, arithmetic, astronomy, and other branches of natural knowledge, Mary excels and becomes a model student. In diligence, "in courage, in spirit, in dexterity, and resource," she is equal to or perhaps slightly ahead of William, whom Mr. Raymond tutors (9).

In her *Appeal to the Men of Great Britain in Behalf of Women* which was co-written with her sister, Hays remarked that the "abilities and capacities of sexes are so alike, that with equal advantages it were difficult to determine to whom the palms were due."[21] In this treatise, she complained that women have been "bound by chains" and "subjected as a race."[22] Similarly, in a letter published in July 1796 in *The Monthly Magazine*, Hays, writing as "A Woman," complained about the way women were excluded from certain activities:

> That one half of the human species, on a self-erected throne, should prescribe bounds to, and impose intellectual fetters on, the other half; and dictate to them to what purposes they are to apply, and how far they are to be allowed to exercise, their common faculties, is not more intolerable than vain.[23]

She pointed out that "because the education of women has been uniformly *perverted*, as well as neglected, than that of men, their general inferiority then follows as a consequence."[24] In *The Victim of Prejudice*, what she tries to demonstrate is the loss of possibilities for intelligent women such as her heroine. The fact that Mary Raymond had the mental and physical potential, but fails to transcend the customary social prejudices and limitations makes her narrative all the more tragic. Her initial aspirations and desires to live a life of liberty and independence are thwarted by many "prejudices" of society.

Although she has been unfettered by gender in her childhood and early adolescence, Mary soon encounters what Hays has called the "tyranny of custom."[25] During her seventeenth year, when she is "tall, healthful, glowing," and beginning to "display all the graces and the bloom of womanhood," her guardian reluctantly acquaints her with "the manners and maxims of the world" (25). He informs her that because of her lack of a good family, she can "never be the wife of William Pelham" who had been her childhood playmate and companion (32). William's father wishes him to be "preserved from humiliating connections," and Mary's "poverty, obscure birth, and the want of splendid connections" overshadow her "beauty, " "virtue," and "talents" (32). She is obliged to separate from William at the request of her guardian. This injunction has the paradoxical effect of awakening previously unarticulated desires and feelings in Mary. After their conversation, she thinks:

> Many of the sentiments and reflections of my patron struck me as at once new, extraordinary, and inconsistent. My ideas were confused, my reasoning powers suspended: undefined apprehensions and suspicions arose in my mind; my principles were unhinged and my passions thrown into disorder. (33)

What Hays demonstrates is the contradiction between social practices and reason which suggested that she and William were compatible. For the first time in her life, her heroine's "reasoning powers" were "suspended," and her "principles . . . unhinged" (33). Sandra Sherman points out that throughout the novel, Hays depicts "women's reason as constituted by ideology premised on women's subjection."[26] Sherman argues that "in Hays's postrevolutionary epistemology, women's mental exertion is subject to distortion by affective imperatives that reinscribe patriarchal limits, subverting strategies—represented in hopeful, revolutionary terms of 'reason'—through which women might become autonomous subjects."[27] Here the prohibition has a disruptive effect on her emotions as well as her body:

> Mr. Raymond's discourse had awakened in my heart new desires and new terrors, to which, till that moment, it had been a stranger. The novelty of my sensations at once surprised and alarmed me. . . . If nature had yet spoken in my heart, so soft and gentle were her whispers, that her voice had hitherto been unheeded. The caution of my patron appeared to have given a sudden and premature existence to the sentiment against which he sought to arm me. (34)

Here Hays is doing what Michel Foucault would call a genealogical analysis of female sexuality and desire. Hays reveals that it is not "nature" that speaks to Mary's heart, but the "caution" of her guardian. In other words, language, in the form of the prohibition of Mr. Raymond, creates sexual desires in Mary: "his discourse awakened . . . new desires" and gave a "sudden and premature existence" to the very sentiment which she is forbidden to experience (34).

In *The History of Sexuality*, Foucault argued that it was in the eighteenth century that there was a "hysterization of women's bodies, where the feminine body was analyzed . . . as being thoroughly saturated with sexuality."[28] As Hays shows, previous to Mr. Raymond's injunction, Mary did not view her body as a sexualized one. She had not ever thought of William as anything more than a companion and friend. However, the day after the prohibition, Mary begins to lament that she can "never be the wife of William Pelham," a wish she had not articulated before (35). She begins to see herself as a sexual being, and the energies she previously devoted to intellectual and physical pursuits are henceforth channeled into feminine ones that conform to social expectations of what a woman should be. Mary admits to William: "I knew not, that the regard I felt for you differed, in any respect, from our mutual and infantine fondness, till Mr. Raymond awakened my fears, and alarmed my tenderness, by telling me that I must separate myself from you, that 'I must never be the wife of William Pelhlam'" (53). In representing Mary as a dangerous threat because of her sexuality or reproductive capacity, Mr. Raymond then succeeds in colonizing and shaping Mary's body. Through language, her body is invested with ideological meanings previously unknown to her. Well-intentioned as he is, Raymond nevertheless instills in Mary the notion that her desire and her body are perverse and unacceptable to respectable society.

This scene also illustrates the relationship between power and desire. Foucault notes that "the law is what constitutes both desire and the lack on which it is predicated. Where there is desire, the power relation is already present."[29] He points out that "power's hold on sex is maintained through language, or rather through the act of discourse that creates, from the very fact that it is articulated, a rule of law."[30] In *The Victim of Prejudice*, Hays makes us aware that Mary's body becomes a highly-charged *topos* and becomes inseparable from her social identity, from her intellectual and psychic self. It is not only Mr. Pelham and Mr. Raymond, the father-figures of the novel, who construct her as sexualized being. Other men, such as her friend William, and the Gothic villain, Sir Peter Osborne, also construct Mary's identity and objectify her. Though they have very different intentions—one wishes initially to be her husband, and the other wishes to seduce her—the end result is the same for Mary. Whereas in her youth, with her "active mind," "ardent curiosity," and "an enthusiastic love of science and literature," she had been a serious student, she is increasingly unable to see herself apart from the feminized and sexualized position of wife and mistress (24–25).

William plays a much smaller role in the construction of Mary into a feminine subject than Sir Peter Osborne. Early on, he naively proposes to "purchase a cottage, and hide . . . from the world" with Mary. In a reckless moment, Mary compares their youthful passion to the sublime love between Emilius and Sophia who she thinks experienced the "most exquisite rapture" and the most "bewitching delirium" that the human mind is capable of enjoying (55–56). This is an interesting and suggestive reference because both Wollstonecraft and Hays disagreed with Rousseau's principles of education which maintained that a soft, gentle, and feminine Sophie was perfectly formed to be Emile's companion. Rousseau believed that "woman is framed particularly for the delight and pleasure of man."[31] That Mary alludes to this problematic text at a moment when she contemplates an implausible act is significant. She sees the impossibility of her relationship with William, and calls their future an "undefinable contradiction" (55). The allusion to *Emile* acts as a forewarning of what comes subsequently. For much later in the novel, William meets Mary again and proposes to restore to her all his "affections" despite the fact that he is married to another. While he claims to be following the "dictates of nature and virtue" rather than the "factitious relations of society," Mary can only interpret his proposal as an attempt to "seduce" her "judgement" (127). She refuses to become his mistress, his object of "delight and pleasure," and would rather brave "dishonour, death," than "self-reproach" (129). Though he is certainly not as villainous as Sir Peter Osborne, what he offers Mary is similarly sinister. Both William and Osborne view the seduced woman as a vulnerable and easily penetrable body.

Of all the characters in the novel however, it is Sir Peter Osborne, representative of aristocratic decadence, who wields the most power over Mary and her body. Through physical, linguistic, psychic, and economic violence, he single-handedly transforms Mary into a socially acceptable docile body. His relentless pursuit of Mary takes many forms. At their first meeting, he catches Mary trying to steal grapes from his garden and immediately calls her "a true daughter of Eve," as well as pronouncing her to be "a little beauty," "a Hebe," and "a wood-nymph" (14). These names and mythical allusions are representations of woman which are culturally constructed and instilled. They are meant to reflect man's ideals or fears of sexuality or mortality which have historically been projected unto women. Twentieth-century feminist Luce Irigaray has pointed out that feminine roles like these are difficult for women to play:

> The value of a woman would accrue to her from her maternal role, and, in addition, from her 'femininity.' But in fact that 'femininity' is a role, an image, a value, imposed upon women by male systems of representation. In this masquerade of femininity, the woman loses herself, and loses herself by playing on her femininity. The fact remains that this masquerade requires an *effort* on her part for which she is not compensated. Unless her pleasure comes simply from being chosen as an object of consumption or of desire by masculine 'subjects.'[32]

From his first meeting with her, Sir Peter sees Mary as "an object of consumption or of desire." He demands a kiss from her at this and their next encounter and assaults her with violence both times. Though Mary is unharmed by these escapades, their effect is to create terror in her where there previously was none. These incidents force Mary to view her body as a vulnerable and weak one even though earlier on in her youth she had boasted that she was equal to William in "boldness and agility" and even "daring" (9). Though Mary resists these roles and refuses to play the "masquerade" of femininity for a long time, these scenes, isolated as they seem, are part of the ways in which a woman is disciplined and punished into conforming to what society expects of her.

The most overt way in which Sir Peter Osborne forces his will upon Mary is to rape her. That Hays was thinking of *Clarissa* as she wrote her novel is evident from the somewhat similar circumstances of the characters and of the rape.[33] The *Anti-Jacobin Review* had observed that in the "dishonour" of Mary there was an imitation of Clarissa, but that the heroines were quite different in the way they handled their loss of chastity. More than once in her letters, both in private and published ones, Hays has discussed the over-valuation of chastity by society. In a letter to William Godwin dated 6 February 1796, Hays wrote: "It is from chastity having been render'd a *sexual virtue*, that all these calamities have flow'd—Men are by this means render'd sordid and dissolute in their pleasures; their affections blunted and their feelings petrified; they are incapable of satisfying the *heart of a woman* of sensibility and virtue."[34] Similarly, in an essay entitled "Improvements Suggested in Female Education," Hays wrote: "Sexual distinctions respecting chastity, an important branch of temperance, have served but to increase the tide of profligacy, and have been the fruitful source of the greater part of the infelicity and corruption of society."[35] Hays was not advocating that women be lascivious, but did not approve of the way a woman's whole life and reputation were dependent upon her virginity. In her view, chastity had become a highly sought prize for men who then were unable to view women through other terms. In *The Victim of Prejudice*, Mary attempts, albeit unsuccessfully, to convince the people around her that her honour and virtue are intact despite the fact that she has lost her virginity.

Hays's concept of virtue is unlike Richardson's in *Pamela*, where virtue is equated with the guarding of the heroine's chastity. In addition, contrary to the hagiographic tendencies in *Clarissa*, what Hays highlights in her novel are physical and economic effects of the violation. She uses the narrative to make observations about women's liberty, by linking the restraints on Mary's liberty and rights after her rape to those of powerless creatures such as the hare. The hare, like her, is hunted and trapped by Osborne. In both cases, Osborne, the pursuer, uses his position and power—as a man and a member of the aristocracy to sport with the weaker. Even before the actual rape, Osborne torments Mary in the village where she resided, and even invades the privacy of the home where she stayed: "he beset my paths, haunted me daily, and overwhelmed me with adulation and offensive gallantry" (51). I point out these earlier instances of harassment because they show that the rape was not a single act of violence but the culmination of systemic abuses and injustices that men in positions of power were culturally encouraged to act out against women. In her poststructuralist analysis of rape, Sharon Marcus points out that "rape is structured like a language, a language which shapes both the verbal *and* physical interactions of a woman and her would-be assailant. . . . The language of rape solicits women to position ourselves as endangered, violable, and fearful and invites men to position themselves as legitimately violent and entitled to women's sexual services."[36] In the eighteenth century, more so than today, this attitude of weakness and vulnerability in women versus physical violence in men would have been even more pronounced.[37] In *The Victim of Prejudice*, Osborne taunts Mary not only by his body, but also through language and his economic power. After the rape, he is confident that the authorities, the law, and the members of the community would support him rather than Mary, because she is a woman with no family and because she admits to having lost her chastity. He tells her, "No one . . . will now receive you . . . even were it more worthy of you; such are the stupid prejudices of the world. What is called, in your sex, honour and character, can, I fear, never be restored to you" (119). Though Mary at first believes that she can transcend these social prejudices, she learns that the loss of reputation in woman in eighteenth-century society is destructive. Despite her best efforts, she is unable to find employment suitable to her condition.

What the last part of the novel stresses is not so much the defeat of the heroine, though such a reading is certainly possible, but the difficulty for a woman to ignore her sexed body. In *Volatile Bodies*, feminist Elizabeth Grosz points out that in Western philosophy from Plato to Descartes there has been a tradition of separating the mind from the body. This dualism is often gendered and hierarchized so that women are associated with the body, while men are linked to the mind or reason. Grosz sees an urgent need to break down the dichotomy and to "refigure" bodies. She argues, "Only when the relation between mind and body is adequately retheorized can we understand the contributions of the body to the production of knowledge systems, regimes of representation, cultural production, and socioeconomic exchange."[38] In *The Victim of Prejudice,* Hays demonstrates the way discursive constructions of woman affect the heroine physically and psychically. In other words, she highlights the near impossibility for a woman to separate her mind or spirit from her body, to live outside codes of propriety, femininity, and chastity expected of her gender.

There are a number of incidents in the novel which show the link between language, representation, and a woman's corporeal existence. Three examples here should suffice. In one of her attempts to find employment, Mary applies to a lady in London recommended by her deceased guardian. Upon checking Mary's references, the woman finds out scandalous information about her past from William's father: that Mary had attempted to seduce William; that her birth was infamous; that she was brought up by charity (135). Mary's reaction to this biased version of her past is passionate. She recounts: "O God! how terrible were the first indignant feelings that rent my heart on the perusal of this barbarous recital!" (135). Here it is the recital or narrative that creates much emotion and anguish in her. In addition, because of these representations of Mary, the woman adamantly refuses to have any further contact with her. Upon hearing this, Mary has a strong physical reaction: "Unable to say more, my tottering limbs failed me; a mist overspread my eyes; while, overpowered by the passions that crowded tumultuously upon my heart, I sunk into a swoon, and should have fallen to the bottom of the stairs but for the support of the servant" (136). In this example, we see how words can modify a woman's sense of her self. Despite her youthful claims of physical and mental agility, Mary is slowly beginning to be overcome by her sense of powerlessness and vulnerability. This negative representation also adversely influences her prospects of employment. Without giving Mary a chance to tell her story, the woman makes a decision based on Mary's loss of "reputation," rather than on her capabilities or intrinsic moral worth. Unlike Clarissa and the young maiden in Moore's fable, Mary is unable to simply ignore the world's opinion of her and turn to heaven. For

Hays who also had problems with her own reputation, the realities of day-to-day living had much to do with the way people perceived a woman's sexual self. In the novel she reveals the way Mary's economic situation became dependent upon the way others chose to read her body.

In two other incidents, Mary is again defeated by malicious representations of her. In one instance, at the print shop, the master makes sexual advances towards Mary because he has heard rumors about her involvement with Sir Peter Osborne and William Pelham. When Mary resists him, he only insults her: "My dear little angel, why this distress? why these pretty romantic airs?" (140). As she escapes from his arms, she hears the "ribaldry and cruel comments of the young men employed in the business" (140). Mary makes the connection between the representation of her and her desire for liberty: "I perceived that the fatal tale of my disgrace pursued and blasted all my efforts" (140). Despite her efforts to exist as an independent woman, she is forced to acknowledge her sexuality, her femininity, and her powerlessness in combating what people expect of a woman in her circumstance. This experience is repeated when she later finds a comfortable home with James on a farm. After six months of peaceful living, Osborne discovers their rural retreat and misrepresents her past to the villagers:

> Suddenly I found myself shunned by my acquaintance, as one infected by a pestilence: every eye scowled on me, every neck was scornfully averted on my approach. The young peasants, who had been accustomed to pay me homage, leered and tittered as I passed; and the village-maidens, bridling, shunned every familiar courtesy or advance. (162)

As in the previous example, Mary's body and her sexuality are overcharged with significance. All her actions are read from her sexualized position, and her body is no longer private, but becomes a site for public viewing, for comparison, for abjection and horror. Her female body imprisons her; she becomes simply body and no mind in others' eyes. This example may be fairly extreme, but it illustrates the way women's bodies have traditionally been viewed in patriarchy. Women's bodies are inscribed with reproductive and sexual functions, and often used as a means of socioeconomic exchange.

It is not surprising that Hays ends her novel with the female body in the penitentiary. It is an appropriate metaphor for the social and cultural restrictions placed on women in the eighteenth century. What John Bender says of Defoe's contribution to the rise of the penitentiary could equally apply to Hays's work: "he showed how, in confinement, the internal forces of psychological motivation fuse dynamically with the physical details of perceptual experience. Here is the penitentiary imagined as the meeting point of the individual mind and material causes."[39] In prison, Mary writes in a fatalistic tone which echoes the language of her mother:

> Almighty Nature, mysterious are thy decrees!—The vigorous promise of my youth has failed. The victim of a barbarous prejudice, society has cast me out from its bosom. The sensibilities of my heart have been turned to bitterness, the powers of my mind wasted, my projects rendered abortive, my virtues and my sufferings alike unrewarded, *I have lived in vain!* unless the story of my sorrows should kindle in the heart of man, in behalf of my oppressed sex, the sacred claims of humanity and justice. (174)

Though this conclusion may sound extremely pessimistic, what Hays has delineated in her novel is the way material causes affect the mind or the psyche of a woman. Although Mary's story seems similar to that of her mother's and to the narratives of other seduced women, the difference is that we are made aware of the way society's "barbarous prejudice" works to construct and delimit the female subject through the details of Mary's memoirs. It is this hope of awakening the consciousness of humanity that motivates the author and her heroine into writing this compelling account.

Notes

1. Mary Hays, *The Victim of Prejudice,* ed. Eleanor Ty (Peterborough, Ontario: Broadview Press, 1994), 1.

2. Mary Wollstonecraft, *A Vindication of the Rights of Woman,* 2nd ed., ed. Carol H. Poston (New York: Norton Critical Edition, 1988), 131, 133.

3. See my introduction to *Unsex'd Revolutionaries: Five Women Writers of the 1790s* (Toronto: University of Toronto Press, 1993), 3–30.

4. Hays, *Victim of Prejudice,* 1. For a discussion of desire, see my introduction to Mary Hays, *Memoirs of Emma Courtney,* ed. Eleanor Ty (Oxford: Oxford World's Classics, 1996), vii–xxxvii.

5. I am using the term "proper lady" to designate the tractable, obedient woman and wife as described in conduct books of the 17th and 18th centuries. See Chapter 1 of *Mary Poovey, The Proper Lady and the Woman Writer: Ideology as Style in the Works of Mary Wollstonecraft, Mary Shelley, and Jane Austen* (Chicago: University of Chicago Press, 1984).

6. Lois McNay, *Foucault and Feminism: Power, Gender and the Self* (Boston: Northeastern University Press, 1992), 23.

7. Michel Foucault, *Discipline and Punish: The Birth of the Prison,* trans. Alan Sheridan (New York: Vintage, 1979), 10.

8. Foucault, *Discipline and Punish,* 11.

9. Sharon Marcus, "Fighting Bodies, Fighting Words: A Theory and Politics of Rape Prevention," in *Feminists Theorize the Political,* ed. Judith Butler and Joan W. Scott (New York: Routledge, 1992), 389.

10. Susan Staves, "British Seduced Maidens," *Eighteenth-Century Studies* 14, no. 2 (1980–81): 110.

11. Staves, "British Seduced Maidens," 110.

12. Ibid.

13. Gary Kelly, "Jane Austen and the English Novel of the 1790s," in *Fetter'd or Free? British Women Novelists, 1670–1815,* ed. Mary Anne Schofield and Cecilia Macheski (Athens, Ohio: Ohio University Press, 1986), 287, 286. Kelly notes that Anti-Jacobin novels tended to employ an omniscient narrator, and used wit and satire to expose the follies of youth and the New Philosophy, 289.

14. Edward Moore, *Fables for the Female Sex,* in *The Young Lady's Pocket Library, or Parental Monitor* (London: 1790; facsimile rprt. Bristol: Thoemmes Press, 1995), 268.

15. Moore, "The Female Seducers," 273, 277.

16. Nancy Armstrong, *Desire and Domestic Fiction: A Political History of the Novel* (New York: Oxford University Press, 1987), 23.

17. Vivien Jones, *Introduction to The Young Lady's Pocket Library, or Parental Monitor* (1790, facsimile rprnt. Briston: Thoemmes Press, 1995), vi.

18. See the introduction to *The Victim of Prejudice,* xxii–xxiv.

19. *The Anti-Jacobin Review and Magazine* 3 (April–Aug. 1799): 57.

20. Mary Wollstonecraft, *A Vindication of the Rights of Woman,* ed. Carol Poston (New York: Norton Critical Edition, 1988), 9.

21. Mary Hays, *Appeal to the Men of Great Britain in Behalf of Women* (London: J. Johnson, 1798; facsimile rprt. New York: Garland, 1974), 45.

22. Hays, *Appeal to the Men of Great Britain,* 70.

23. A Woman, "Remarks on A. B. Strictures on the Talents of Women," *The Monthly Magazine* (July 1796): 469. Burton Pollin, in "Mary Hays on Women's Rights in the Monthly Magazine," *Etudes Anglaises* 24, no. 3 (1971): 271–82, first noted that these articles and those signed M. H. were probably written by Mary Hays.

24. A Woman, "Remarks on A. B.," 469.

25. Mary Hays, *Letters and Essays, Moral and Miscellaneous* (London: 1793; facsimile rprnt. New York: Garland, 1974) I: 9. Hays comments, "The truth is, the modes of education, and the customs of society are degrading to the female character and the tyranny of custom is sometimes worse than the tyranny of government."

26. Sandra Sherman, "The Feminization of 'Reason' in Hays's The Victim of Prejudice," *The Centennial Review* XLI, no. 1 (1997): 144.

27. Sherman, "Feminization of 'Reason,'" 143.

28. Michel Foucault, *The History of Sexuality: An Introduction, vol. I,* trans. Robert Hurley (New York: Vintage, 1990), 104.

29. Foucault, *History of Sexuality,* 81.

30. Foucault, *History of Sexuality,* 83.

31. Jean-Jacques Rousseau, *Emilius; or, A Treatise of Education, 3 vols.* (Edinburgh: J. Dickson, 1773), III, v, 7.

32. Luce Irigaray, *This Sex Which Is Not One,* trans. Catherine Porter (Ithaca, N.Y.: Cornell University Press, 1985), 84.

33. In my introduction to *The Victim of Prejudice,* I noted that, "like Clarissa, Mary is from an untitled middle-class family and is courted by an aristocrat. Both heroines are transported from their homes by deceit to the London residences of the villain and rakes. Both are raped and dishonoured by their abductors, and live long enough to exclaim against their fate in writing," xxiii.

34. Mary Hays, letter #12 to William Godwin, 6 February 1796, New York Public Library, New York.

35. M. H., "Improvements Suggested in Female Education," *The Monthly Magazine* (March 1797): 194.

36. Sharon Marcus, "Fighting Bodies, Fighting Words: A Theory and Politics of Rape Prevention," *Feminists Theorize the Political,* ed. Judith Butler and Joan W. Scott (New York: Routledge, 1992), 390.

37. Margaret Hunt, in "'The Great Danger She Had Reason to Believe She Was in:' Wife-Beating in the Eighteenth Century," *Women & History: Voices of Early Modern England,* ed. Valerie Frith (Toronto: Coach House Press, 1995), 86, notes that "Eighteenth-century English society was profoundly hierarchical, explicitly committed to male supremacy and accustomed to the belief that the use of violence was essential for the maintenance of order among subordinate groups."

38. Elizabeth Grosz, *Volatile Bodies: Toward A Corporeal Feminism* (Bloomington: Indiana University Press, 1994), 19.

39. John Bender, *Imagining the Penitentiary: Fiction and the Architecture of Mind in Eighteenth-Century England* (Chicago: University of Chicago Press, 1987), 43.

Masculinity and Morality in Elizabeth Inchbald's Nature and Art

Shawn Lisa Maurer

The fiction of the Jacobin novelist Elizabeth Inchbald, like that of many of her contemporaries, is notably concerned with family plots. *A Simple Story* (1791) takes its structural framework and ideological valence from the sequential narrative of a mother and daughter, while her final novel, *Nature and Art* (1796), tells the story of two contrasting brothers and their equally disparate sons. However, whereas *A Simple Story* is readily available and widely discussed, *Nature and Art* has, until quite recently, remained out of print and comparably unknown.[1] There are a number of reasons why Inchbald's second novel may have confounded critical expectations, including its marked differences from the rapidly acclaimed *A Simple Story* and its failure to fit solidly within any single generic category. Yet I would speculate that *Nature and Art*, despite its legitimate claim to a significant place both in literary history and in Inchbald's oeuvre, has remained relatively obscure in large part because it tells the story of generations of men.[2]

Inchbald's view of masculinity as a familial as well as social construction goes against the grain of a critical tendency that, whether deliberately or unwittingly, claims to analyze the female sex as detached from the male half of the species except in the latter's exclusive role as women's oppressors. Attention to the work of two of the few critics who have recently dealt at some length with *Nature and Art* provides insight into the ways in which the constructed and dialectic nature of masculinity can often be obscured within the dynamics of feminist criticism. In *Her Bread to Earn: Women, Money and Society from Defoe to Austen,* Mona Scheuermann consistently elides gender with the construction of a feminine gendered identity. While I agree with Scheuermann's assessment of class as a dominant aspect of the novel, her contention that "Inchbald sees class rather than gender as the determinant of victimization"[3] inevitably erases the victimization done to men by their own increasingly oppressive gender roles, thus marginalizing an understanding of masculinity as a socially constructed identity. Whereas the Lacanian psychoanalytic perspective offered by Eleanor Ty's *Unsex'd Revolutionaries: Five Women Novelists of the 1790s* would seem to take the opposite tack by emphasizing gender construction and gendered relations, her sometimes essentialized view of gender serves, ironically, to reify masculinity and thereby expunge it from critical view. By arguing that the younger Henry's naiveté and benevolence associate him "with the literal," and thus "the maternal or the pre-symbolic," Ty accepts as static, given, indeed "natural" the very gendered categories that Inchbald's novel, I will argue, attempts to interrogate.[4] Ty's analysis moots Inchbald's important choice of male protagonists and obfuscates the fact that *as men* Henry's and his son's possession of such qualities as nurturance or benevolence acts not to feminize them, but to open up, and thus to redefine, what it means to be a man.

In this essay, I examine the ways in which Inchbald's male characters function as a kind of masculine continuum that necessarily militates against any easy assimilation of masculinity into some monolithic and ahistoric patriarchy. Through her protagonists and their sons she astutely exposes the development of the masculine breadwinner role and its concomitant dependence upon an ideology of separate spheres. While William's rags-to-riches story is the stuff of fairy tale, his dramatic rise also reflects a historical moment when the growth of trade and the professions significantly increased men's opportunities for social advancement;[5] moreover, Inchbald shows that such economic activity does not transpire in a public sphere ostensibly separate from hearth and home, but is inextricably bound to family and personal life. For William as for his son, worldly aspirations both necessitate and attempt to assuage, albeit unsuccessfully, emotional loss. Emphasizing the fact that gender is constructed in association with other relational categories, including class, family, education, privilege, and power, Inchbald's approach to masculinity is both historical and psychological as it traces the complex factors that contribute to making men.[6]

* * *

The plot of *Nature and Art* centers upon two brothers, William and Henry Norwynne, who are forced to make their way in the world upon the death of their shopkeeper father. Henry, the younger and seemingly more decent of the brothers, supports both himself and his more prideful sibling by playing the fiddle; in his generosity, Henry provides William with an education and a living—a deanery at £500 per year. The brothers marry women comparable to themselves: Henry a virtuous and humble public singer and William a vain and haughty noblewoman. The excessive pride of William and his new spouse estranges Henry; after the sudden death of his own wife Henry takes his infant son, named Henry as well, to an African island. William successfully pursues his ecclesiastical career and raises a child, also called after himself. After thirteen years of silence between the brothers, an uprising among the island's native inhabitants causes Henry to send his boy to England, where he is raised as a second son by his uncle William. Eventually, both cousins fall in love: William seduces Hannah Primrose, a cottager's daughter in Anfield, the village where his father has purchased an estate, while Henry falls chastely in love with the local curate's daughter, Rebecca Rymer. William forsakes Hannah to make an unhappy marriage to an upper-class woman; Hannah bears a son, whom she first attempts to kill and then abandons. Henry finds the infant and brings him to Rebecca to raise. Her family soon discovers the child and, taking Rebecca for his mother, erupts in furor. Hannah later reclaims her son, and together they wander the countryside. She ends up in London, where she falls "innocently" into a life of crime and is there condemned to death by her former lover, the younger William, now a London magistrate. Henry, meanwhile, has left Rebecca behind in an effort to rescue his father; after eighteen years of travails the two men return to England where, reunited with the faithful Rebecca, they live happily ever after.

The novel's dualistic framework seems to set up a clear antithesis between nature, exemplified by the charitable Henry and his son, a "child of nature" who has been raised without books on an African island, and art, in the form of artifice, represented by the hypocritical standards and conventions of the eighteenth-century upper classes espoused by William and drilled relentlessly into his own child. Yet in contrast to this perceived dichotomy between nature and art epitomized by the two brothers and their sons, I contend that the characters and the positions they represent operate rather as a dialectic. That is, the actions of all four men gain meaning only relationally; in both narrative and moral terms, each character can function only in explicit connection to his counterpart. Time and again, brothers or cousins react to the same situation in diametrically opposed ways, with each Henry's "goodness" serving as the necessary foil to each William's "evil." Without the savage country that is England, the younger Henry's island existence could have little point; at the same time, Henry's naive exposure of upper-class attitudes gains power in relation to his cousin William's unthinking assimilation of such beliefs.

On the one hand, Inchbald's spectrum of masculinity challenges tradition by refusing to dichotomize along customary gender lines. In other words, Inchbald does not delineate the exemplary man in relation to—and often in distinction from—the ideal woman; rather, goodness in any character, whether male or female, is marked by that character's possession of significant attributes, including generosity, nurturance, compassion, the capacity for intimacy, and the ability to think of others before oneself. Conversely, and without exception, Inchbald represents the characters who possess wealth, privilege, status, and power as corrupt, whether male or female. The author's depiction of virtue as an ungendered category stands, of course, in explicit contrast to such influential works as the periodicals of Joseph Addison and Richard Steele in the early eighteenth century or the mid-century novels of Samuel Richardson, which promulgated, with regard to gender, an incommensurability of both bodies and spirits. In *Tatler* No. 172, Steele writes that "there is a sort of Sex in Souls" and that "the Soul of a Man and that of a Woman are made very unlike, according to the Employments for which they are designed," so that even "the Virtues have respectively a Masculine and a Feminine Cast."[7] Instead of defining ideal (and thus normative) masculinity as that which is not feminine, Inchbald represents virtuous men and women as those who function outside the dominant class structure.[8] Moreover, these characters generously endanger their own lives, livelihoods, or security in order to assist others. The privileged characters, by comparison, care only to maintain or enhance their own position. Pride and vanity are the qualities most often attributed to the nobility—all of the nobility—in this novel, just as benevolence and compassion distinguish the characters who are virtuous in spite of, or because of, their relative lack of affluence.

On the other hand, and despite its radical elements, Inchbald's approach is also problematic, for she seems unaware that there can be no such category as pure nature: like Rousseau's character Emile, the younger Henry's natural man is as much a construct as the younger William's civilized and thus artificial one. Ironically, the younger Henry is more a product of nurture than nature, for his goodness stems from a specific education in the basic principles of Christianity—in particular the principle of "Do unto others." Henry sees through aristocratic forms not only because he has not yet become inured to them, but also because the values they represent contradict the principles he has been taught by his father. More type than character, Henry, in his inability to stand solidly as the novel's center of interest, provides a key to Inchbald's complex depiction of gender. The novel's ultimate power resides not in the portrait of the compassionate Henry and his father, but in Inchbald's more complex, more ambivalent, and ultimately more interesting depiction of William and his son. Ironically, then, the fundamental opposition on which the novel rests—between the benign qualities available to human nature per se and the debasement of those qualities in a corrupt and artificial society—ultimately collapses upon itself when confronted with Inchbald's forceful and sympathetic portrait of William: a father condemned by circumstances to bequeath to his son a legacy of bitter unhappiness.

* * *

While the novel's framework is unavoidably schematic, Inchbald does not present her protagonists, like Henry Fielding's Blifil and Tom Jones, as simply born that way. Rather, she provides cogent psychological justification for her characters' behaviors and choices. The novel opens when two brothers, like the sons in a fairy tale, are forced into the world to seek their fortunes after the death of their father, "a country shopkeeper."[9] They begin as compatriots, equally destitute, equally able and willing to work,[10] and both suffer under the inequities of a system that scorns talent without capital: "If they applied for the situation of a clerk to a man of extensive concerns, their qualifications were admitted; but there must be security given for their fidelity:—they had friends, who would give them a character, but who would give them nothing else" (5). The brothers are eventually saved from starvation by the recollection of Henry's musical talent—"Reader—Henry could play upon the fiddle" (Ibid.)—a skill that not only supports them, but also pays for William's higher education and, through patronage, obtains him a lucrative church living.

While Henry is clearly generous, sympathetic, and kind-hearted (he sheds tears of "fraternal pride and joy" at William's investiture as dean [9]) and his brother haughty, prideful, and downright mean at times, it would be inaccurate to see these characteristics as simply part of their personalities. Rather, I would contend that those very personalities are to no small degree constructs shaped by the relation between gender and economics. To begin with, their father has died "insolvent" (3). While the charitable Henry can feel grateful that his death had allowed him to "'escape[ ] from his creditors,'" Henry also notes that if their father were alive, "'he would not have suffered us to begin this long journey [to London] without a few more shillings in our pockets'" (Ibid.). A failure as provider, their father leaves his sons with no money for further education, apprenticeship fees, or setting themselves up in business. Customarily William, as older brother, would take his father's place, but both brothers are rendered equal under the destitute circumstances in which neither can find work. It is finally Henry who assumes the paternal role, by providing their day-to-day support and by paying for the education that will allow William to assume his position in the church.

Yet rather than being grateful to his brother, or perhaps in conjunction with his thankfulness, William feels humiliated by his own impotence: "William was not without joy; neither was he wanting in love or gratitude to his brother— but his pride was not completely satisfied" (9). William assuages his battered ego by emphasizing the differences between himself and his brother: in one of the novel's many ironies, William uses the very education that Henry's fiddle-playing has made possible as justification for criticism: "'I am the elder,' thought he to himself, 'and a man of literature; and yet am I obliged to my younger brother, an illiterate man'" (Ibid.). Moreover, that very education, by raising William to the professional ranks, enables him further to appease his bruised sense of self-importance by marrying Lady Clementina, a "woman of family" (11). Vain, shallow, self-centered, and pretentious, Lady Clementina, "the daughter of a poor Scotch earl, whom he had chosen, merely that he might be proud of her family; and, in return, suffer that family to be ashamed of his" (Ibid.), provides William with neither sympathy nor companionship, either intellectual or emotional; instead, her excessive pride dooms him to life-long misery.[11] Whereas eighteenth-century literature provides us with numerous portraits of loveless, unhappy, or unsuccessful marriages from the woman's point of view,[12] few authors—male or female—show us the man's side. By knowing William's pain, we are more sympathetic to his choices, even if they are bad ones.

The narrative positions William and Lady Clementina as virtual mirror images: "That, which in a weak woman is called vanity, in a man of sense is termed pride—make one a degree stronger, or the other a degree weaker, and the dean and his wife were infected by the self-same folly" (14). William uses his wife's vanity to shore up a pride that is not intrinsic to his own socioeconomic background: feeling not enough of a man, he marries a woman whose ostensible superiority in class terms allows him, by association, to shun both his "illiterate" brother and his brother's equally humble wife. His pride thus functions as a form of displacement as his turn to class difference is precipitated by the blow to his masculine identity. In William's psychic framework there can be no real place for gratitude, since gratitude for the enormous debt he owes to Henry triggers only humiliation and anxiety—the sense of his own failure.

William adopts a value system based solely upon status—a system shared not only by Lady Clementina, but also by the bishop who is William's church superior and friend, as well as by Lord and Lady Bendham, the first family of the village where William eventually purchases an estate. He passes those values on to his son, who will grow to surpass even his father in obsequiousness, hypocrisy, and misery. The social forms that Frances Burney takes such great delight in exposing throughout her 1778 novel *Evelina* (but which her heroine must learn to negotiate nonetheless) here serve as socially sanctioned excuse for inexcusable behavior. After William hears that Henry's wife has died, his response is still bounded by convention: instead of spurning Henry's wife, he might have allowed her a visit if he had known it was to be the last. Later, however, his regret seems genuine, but it comes, alas, too late: Henry has gone to Africa and taken his infant with him. Largely because he feels unfulfilled by his love-less marriage, William mourns Henry's absence, going so far as to fetishize objects associated with him—a coat, a walking-stick, even a music book. Indeed the narrator comments that "nor would his poor violin, had it been there, have then excited anger" (15)—a displacement ironic in light of his earlier inveterate aversion to the instrument.

William's attention is soon taken up by another displacement: his own child, "a still nearer and dearer relation than Henry had ever been to him" (16). In the relationship between William and his son, Inchbald depicts the painful unravelling of a bond she describes elsewhere as the epitome of human connection.[13] Both directly and through implication, we are shown William's intense and, we will shortly discover, ultimately ruinous involvement in the raising of this boy, who inherits, along with his father's name, "all the pride and ambition of the dean" (40). For William, his son is not a person but a receptacle, a vessel to be filled with the bitter brew of his own unmet and voracious desires. Inchbald shows us that, as with mothering, fathering too can reproduce itself, albeit not through unbounded connection;[14] men pass on the need to categorize and compartmentalize, to deny certain needs at the expense of others, to value external achievement over emotional connection. William attains professional success yet sacrifices romantic happiness; but the child he hopes will fill that emptiness becomes himself an empty vessel. Yet despite the fact that the son William loves so dearly possesses few, if any, redeeming qualities, the unsympathetic William junior is very much his father's child: like his parent, he is not intrinsically bad but made so through circumstances.[15]

Along with his son, William's career fills the emotional vacuum created by the absence of his brother and the presence of his wife. The narrator writes that William had "a domestic comfort highly gratifying to his ambition: the bishop of **** became intimately acquainted with him soon after his marriage, and from his daily visits had become, as it were, *a part of the family*" (16, italics added). Inchbald's coy "as it were" highlights rather than underplays the bishop's place in William's life. The dean's relation to the bishop, who is his direct "superior in the church," allows William to invent a new father, one whose "blood is ennobled by a race of ancestors"; moreover, he is one to whom, the narrator caustically reminds us, "all wisdom on the plebeian side crouches in humble respect" (Ibid.). The bishop frequents William's home not just because he enjoys the latter's company, but out of "the desire of fame, and dread of being thought a man receiving large emolument for unimportant service" (30–31).[16] Indeed the metaphor the narrator uses to describe the dean's practice with regard to the bishop infantilizes William while simultaneously contesting the moral superiority of the church: "The elder William was to his negligent or ignorant superiors in the church, such as an apt boy at school is to the rich dunces—William performed the prelates' tasks for them, and they rewarded him—not indeed with toys or money, but with their countenance, their company, their praise" (31). Even more damning, perhaps, is the fact that William remains virtually unaware of the unethical nature of his actions, a phenomenon that the narrator attributes, at least in part, to William's "humble" background: "so degradingly did William, the shopkeeper's son, think of his own honest extraction, that he was blinded, even to the loss of honour, by the lustre of this noble acquaintance" (Ibid.).

The bishop's unacknowledged ghostwriter, William gives away his self along with his words. This loss of integrity powerfully foreshadows that of his own son, who "was taught to revere such and such persons, however unworthy of his reverence; to believe such and such things, however unworthy of his credit; and to act so and so, on such and such occasions, however unworthy of his feelings" (17). The novel thus presents such false deference as a family trait, passed down from one generation to the next. For William, objects substitute for people and people are turned into objects. In contrast, Henry, like his son after him, exemplifies a masculinity concerned with emotional intimacy and social justice instead of hierarchies of power. The narrator describes the younger Henry as one whose "affectionate heart . . . loved *persons* rather than *things*" (112); he finds happiness at the novel's end in honest poverty with his long-lost father and long-faithful beloved. The ending that has troubled or disappointed critics makes sense when placed in the light of father's and son's ability to do what William and his son patently cannot: eschew "public opinion" in the name of "private happiness" (58). The younger Henry's compassion for the poor, his rescue of the child abandoned by its mother, his decision to search for his own lost father rather than pursue a career—all testify to his valuation of intimate personal relations, "private happiness."[17] Moreover, *pace* Ty, Henry's actions function not to feminize him but rather to pose the characteristics of the private man as important—and often ignored—aspects of desirable masculine identity. The humble and contented Henrys stand in direct contrast to their generational counterparts, whose desire for rank and privilege has led them to prosperous careers but miserable lives.

Yet it is interesting to note that despite Henry's claim to moral exemplarity, the education of the younger William occupies far more of the novel's narrative energy. In explicit contrast with Rousseau's *Emile*, Inchbald's novel provides not the smallest glimpse of the young Henry's life upon the African island; the only description of his upbringing comes obliquely, in a letter that his father has sent to England along with his son:

> I have taught him to love, and to do good to his neighbour, whoever that neighbour might be, and whatever may be his failings. Falsehood of every kind I included in this precept as forbidden, for no one can love his neighbour and deceive him.
>
> I have instructed him too, to hold in contempt all frivolous vanity, and all kinds of indulgences which he was never likely to obtain. (20)

While, on the one hand, these tenets represent an accepted part of Christian doctrine, on the other hand they serve to set up the younger Henry as the seemingly perfect medium for Inchbald's social critique. Henry never learns the customs of his country: throughout the novel, he stands firmly outside the circulation of the signs of English class, educational, and cultural systems. Although Inchbald's satire necessarily rests upon Henry's wise, albeit static, innocence as a means of deconstructing those very systems, she must construct his goodness as artfully—and as artificially—as she does William's corruption. Indeed Inchbald's vividly detailed and condemnatory description of William's education, the best that civilization has to offer, depends crucially upon the existence of a state of nature untainted by culture: "Young William passed his time, from morning till night, with persons who taught him to walk, to ride, to talk, to think like a man—a foolish man, instead of a wise child, as nature designed him to be" (17). Although William's education acts only to dehumanize him—the narrator compares him to "a parrot or magpie—for he merely repeated what had been told to him, without one reflection upon the sense or probability of his report" (Ibid.)—Inchbald clearly believes that William, like his cousin, possesses the capacity to be "natural"—his corruption not inherent in his personality but a result of the needs of those around him.

In Inchbald's conception, both William and Henry begin as a *tabula rasa*, yet while Henry is inscribed by his compassionate and moral father, William is written on by people who have been themselves infected with society's ills. Indeed the narrator states that "with the pedantic folly of his tutors, the blind affection of his father and mother, the obsequiousness of the servants, and the flattery of the visitors, it was some credit to him that he was not an ideot, or a brute" (Ibid.). William's education cannot, however, fail to brutalize him, for the narrator continues, "though when he imitated the manners of a man, he had something of the latter in his appearance—for he would grin and bow to a lady, catch her fan in haste if it fell, and hand her to her coach, as thoroughly void of all the sentiment, which gives grace to such tricks, as a monkey" (Ibid.). Here "sentiment" is construed as the efficacious mixture of mind and body, rationality and emotion. Yet William's only feeling is for the thoughts of others; concerned solely with the impressions he makes and thus impressed exclusively by others' responses, the child William is a puppet manipulated by the strings of convention.

While Inchbald repeatedly employs satire to convey the contemptible and destructive nature of such slavish adherence to outward forms, her portrayal of the younger William's adult behavior partakes of a very different literary mode. As a young man, William exemplifies the tenets of libertinism, enacting them upon the body of the working-class woman, Hannah Primrose. William's thorough immersion in social forms allows him to perpetuate rather than challenge the double standards of both gender and class. William's seduction and abandonment of Hannah and her subsequent destitution are the stuff not of satire but of drama, even of melodrama; Inchbald ups the emotional ante to show the harrowing consequences of such behavior for William as much as for his lover. It is not so much that William separates sex from love (for he does care deeply for Hannah as well as being sexually attracted to her) as that he distinguishes desire from duty: he cannot "love" Hannah because a poor and uneducated woman, despite her evident possession of tremendous sensibility, cannot be a suitable object for his affections. Although during the eighteenth century inter-class marriage—by definition marriage for love—was part of a constellation of changing attitudes related to an ideology of marital companionship, historians have shown that, at least among the elite, status and wealth remained primary criteria for conjugal attachment.[18] Yet Inchbald presents William's utter inability even to consider Hannah a possible, let alone proper mate as a personal failing rather than a cultural one. As evidenced in the following dialogue between William and his cousin, William's unqualified acceptance of his father's superficial values will mean that he, like his father, is doomed to forego the opportunity for any lasting emotional connection:

> The first time he was alone with William, . . . [Henry] mentioned his observation on Hannah's apparent affliction, and asked "Why her grief was the result of their stolen meetings?"
>
> "Because," replied William, "her professions are unlimited, while her manners are reserved; and I accuse her of loving me with unkind moderation, while I love her to distraction."
>
> "You design to marry her then?"
>
> "How can you degrade me by the supposition?"
>
> "Would it degrade you more to marry her than to make her your companion? To talk with her for hours in preference to all other company? To wish to be endeared to her by still closer ties?"
>
> "But all this is still not raising her to the rank of my wife."
>
> "It is still raising her to that rank for which wives alone were allotted."
>
> "You talk wildly!—I tell you I love her; but not enough, I hope, to marry her."
>
> "But too much, I hope, to undo her?" (51)

When Henry then urges William, who "cannot live without" Hannah, to "live with her by the laws of your country; and make her and yourself both happy" (52), his cousin responds that he would make his parents miserable, and be disowned by them. Henry counters with words from William senior's most recent sermon, "upon—*the shortness of this life: contempt of all riches and worldly honours in balance with a quiet conscience—and the assurance he gave us—that the greatest happiness enjoyed upon earth, was to be found under an humble roof with heaven in prospect*" (Ibid.). William's telling response, that his father, "instead of being satisfied with an humble roof, . . . looks impatiently forward to a bishop's palace," exposes the religious hypocrisy that is necessarily tied to the double standards of class and sexual behavior.

The contrasting love lives of the two cousins provide insight into Inchbald's explication of male sexual identity in explicit relation to class position. Just as Inchbald's depiction of Henry's moral self-sufficiency, in comparison with William's pandering to the opinions of others, partakes in the middle-class critique of aristocratic masculine behavior,[19] so too do the different attitudes toward sexuality espoused by each cousin represent different sides of this hegemonic debate. William's feelings for Hannah Primrose, the illiterate daughter of poor cottagers, typify a libertinism traditionally associated with the aristocracy: he "loved" her and "hoped to make her his mistress" (45), whereas Henry's love for Rebecca Rymer, the village curate's educated daughter, represents an ethos of what I have described elsewhere as "chaste heterosexuality"—male sexual desire channeled into monogamous marriage.[20] Henry thinks that what he feels for Rebecca must necessarily "go by a different name" from the love William feels for Hannah, for not only has modesty prevented him from even expressing his feelings, but those feelings would preclude any behavior that might "tend to her dishonour" (Ibid.).

For William, honor consists solely in adherence to outward forms: he will be dishonored, "degraded," not by seducing and then abandoning the hapless Hannah, but by deigning to make her his wife.[21] While Inchbald devotes significant narrative attention to the process as well as consequences of Hannah's "fall," she also, and more unusually, shows us the twists and turns of William's own displacements and denials. Not a stock villain but very much a man, William must "force himself to shake off every little remaining affection, even all pity, for the unfortunate, the beautiful, the sensible, the doting Hannah" (58) in order to cement his alliance with a woman whose "whole person" had never provided even "the least attraction to excite his love" (57). This state of insensibility is soon achieved, for "[c]onnections, interest, honours, were powerful advocates—his private happiness William deemed trivial, compared to public opinion" (58). Bluntly displaying the operation of William's psyche, the narrative ultimately reveals that such a partitioning of intimate needs is, ultimately, not only impossible but also highly destructive. By offering a portrait of the seducer as well as the seduced, and by demonstrating the ultimate entwinement of their fates, Inchbald illustrates the harrowing toll, for both sexes, of subjugating feeling to ambition.

Whereas William can, indeed must, separate head and heart, Hannah's decisions reflect her adamant refusal to choose expediency over intimacy. Despite the exhortations and threats of the senior William, who wishes to "'hush the affair up'" (92) in order to protect the reputation of his recently-married son, Hannah accepts certain poverty rather than give up the child with whom she has been so recently reunited. Hannah's decision to keep her illegitimate child constitutes her a social outcast; after leaving Anfield, the only employer she can find is a farmer who hires her to tend his cattle: "By herding solely with the brute creation, she and her child were allowed to live together; and this was a state she preferred to the society of human creatures, who would have separated her from what she loved so tenderly" (99). Inchbald's terminology, with its reverberation between "brute creation" and "human creatures," implies that civilization can be more savage than the nature it has supposedly been given to tame. The child for whom Hannah sacrifices any broader social existence resembles his father in every aspect but one:

> he loved Hannah with an affection totally distinct from the pitiful and childish gratification of his own self-love—he never would quit her side for all the tempting offers of toys or money—never would eat of rarities given to him, till Hannah took a part—never crossed her will, however contradictory to his own—never saw her smile that he did not laugh—nor did she ever weep, but he wept too. (100)

Inchbald seems to recognize that this mother-child bond cannot be sustained in the real world. Never named, the boy has no existence apart from his mother and must "pine[ ] away" (121) with grief upon her execution. The son's literally selfless love, his explicit attention to his mother's happiness, provides an incriminating contrast to William's egocentric attitude toward Hannah: the narrator writes that when William thinks of Hannah, "it was self-love, rather than love of *her,* that gave rise to these thoughts—he felt the want of female sympathy and tenderness, to soften the fatigue of studious labour; to soothe a sullen, a morose disposition—he felt he wanted comfort for himself, but never once considered, what were the wants of Hannah" (117). Moreover, the boy's pathetic attempt to take his father's place seems only to exacerbate the harmful effects, both psychological and social, of William's denial of his own paternity, as well as to highlight the barrenness of his marriage.

Like his father before him, William handles his lack of emotional satisfaction through displacement. Since he and his wife have no children, William can turn only to his career for compensation. The narrator calls explicit attention to the ways in which William's life reproduces that of his father:

> Young William, though he viewed with contempt Henry's inferior state, was far less happy than he—*His marriage had been the very counterpart of his father's*; and having no child to create affection to his home, his Study was the only relief from that domestic encumbrance, his wife: and though by unremitting application there (joined to the influence of the potent relations of the woman he hated) he at length arrived at the summit of his ambitious desires, still they poorly repaid him, for the sacrifices he had made in early life, of every tender disposition. (112, my italics)

Inchbald, whose own career as a producer of drama and fiction may also have functioned to assuage emotional loss, has given us perhaps the first portrait of the workaholic in English literature. Thus while William's success in the law is such that he finds himself, at thirty-eight, "raised to preferment, such as rarely falls to the share of a man of his short experience—he found himself invested with a judge's robe" (Ibid.), the novel's plotline, in which William unknowingly passes sentence upon Hannah and is doomed to suffer for his action, serves as potent and ironic demonstration of the failure of such methods. William's final words to Hannah—"'Dead, dead, dead.'" (Ibid.)—are recalled a few pages later, when, after having read both Hannah's public confession and a letter written expressly to him, William "envied Hannah the death to which he first exposed, then condemned her—He envied her even the life she struggled through from his neglect—and felt that his future days would be far less happy than her former existence. He calculated with precision" (121).

While Hannah's child loves his mother as himself, and William loves Hannah for himself, the love between Henry and his father, as well as that between the younger Henry and Rebecca, would seem instead to illustrate a different kind of attachment, one in which self is not sacrificed to the Other, or the Other to oneself. By deferring the pleasure of his marriage to Rebecca and returning, in the first act of his majority, to the African island in an attempt to find his father, Henry rescues the man who had earlier saved him—first from the brutalities of English culture, by taking him to the island and educating him in honesty and goodness, then from the possible "savagery" of the island's inhabitants, when he is sent back to England. In a narrative comprised of emotional fracture and fissure—family members die, leave, or are believed dead; lovers are separated or estranged—the book's concluding reunion between father and son manifests, more powerfully than any other event in the novel, a vision of community. Father to his own father, Henry experiences the epitome of filial connection and his father the zenith of happiness. As with her other depictions of father-son relations, Inchbald wrings from this scene every moral and melodramatic drop, emphasizing the value of familial love over any kind of outward achievement. After Henry has rushed from the boat to fall at his father's feet, exclaiming "'My father! oh! my father!,'" the narrator comments: "William! dean! bishop! what are your honours, what your riches, what all your possessions, compared to the happiness, the transport bestowed by this one sentence, on your poor brother Henry?" (110).

By comparison, we are told very little about William's relationship to his own adult son. The younger William is never described as a mourner at his father's funeral; the most powerful emotion he feels is "Remorse" when he discovers that the woman he has just condemned to death is his once-beloved Hannah Primrose. This remorse directly echoes the emotion Hannah had herself felt when, after having been seduced, impregnated, and abandoned by William, she leaves her child to die. Thus William too comes full circle at the novel's end; his living death recapitulates the literal death of his father, just as his life has duplicated the emotional wasteland chosen and endured by his father.

The exemplary "peace of mind" experienced by the two Henrys and Rebecca—unfelt by any of the novel's other characters[22]—is both cause and function of their economic situation: they "planned the means of their future support, independent of their kinsman William—not only of him, but of every person and thing, but their own industry" (134). In her description of their secluded life, Inchbald stresses the link between material and psychological self-sufficiency:

> By forming an humble scheme for their remaining life, a scheme dependent upon their *own* exertions alone; on no light promises of pretended friends, and on no sanguine hopes of certain success; but with prudent apprehension, with fortitude against disappointment, Henry, his son, and Rebecca, (now his daughter) found themselves, at the end of one year, in the enjoyment of every comfort which such distinguished minds knew how to taste.
>
> *Exempt both from patronage and from controul*—healthy—alive to every fruition with which nature blesses the world; dead to all out of their power to attain, the works of art—susceptible of those passions which endear human creatures one to another, insensible to those which separate man from man—they found themselves the thankful inhabitants of a small house or hut, placed on the borders of the sea. (Ibid., my italics)

While critics have condemned the novel's ending as a "failure not only of social but of artistic vision"[23] or a turn to "Pantisocracy," an escape "through the romance of sympathy,"[24] I contend that Inchbald employs the convention of rural retreat as a different kind of social critique, in which the "hut, placed on the borders of the sea" operates not as utopia, but rather as condemnation of the society from which they have withdrawn. After their return to England, Henry and his son engage in conversation with a peasant from William's parish who bitterly describes the bishop's lack of compassion and concern for the poor. The "malicious joy" with which he relays his information makes Henry believe that there was a "want of charity and Christian deportment in the conduct of the bishop's family." Inchbald launches her final comparison: "He almost wished himself back on his savage island, where brotherly love could not be less, than it appeared to be in this civilised country" (129). Thus the characters' final turn to a social, if not "savage" island functions less as a retreat in the classic sense[25] than as an admission of their utter inability to live a life of "charity and Christian deportment" in society as it stands. While I agree with Mona Scheuermann's contention that Henry's final speeches problematically confound "simplicity of lifestyle and poverty,"[26] I would also argue that by making her exemplary characters farmers and fisherman instead of rural landowners, Inchbald redefines the nature of such retreat, for their island is characterized less by its poverty than by its provision of self-sufficiency, both material and emotional.

I have argued that throughout *Nature and Art*, Inchbald demonstrates the links among gendered identity, social standing, and moral turpitude. William senior, like the aptly named Bendhams, panders self-worth for status; his psychological manipulations, like those of his son, mirror the distortions necessary to such an existence. Inchbald's civilized world is one of anomie and chaos, peopled by chameleons who take their sickly hue from the corruption that surrounds—and sustains—them. Henry and his family, by contrast, live "[e]xempt both from patronage and from controul." Yet their island existence should not be seen to function as a social blueprint; indeed the hut and the self-sufficient existence it allows represent a move outside of class relations per se, a passage into a pre-lapsarian world of Edenic hunter-gatherers, concerned with survival instead of with the production and ownership of goods. Indeed Henry and his family might be said to partake in a privileged form of economic relations, one in which they possess the means of production, simple though that means might be. We are never told how Henry and his son, who have spent nearly two decades in an attempt to return to England, or the impoverished Rebecca, who has passed the years waiting for Henry's return by eking out a simple living with sewing and spinning, managed to purchase, or even lease, their hut. The novel's final retreat is as much an artificial construction as the supposedly natural Henry; as such, it cannot stand independent of the society it is designed to correct. Thus while the powerful political implications of this novel derive in large part from Inchbald's juxtaposition of nature and artifice, uncivilized goodness and societal corruption, her project ultimately ruptures upon the reef of this false dichotomy.

For by positing Henry as a character who is able to live only outside of society, Inchbald affirms the existence of a pure and untainted human nature. Yet the novel's penetrating psychological portraits of William and his son demonstrate that there is no such thing as nature unmediated by culture. As in the film *A Few Good Men*, where the protagonist's exposure of the unconscionable behavior of a certain commander in the Navy allows the system as a whole to remain unquestioned, even to be exonerated, Henry's movement outside of "corrupt" society unwittingly reconfirms the status quo by presenting an alternative that is inviable. Thus while the novel presents, on the one hand, a powerful, indeed radical critique of gender and class oppression, Inchbald's depiction of masculinity as torn between the poles of the natural and the artificial, between morality and corruption, acts to cushion the fist that strikes the blow. Like the earlier *A Simple Story*, *Nature and Art* furnishes no easy answers to the problematic issues it raises. Yet in its complex depictions of masculine professional, sexual, and familial identities, Inchbald's final novel provokes and enlightens.

Notes

1. After a more than hundred-year hiatus, Wordsworth Books published a facsimile of the novel's first edition (Oxford and New York: Wordsworth Books, 1994), while the following year Routledge/Thoemmes issued a facsimile of the novel's revised second edition. Most recently, Shawn Lisa Maurer has edited a modern critical edition of the novel, based upon the novel's second edition, for Pickering Women's Classics (London: Pickering & Chatto, 1997).

2. For an analysis of the problems surrounding the critical reception of *Nature and Art* from the time of its publication to the present, see Maurer, Introduction to the Pickering edition, cited above; the introduction also discusses the novel's aesthetic and political importance.

3. Mona Scheuermann, *Her Bread to Earn: Women, Money and Society from Defoe to Austen* (Lexington: University Press of Kentucky, 1993), 169.

4. Eleanor Ty, *Unsex'd Revolutionaries: Five Women Novelists of the 1790s* (Toronto: University of Toronto Press, 1993), 101.

5. See Scheuermann's insightful reading of the brothers' situation in *Social Protest in the Eighteenth-Century Novel* (Athens: Ohio State University Press, 1985), 170–72.

6. Here Inchbald concurs with other Jacobin novelists in elucidating the ways in which even potentially good men are debauched by the exigencies and opportunities of a

corrupt system. Perhaps the most virulent example of this process occurs in William Godwin's novel, *Caleb Williams; or, Things As They Are* (1794), in which Falkland, the initially benevolent squire, turns into a murderer and a tyrant to protect his own honor. For Inchbald's response to this novel, see Maurer, Introduction, xviii.

7. *The Tatler*, Ed. Donald F. Bond, 3 vols. (Oxford: Clarendon Press, 1987).

8. However, characters' relation to that structure is often depicted differently according to sex: Henry and his son are consistently represented in noble opposition to such systems of power and privilege as the church and the law, while the two virtuous female characters, Hannah and Rebecca, are more often represented as legal and religious victims.

9. Elizabeth Inchbald, *Nature and Art* (London: Pickering & Chatto, 1997), 3. All further quotations will be included in the text. Italics are original unless otherwise noted.

10. Whereas the classic female plot might be self-discovery culminating in marriage (see Marilyn Butler's reading of *Emma* in *Jane Austen and the War of Ideas* [Oxford, 1975]), the male narrative might be said to begin with self-discovery through labor.

11. For a similar tale of marital discontent, see *Spectator* No. 299: the story of "plain Jack Anvil" who becomes "Sir John Enville."

12. I am thinking, among other examples, of Roxana's marriage to the brewer in Daniel Defoe's *Roxana* (1724), the marriage described in "The Memoirs of a Lady of Quality" in Tobias Smollett's *Peregrine Pickle* (1751), Betsy Thoughtless's marriage to Mr. Munden in Eliza Haywood's *The Adventures of Miss Betsy Thoughtless* (1751), Mrs. Morgan's forced marriage in Sarah Scott's *Millennium Hall* (1762), and Maria's marriage to the venal George Venables in Mary Wollstonecraft's *The Wrongs of Woman* (1798).

13. Powerful examples of filial piety may be found not only in the example of Henry Norwynne in this novel, but also in his possible antecedent, Henry Willford, in Inchbald's play *Next Door Neighbours* (1791). An especially moving instance of a father's love for his son occurs in Inchbald's suppressed play, *The Massacre* (1792), in which old Tricastin attempts to impersonate his son in order to save him from death at the hands of a mob.

14. See Nancy Chodorow's influential study, *The Reproduction of Mothering* (Berkeley: University of California Press, 1978).

15. This point is emphasized in the novel's earlier title: "The Prejudice of Education," cited in Gary Kelly, *The English Jacobin Novel 1780–1805* (Oxford: Clarendon Press, 1976), 99; James Boaden, *The Memoirs of Mrs. Inchbald*, 2 vols. (London: Bentley, 1833), I: 346.

16. Inchbald's bishop seems to invite comparison to Dr. Blick, the unctuous and mercenary rector in Robert Bage's *Hermsprong*, published in the same year as *Nature and Art*. Dr.

Blick receives £1000 a year for doing virtually nothing, while his poor and virtuous curate, Mr. Woodcock, is paid only £40 to perform the community's spiritual and emotional services. The bishop's willingness to claim William's writing as his own also likens him to the plagiarizing bishop in Thomas Holcroft's novel, *Hugh Trevor* (1794–97). According to Gary Kelly, both Holcroft's and Inchbald's bishops, as well as Dr. Blick, were based upon an actual man, the reactionary bishop Samuel Horsley (*The English Jacobin Novel*, 105).

17. While this process might not, at first glance, seem to be a gendered one, since the novel's female characters both court and eschew public opinion, the ramifications for men seem nevertheless different, as public opinion is inextricably bound to profession rather than person.

18. See Randolph Trumbach, *The Rise of the Egalitarian Family: Aristocratic Kinship and Domestic Relations in Eighteenth-Century England* (New York: Academic Press, 1978) and Lawrence Stone and Jeanne C. Fawtier Stone, *An Open Elite? England 1540–1880* (Oxford: Oxford University Press, 1986).

19. For a discussion of the background and implications of this debate, see Chapter 4, "Reconstructing Honor," in my book entitled *Proposing Men: Dialectics of Gender and Class in the Eighteenth-Century English Periodical* (Stanford, Calif.: Stanford University Press, 1998).

20. See Shawn Lisa Maurer, "'Chaste Heterosexuality' in the Early English Periodical" *Restoration* 16, no. 1 (1992): 39–52.

21. Ironically, William uses the very concept of "honour" to break off relations with Hannah. See the analysis of Inchbald's critique of aristocratic honor in Maurer, Introduction, xxv–xxvi.

22. After Henry and his father return to England in time for William's funeral, they learn that the other characters have been retributively destroyed by their own vices: Lady Clementina by vanity, Lord Bendham by intemperance, and his wife by gaming; William, moreover, has been divorced from his adulterous wife.

23. Scheuermann, *Social Protest*, 200.

24. Kelly, 111, 112: "But like all the other woman novelists of the decade, and some of the men, [Inchbald] turned away from the failed Revolution and escaped through the romance of sympathy."

25. I am thinking, for example, of *Spectator* No. 15 (1711); Alexander Pope's *Epistle to Burlington* (1731); the character of Lord Munodi in Part III of Swift's *Gulliver's Travels* (1726); Samuel Johnson's poem "London" (1738); the rural retirement of Joseph, Fanny,

and the Wilsons at the end of Henry Fielding's *Joseph Andrews* (1742); and the conclusions of Johnson's *Rasselas* (1759), Voltaire's *Candide* (1759), and Tobias Smollett's *Humphry Clinker* (1771).

26. Scheuermann, *Social Protest,* 199.

Bibliography

Primary Sources

Bage, Robert. *Hermsprong, or Man As He Is Not.* 1796. Oxford: Oxford University Press, 1985.

Bowstead, Diana. "Charlotte Smith's *Desmond:* The Epistolary Novel as Ideological Argument." In *Fetter'd or Free? British Women Novelists, 1670–1815.* Ed. Mary Anne Schofield and Cecilia Macheski. Athens, Ohio: Ohio University Press, 1986.

Burke, Edmund. *Reflections on the Revolution in France.* 1790. Ed. C. O'Brien. London: Penguin, 1968.

Burney, Frances. *Camilla or A Picture of Youth.* 1796. Ed. Edward Bloom and Lillian Bloom. Oxford: Oxford University Press, 1983.

Fenwick, Eliza. *Secresy; or The Ruin on the Rock.* 1795. London: Pandora Press, 1989.

Foster, Hannah W. *The Coquette.* 1799. Ed. Cathy N. Davidson. New York: Oxford University Press, 1986.

Godwin, William. *Caleb Williams.* 1794. Ed. David McCracken. New York: W. W. Norton, 1977.

——. *An Enquiry Concerning Political Justice.* 1793. 3 vols. Ed. F. E. L. Priestley. Toronto: University of Toronto Press, 1946.

——. *Memoirs of the Author of A Vindication of the Rights of Woman.* 1798. Vol. 1 of *Collected Novels & Memoirs of William Godwin.* Ed. Mark Philips. London: William Pickering, 1992. 85–143.

——. *St. Leon.* 1799. Oxford: Oxford University Press, 1994.

Hays, Mary. *Memoirs of Emma Courtney.* 1796. New York: Garland, 1974.

——. *The Victim of Prejudice*. 1799. Ed. Eleanor Ty. Peterborough, Ontario: Broadview, 1994.

Holcroft, Thomas. *Anna St. Ives*. 1792. Ed. Peter Faulkner. London: Oxford University Press, 1970.

Inchbald, Elizabeth. *Nature and Art*. 1796. Ed. Shawn L. Maurer. London and Brookfield, Vt.: Pickering and Chatto Publishers, 1999.

Kelly, Gary, ed. *Bluestocking Feminism: Writings of the Bluestocking Circle, 1738–1790*. 6 vols. Brookfield, Vermont: Pickering & Chatto Publishers, 1999.

Lewis, Matthew Gregory. *The Monk*. 1796. Ed. Emma McEvoy. 2d ed. New York: Oxford University Press, 1996.

Malthias, Thomas. *Pursuit of Literature: A Satirical Poem*. Dublin, 1798.

Mulford, Carla, ed. *"The Power of Sympathy" by William Hill Brown and "The Coquette" by Hannah Foster*. New York: Penguin, 1996.

Opie, Amelia. *Adeline Mowbray: or, the Mother and Daughter*. 1804. Boston: Pandora Reprint, 1986.

——. *The Works of Mrs. Amelia Opie*, 2 vols. New York: AMS Press, 1974.

Polwhele, Richard. *The Unsex'd Females: A Poem*. 1798. New York: Garland, 1974.

Radcliffe, Ann. *The Italian, or the Confessional of the Black Penitents*. 1797. Ed. Frederick Garber. London: Oxford University Press, 1968.

——. *The Mysteries of Udolpho*. 1794. Ed. Bonomy Dobrée. New York: Oxford University Press, 1970.

Robinson, Mary. *Walsingham; or, the Pupil of Nature. A Domestic Story*. 1797. New York: Garland, 1974.

Rogers, Deborah D., ed. *Two Gothic Classics by Women*. New York: Penguin, 1995.

Sade, Marquis de. *Justine, Philosophy in the Bedroom, and Other Writings*. Ed. and trans. by Austryn Wainhouse and Richard Seaver. New York: Grove, 1965.

Smith, Charlotte. *Desmond: A Novel*. 1792. New York: Garland Reprint, 1975.

——. *Desmond*. 1792. Ed. Antje Blank and Janet Todd. London and Brookfield, Vt.: Pickering and Chatto Publishers, 1997.

——. *The Young Philosopher*. 1798. New York: Garland Reprint, 1975.

West, Jane. *A Tale of the Times*. 1799. 3 vols. New York: Garland Reprint, 1974.

Williams, Helen Maria. *An Eye-Witness Account of the French Revolution by Helen Maria Williams: Letters Containing a Sketch of the Politics of France*. Ed. Jack Fruchtman, Jr. New York: Peter Lang, 1997.

——. *Julia: A Novel*. 1790. Ed. Peter Garside. 2 vols. London: Routledge/Thoemmes Press, 1995.

——. *Letters From France*. Ed. with an Introduction by Janet Todd. 2 vols. Delmar, N.Y.: Scholars' Facsimiles and Reprints, 1975.

Wollstonecraft, Mary. *The Works of Mary Wollstonecraft*. Ed. by M. Butler & J. Todd. 7 vols. London: William Pickering, 1989.

——. *The Wrongs of Woman: or, Maria, A Fragment*. 1798. Ed. Gary Kelly. Oxford: Oxford World Classics, 1976.

Secondary Sources

Adams, M. Ray. *Studies in the Literary Backgrounds of English Radicalism, with Special Reference to the French Revolution*. Lancaster, Pennsylvania: Franklin & Marshall College Studies, 1947.

Adickes, Sandra. *The Social Quest: The Expanded Vision of Four Women Travelers in the Era of the French Revolution*. New York: Peter Lang, 1991.

Armstrong, Nancy. *Desire and Domestic Fiction: A Political History of the Novel*. New York: Oxford University Press, 1987.

Armstrong, Nancy and Leonard Tennenhouse, eds. *The Ideology of Conduct: Essays on Literature and the History of Sexuality*. New York: Methuen, 1987.

Backscheider, Paula R. and Timothy Dykstal. *The Intersections of the Public and Private Spheres in Early Modern England*. London: Frank Cass, 1996.

Baker, Ernest A. *The History of the English Novel*. Vol.5. 1929. Reprint, London: H. F. and G. Witherby, Ltd., 1967.

Barker-Benfield, G. J. *The Culture of Sensibility: Sex and Society in Eighteenth-Century Britain*. Chicago: University of Chicago Press, 1992.

Bate, Jonathan. "Faking It: Shakespeare and the 1790s." *Essays and Studies* 46 (1993): 63-80.

Beer, John. *Romantic Influences: Contemporary, Victorian, Modern*. New York: St. Martin's, 1993.

Bender, John. *Imagining the Penitentiary: Fiction and the Architecture of Mind in Eighteenth-Century England*. Chicago: University of Chicago Press, 1987.

——. "Impersonal Violence: The Penetrating Gaze and the Field of Narration in *Caleb Williams*." In *Vision & Textuality*. Durham, N.C.: Duke University Press, 1995.

Benedict, Barbara. "The 'Curious Attitude' in Eighteenth-Century Britain; Observing and Owning" *Eighteenth-Century Life* 14, no. 3 (1990): 59–98.

——. *Framing Feeling: Sentiment and Style in English Prose Fiction, 1745–1800*. New York: AMS Press, 1994.

——. "Literary Miscellanies: The Cultural Mediation of Fragmented Feeling." *ELH* 57, no. 2 (1990): 407–30.

——. *Making the Modern Reader: Cultural Mediation in Early Modern Literary Anthologies*. Princeton, N.J.: Princeton University Press, 1996.

——. "Pictures of Conformity: Sentiment and Structure in Ann Radcliffe's Style." *Philological Quarterly* 68, no. 3 (1989): 363–77.

——. "Reading Faces: Physiognomy and Epistemology in Late Eighteenth-Century Sentimental Novels." *Studies in Philology*. 92, no. 3 (1995): 311–28.

Bernstein, Stephen. "Form and Ideology in the Gothic Novel." *Essays in Literature* 18, no. 2 (1991): 151–65.

Bilger, Audrey. *Laughing Feminism: Subversive Comedy in Frances Burney, Maria Edgeworth, and Jane Austen*. Detroit: Wayne State University Press, 1998.

Blaine, Rodney. *Thomas Holcroft and the Revolutionary Novel*. Athens: University of Georgia Press, 1965.

Bradbrook, Frank W. *Jane Austen and Her Predecessors*. Cambridge: Cambridge University Press, 1966.

Bradfield, Scott. *Dreaming Revolution: Transgression in the Development of American Romance*. Iowa City: University of Iowa Press, 1993.

Bray, Matthew. "Helen Maria Williams and Edmund Burke: Radical Critique and Complicity." *Eighteenth-Century Life* 16 (1992): 1–24.

Brissenden, R. F. *Virtue in Distress: Studies in the Novel of Sentiment from Richardson to Sade*. London: MacMillan and New York: Barnes & Noble, 1974.

Brophy, Elizabeth Bergen. *Women's Lives and the 18th Century English Novel*. Tampa: University of South Florida Press, 1991.

Brown, Homer Obed. *Institutions of the English Novel: From Defoe to Scott*. Philadelphia: University of Pennsylvania Press, 1997.

——. "Of the Title to Things Real: Conflicting Stories." *ELH* 55 (1988): 917–54.

Butler, Marilyn. *Burke, Paine, Godwin and the Revolution Controversy*. Cambridge: Cambridge University Press, 1984.

——. *Jane Austen and the War of Ideas*. Oxford: Clarendon, 1975.

——. "Telling it Like a Story: The French Revolution as Narrative." *Studies in Romanticism* 28, no. 3 (1989): 345–64.

Cameron, Kenneth Neill, ed. *Shelley and his Circle, 1773–1822.* Vol. 1 and 2. Cambridge, Mass.: Harvard University Press, 1961.

Castle, Terry. *Masquerade and Civilization: The Carnivalesque in Eighteenth-Century Culture and Fiction.* Stanford: Stanford University Press, 1986.

Cavaliero, Glen. *The Supernatural and English Fiction.* Oxford: Oxford University Press, 1995.

Claeys, Gregory, ed. *Political Writings of the 1790s.* London: William Pickering, 1995.

Clark, Anna. *Women's Silence, Men's Violence: Sexual Assault in England, 1770–1845.* London: Pandora, 1987.

Clemit, Pamela. *The Godwinian Novel: The Rational Fictions of Godwin, Brockden Brown, Mary Shelley.* Oxford: Clarendon, 1993.

Colley, Linda. *Britons: Forging the Nation 1707–1837.* New Haven: Yale University Press, 1992.

Cone, Carl B. *The English Jacobins: Reformers in Late 18th Century England.* New York: Charles Scribner's Sons, 1968.

Conger, Syndy McMillen. "Austen's Sense and Radcliffe's Sensibility." *Gothic* 2 (1987): 16–24.

———. *Mary Wollstonecraft and the Language of Sensibility.* Toronto: Associated University Press, 1994.

———, ed. *Sensibility in Transformation.* London: Associated Press, 1990.

Conway, Alison. "Nationalism, Revolution, and the Female Body: Charlotte Smith's *Desmond.*" *Women's Studies: An Interdisciplinary Journal.* 24, no.5 (1995): 395–409.

Copley, Stephen and John Whale, eds. *Beyond Romanticism: New Approaches to Texts and Contexts, 1780–1832.* Syracuse: Syracuse University Press, 1991.

Cott, Nancy F. *The Bonds of Womanhood: "Woman's Sphere" in New England, 1790–1835.* New Haven: Yale University Press, 1977.

Craft-Fairchild, Catherine. *Masquerade and Gender: Disguise and Female Identity in Eighteenth-Century Fictions by Women.* University Park, Pennsylvania: Pennsylvania State University Press, 1993.

Crossley, Ceri, and Ian Small, eds. *The French Revolution and British Culture.* Oxford: Oxford University Press,1989.

Dabundo, Laura, ed. *New Essays: Women Novelists of the Romantic Period.* Dallas: ContemporaryResearch Press, 1994.

Davenport-Hines, Richard. *Gothic: 400 Years of Excess, Horror, Evil and Ruin.* New York: North Point Press, 1999.

Davidson, Cathy N. *Revolution and the Word: The Rise of the Novel in America.* New York: Oxford University Press, 1986.

Davis, Lennard. *Factual Fictions: The Origins of the English Novel*. New York: Columbia University Press, 1983.

Dickenson, H.T. *British Radicalism and the French Revolution, 1789–1815*. New York: Blackwell, 1985.

Doody, Margaret. "English Women Novelists and the French Revolution." In *La Femme en Angleterre et dans les colonies américaines aux XVIIe et XVIIIe siècles*. Lille: Publications de l'Université de Lille III, 1976. 176–98.

——. *Frances Burney: The Life in the Works*. New Brunswick: Rutgers University Press, 1988.

Ellis, Markman. *The Politics of Sensibility: Race, Gender and Commerce in the Sentimental Novel*. Cambridge: Cambridge University Press, 1996.

Ellison, Julie. "Redoubled Feeling: Politics, Sentiment, and the Sublime in Williams and Wollstonecraft." *Studies in Eighteenth-Century Culture* 20 (1990): 197–215.

Epstein, Julia. *The Iron Pen: Frances Burney and the Politics of Women's Writing*. Madison: The University of Wisconsin Press, 1989.

Everest, Kelvin. *Revolution in Writing: British Literary Responses to the French Revolution*. England: Milton Keynes; Philadelphia: Open University Press, 1991.

Favret, Mary. *Romantic Correspondence: Women, Politics and the Fiction of Letters*. Cambridge: Cambridge University Press, 1993.

——. "Spectatrice as Spectacle: Helen Maria Williams at Home in the Revolution." *Studies in Romanticism* 32 (Summer 1993): 273–295.

Feldman, Paula R., and Theresa M. Kelley, eds. *Romantic Women Writers: Voices and Countervoices*. Hanover, N.H.: New England University Press, 1995.

Fergus, Jan, and Janice Farrar Thaddeus. "Women, Publishers, and Money, 1790–1820." *Studies in Eighteenth-Century Culture* 3 (1987): 191–207.

Ferguson, Frances. "Sade and the Pornographic Legacy." *Representations* 36 (Fall 1991): 1–21.

Fitzgerald, Laurie. *Shifting Genres, Changing Realities: Reading the Late-Eighteenth-Century Novel*. New York: P. Lang, 1995.

Folkenflik, Robert, ed. *The English Hero, 1660–1800*. Newark: University of Delaware Press, 1982.

——. "The Heirs of Ian Watt." *Eighteenth-Century Studies* 25 (1991-92): 203–17.

Forbes, Joan. "Anti-Romantic Discourse as Resistance: Women's Fiction 1775–1820." *Romance Revisited*. Ed. Jackie Stacey and Lynne Pearce. New York: New York University Press, 1995.

Fort, Bernadette ed. *Fictions of the French Revolution*. Evanston, Illinois: Northwestern University Press, 1991.

Frautschi, Richard L. "Nationalisms Placed and Displaced in French Fiction of the 1790s." *Studies on Voltaire and the Eighteenth Century* 304 (1992): 987–94.

Fry, Carrol L. *Charlotte Smith*. Twayne's English Authors Series. New York: Twayne, 1996.

Frye, Northrop. "Towards Defining an Age of Sensibility." In *Eighteenth Century English Literature: Modern Essays in Criticism*. Ed. James L. Clifford. New York: Oxford University Press, 1959.

Garside, P. D. "Jane Austen and Subscription Fiction." *British Journal for Eighteenth Century Studies* 10, no. 2 (1987): 175-88.

Green, Katherine Sobba. *The Courtship Novel, 1740–1820: A Feminized Genre*. Lexington; University Press of Kentucky, 1991.

Gregory, Allene. *The French Revolution and the English Novel*. New York: Haskell House, 1966.

Gutwirth, Madelyn. *The Twilight of the Goddesses: Women and Representation in the French Revolutionary Era*. New Brunswick: Rutgers University Press, 1992.

Hanley, Keith, and Raman Selden, eds. *Revolution and English Romanticism*. New York: St. Martin's, 1990.

Harasym, S. D. "Ideology and Self: A Theoretical Discussion of the 'Self' in Mary Wollstonecraft's Fiction." *English Studies in Canada* 12, no. 2 (June 1986): 163–177.

Heffernan, James, ed. *Representing the French Revolution: Literature, Historiography, and Art*. Hanover, N.H.: University Press of New England, 1992.

Hemlow, Joyce. "Fanny Burney and the Courtesy Books." *PMLA* 65 (1950): 732-61.

Henderson, Andrea. "Commerce and Masochistic Desire in the 1790s: Frances Burney's *Camilla.*"*Eighteenth-Century Studies*. 31, no. 1 (1997): 69.

Hilbish, Florence May Anna. *Charlotte Smith, Poet and Novelist (1749–1806)*. Philadelphia: University of Pennsylvania Press, 1941.

Hill, Bridget. *Women, Work, and Sexual Politics in Eighteenth-Century England*. Oxford: Basil Blackwell, 1989.

Hoagwood, Terence Allan. Introduction to *The Victim of Prejudice,* by Mary Hays. Delmar, N.Y.: Scholars' Facsimiles and Reprints, 1990.

Hone, J. Ann. *For the Cause of Truth: Radicalism in London, 1796–1821*. Oxford: Clarendon, 1982.

Hunt, Lynn, ed. *The Invention of Pornography: Obscenity and the Origins of Modernity, 1500–1800*. New York: Zone, 1993.

——. *The Family Romance and the French Revolution*. Berkeley: University of California Press, 1992.

——. "The Unstable Boundaries of the French Revolution." In *From the Fires of the Revolution to the Great War*. Ed. Michelle Perot. Vol. 4 of *A History of Private Life*. General ed. Phillippe Aries and Georges Duby. Trans. Arthur Goldhammer. Cambridge, Mass.: Belknap Press, 1990.13–45.

Hunter, J. Paul. *Before Novels: The Cultural Contexts of Eighteenth-Century Fiction*. New York and London: Norton, 1990.

Jacobus, Mary. "The Difference of View." In *Women, Writing and Writing about Women*. Ed. Mary Jacobus. New York: Harper & Row, 1979. 10–21.

Johnson, Claudia L. *Equivocal Beings: Politics, Gender, and Sentimentality in the 1790s. Wollstonecraft, Radcliffe, Burney, Austen*. Chicago: University of Chicago Press, 1995.

Jones, Chris. *Radical Sensibility: Literature and Ideas in the 1790s*. New York: Routledge, 1993.

Jones, Vivien, ed. *Women in the Eighteenth Century: Constructions of Feminity*. London: Routledge, 1990.

Kelly, Gary. *The English Jacobin Novel: 1780–1805*. Oxford: Clarendon, 1976.

——. *Revolutionary Feminism: The Mind and Career of Mary Wollstonecraft*. New York: St. Martin's, 1996.

——. "Women Novelists and the French Revolution Debate: Novelizing the Revolution/Revolutionizing the Novel." *Eighteenth-Century Fiction* 6, no. 4 (1994): 369–88.

——. "Women Writers and Romantic Nationalism in Britain." In *Literature of Region and Nation: Proceedings of the 6th International Literature of Region and Nation Conference*. Ed. Winnifred W. Bogaards. Saint John, New Brunswick: University of New Brunswick, 1998.

——. *Women, Writing, Revolution: 1790–1827*. Oxford: Clarendon, 1993.

Kiely, Robert. *The Romantic Novel in England*. Cambridge: Harvard University Press, 1972.

Klein, Lawrence E. "Gender and the Public/Private Distinction in the Eighteenth Century: Some Questions about Evidence and Analytic Procedure." *Eighteenth-Century Studies*. 29, no. 1 (1995): 97–109.

Landes, Joan B. *Women and the Public Sphere in the Age of Revolution*. Ithaca: Cornell University Press, 1988.

Lang-Peralta, Linda. "Clandestine Delight: Frances Burney's Life Writing." In *Women's Life-Writing: Finding Voice/Building Community*. Ed. Linda S. Coleman. Bowling Green: Bowling Green State University Popular Press, 1997. 23–43

Looser, Devoney, ed. *Jane Austen and Discourses of Feminism*. Basingstoke, England: MacMillan, 1995.

Luria, Gina M. "Mary Hays's Letters and Manuscripts." *Signs: Journal of Women in Culture and Society* 3, no. 2 (Winter 1977): 524–30.

Mackenzie, Catriona. "Reason and Sensibility: The Ideal of Women's Self-Governance in the Writings of Mary Wollstonecraft." *Hypatia* 8, no. 4 (Fall 1993): 35–55.

Martin, Philip W., and Robin Jarvis, eds. *Reviewing Romanticism*. New York: St. Martin's, 1992.

Mayo, Robert D. *The English Novel in the Magazines, 1740–1815*. Oxford: Oxford University Press, 1962.

McKee, Patricia. *Public and Private: Gender, Class, and the British Novel, 1764–1878*. Minneapolis: Minnesota University Press, 1997.

McKeon, Michael. *The Origins of the English Novel, 1600–1740*. Baltimore: Johns Hopkins University Press, 1987.

Mee, Jon. "'Examples of Safe Printing': Censorship and Popular Radical Literature in the 1790s." *Essays and Studies* 46 (1993): 81–95.

Mellor, Anne K. "A Novel of Their Own: Romantic Women's Fiction, 1790–1830." In *The Columbia History of the British Novel*. Ed. John Richetti, et al. New York: Columbia University Press,1994. 327–51

———. *Romanticism and Feminism*. Ed. Anne K. Mellor. Bloomington: Indiana University Press, 1988.

Melzer, Sara E., and Leslie Rabine, eds. *Rebel Daughters: Women and the French Revolution*. Oxford: Oxford University Press, 1992.

Mishra, Vijay. *The Gothic Sublime*. New York: University of New York Press, 1994.

Mullan, John. *Sentiment and Sociability: The Language of Feeling in the Eighteenth Century*. Oxford: Clarendon, 1988.

Myers, Mitzi. "Unfinished Business: Wollstonecraft's *Maria*." *The Wordsworth Circle* 11.2 (1980): 107–14.

Napier, Elizabeth R. *The Failure of the Gothic: Problems of Disjunction in an Eighteenth-Century Literary Form*. Oxford: Clarendon Press, 1987.

Nussbaum, Felicity, and Laura Brown, eds. *The New Eighteenth Century: Theory, Politics, English Literature*. New York: Methuen, 1987.

Parameswaran, Uma, ed. *Quilting a New Canon: Stitching Women's Words*. Toronto: Sister Vision, 1996.

Paulson, Ronald. *Representations of Revolution (1789–1820)*. New Haven: Yale University Press, 1983.

Perry, Ruth. "The Contributions of Gender to the Evolution of the Novel." *Modern Language Quarterly* 57, no. 4 (1996): 633–43.

——. *Women, Letters and the Novel.* New York: Garland, 1980.

Philps, Mark. *Godwin's Political Justice.* London: Gerald Duckworth, 1986.

Poovey, Mary. *The Proper Lady and the Woman Writer: Ideology as Style in the Works of Mary Wollstonecraft, Mary Shelley, and Jane Austen.* Chicago: University of Chicago Press, 1984.

Punter, David. *The Literature of Terror: A History of Gothic Fiction from 1765 to the Present Day.* London and NewYork.: Longman, 1980.

Rajan, Tilottama. "Autonarration and Genotext in Mary Hays' *Memoirs of Emma Courtney.*" *Studies in Romanticism* 32 (1993): 146–76.

Rajan, Tilottama, and Julia M. Wright, eds. *Romanticism, History, and the Possibilities of Genre.* New York: Cambridge University Press, 1998.

Rajan, Tilottama. "Wollstonecraft and Godwin: Reading the Secrets of the Political Novel." *Studies in Romanticism* 27, no. 2 (1988): 221–51.

Rendall, Jane. *The Origins of Modern Feminism: Women in Britain, France and the United States, 1780–1860.* London: MacMillan, 1985.

Renwick, W. L. *English Literature 1789–1815.* Vol. 9. *The Oxford History of English Literature.* Oxford: Clarendon, 1963.

Richardson, Alan. *Literature, Education, and Romanticism: Reading as Social Practice, 1780-1832.* Cambridge: Cambridge University Press, 1994.

Richter, David H. *The Progress of Romance: Literary Historiography and the Gothic Novel.* Columbus: Ohio State University Press, 1996.

Roberts, Bette B. "The Horrid Novels: The Mysteries of *Udolpho* and *Northanger Abbey.*" In *Gothic Fictions: Prohibition/Transgression.* New York: AMS, 1989. 89–111.

Rogers, Katherine. *Ann Radcliffe: A Bio-Bibliography.* Westport, Conn.: Greenwood, 1996.

——. "The Contribution of Mary Hays." *Prose Studies* 10, no. 2 (1987): 131–42.

Ross, Deborah. *The Excellence of Falsehood: Romance, Realism, and Women's Contribution to the Novel.* Lexington: University Press of Kentucky, 1991.

Rothstein, Eric. Review of Michael McKeon, *The Origins of the English Novel, 1600-1740. Eighteenth-Century Studies* 21 (1987–88): 228–31.

——. *Systems of Order and Inquiry in Later Eighteenth-Century Fiction.* Berkeley and Los Angeles: University of California Press, 1975.

Sage, Victor. *Horror Fiction in the Protestant Tradition.* New York: St. Martin's, 1988.

Sapiro, Virginia. *A Vindication of Political Virtue: The Political Theory of Mary Wollstonecraft.* Chicago: University of Chicago Press, 1993.

Scheuermann, Mona. *Her Bread to Earn: Women, Money, and Society from Defoe to Austen.* Lexington: University Press of Kentucky, 1993.

———. *Social Protest in the Eighteenth-Century Novel.* Columbus: Ohio State University Press, 1985.

Schofield, Mary Anne and Cecilia Macheski, eds. *Fetter'd or Free? British Women Novelists, 1670–1815.* Athens, Ohio: Ohio University Press, 1986.

Schofield, Mary Anne, ed. *Masking and Unmasking the Female Mind: Disguising Romances in Feminine Fiction, 1713–1799.* Newark: University of Delaware Press, 1990.

Spacks, Patricia Meyer. "Energies of Mind: Plot's Possibilities in the 1790s." *Eighteenth-Century Fiction* 1, no. 1 (1988): 37–51.

———. "Energies of Mind: Novels of the 1790s." In *Desire and Truth: Functions of Plot in Eighteenth-Century English Novels.* Chicago: University of Chicago Press, 1990. 175–202.

———. "Novels of the 1790s: Action and Impasse." In *The Columbia History of the British Novel.* Ed. John Richetti, et al. New York: Columbia University Press, 1994. 247–74.

Spencer, Jane. *The Rise of the Woman Novelist: From Aphra Behn to Jane Austen.* Oxford: Basil Blackwell, 1986.

Spender, Dale, ed. *Feminist Theorists: Three Centuries of Women's Intellectual Traditions.* London: The Women's Press, 1983.

———, ed. *Living by the Pen: Early British Women Writers.* The Athene Series. New York: Teachers College, 1992.

———. *Mothers of the Novel: 100 Good Women Writers before Jane Austen.* London and New York: Pandora, 1986.

Stafford, William. "Narratives of Women: English Feminists of the 1790s." *History: The Journal of the Historical Association* 82 (1997): 2443.

Stanton, Judith Phillips. "Charlotte Smith's 'Literary Business': Income, Patronage, and Indigence." *The Age of Johnson.* Ed. Paula Korshin. New York: AMS Press, 1987. 375–401.

Stern, Julia A. *The Plight of Feeling: Sympathy and Dissent in the Early American Novel.* Chicago: Chicago University Press, 1997.

Suleiman, Susan Rubin. *Authoritarian Fictions: The Ideological Novel as a Literary Genre.* New York: Columbia University Press, 1983.

Sullivan, Garrett. A. Jr., "'A Story to Be Hastily Gobbled Up': *Caleb Williams* and Print Culture." *Studies in Romanticism* 32, no. 3 (1993): 323–37.

Tabor, Eve. *Skepticism, Society and the Eighteenth-Century Novel*. New York: St. Martin's Press, 1987.

Thompson, James. *Models of Value: Eighteenth-Century Political Economy and the Novel*. Durham: Duke University Press, 1996.

Todd, Janet. *Sensibility: An Introduction*. New York: Methuen, 1986.

———. *The Sign of Angellica: Women Writing and Fiction, 1660–1800*. London: Virago, 1989.

Tompkins, J. M. S. *The Popular Novel in England: 1770–1800*. London: Constable and Co., 1932.

Turner, Cheryl. *Living By the Pen: Women Writers in the Eighteenth Century*. New York: Routledge, 1992.

Turner, James Grantham. "The Whore's Rhetorick: Narrative, Pornography, and the Origins of the Novel." *Studies in Eighteenth-Century Culture*. Vol. 24. Ed. Carla Hay. (1995): 297–306.

Ty, Eleanor. *Empowering the Feminine: The Narratives of Mary Robinson, Jane West, and Amelia Opie, 1796–1812*. Toronto: University of Toronto Press, 1998.

———. *The Unsex'd Revolutionaries: Five Women Novelists of the 1790s*. Toronto: University of Toronto Press, 1993.

Uphaus, Robert, ed. *The Idea of the Novel in the Eighteenth Century*. East Lansing: Colleagues Press, 1988.

Van Sant, Ann Jessie. *Eighteenth-Century Sensibility and the Novel: The Sense in Social Context*. Cambridge: Cambridge University Press, 1993.

Warner, William B. "The Elevation of the Novel in England: Hegemony and Literary History." *ELH* 59 (1992): 577–96.

Watson, Nicola. *Revolution and the Form of the British Novel, 1790–1825*. Oxford: Clarendon, 1994.

Watt, Ian. *The Rise of the Novel*. Berkeley and Los Angeles: University of California Press, 1957.

———. "Serious Reflections on *The Rise of the Novel*." *A Forum on Fiction* 1 (Spring 1968): 205–18.

Wehrs, Donald R. "Rhetoric, History, Rebellion: *Caleb Williams* and the Subversion of Eighteenth-Century Fiction." *Studies in English Literature, 1500–1900* 28, no. 3 (1988): 497–511.

White, Devon. "Contemporary Criticism of Five Early American Sentimental Novels, 1970–1994: An Annotated Bibliography." *Bulletin of Bibliography* 52, no. 4 (1995): 293–305.

Wiesenfarth, Joseph. *Gothic Manners and the Classic English Novel*. Madison: The University of Wisconsin Press, 1988.

Wilson, Carol Shiner, and Joel Haefner, eds. *Re-visioning Romanticism: British Women Writers, 1776–1837*. Philadelphia: University of Pennsylvania Press, 1994.

Wilson, R. McNair. *Women of the French Revolution*. Port Washington, N.Y.: Kennikat, 1936.

Winter, Kari J. "Sexual/Textual Politics of Terror: Writing and Rewriting the Gothic Genre in the 1790s." In *Misogyny in Literature: An Essay Collection*. New York: Garland, 1992. 89–103.

Worrall, David. *Radical Culture: Discourse, Resistance and Surveillance, 1790–1820*. New York: Harvester Wheatsheaf, 1992.

Yarrington, Alison, and Kelvin Everest, eds. *Reflections on Revolution: Images of Romanticism*. London: Routledge, 1993.

Zaczek, Barbara Maria. *Censored Sentiments: Letters and Censorship in Epistolary Novels and Conduct Material*. Newark: Delaware University Press, 1997.

Zimmerman, Everett. *The Boundaries of Fiction: History and the Eighteenth-Century British Novel*. Ithaca: Cornell University Press, 1996.

Zlotnick, Susan. *Women, Writing and the Industrial Revolution*. Baltimore: Johns Hopkins University Press, 1998.

Zonitch, Barbara. *Familiar Violence: Gender and Social Upheaval in the Novels of Frances Burney*. Canbury, N.J.: Associated University Press, 1997.

Contributors

BARBARA M. BENEDICT, Associate Professor of English at Trinity College, Conn., is the author of *Framing Feeling: Sentiment and Style in English Prose Fiction, 1745–1800* (New York: AMS Press, 1994), and *Making the Modern Reader: Cultural Mediation in Early Modern Literary Anthologies* (Princeton, N.J.: Princeton University Press, 1996). She has also written on eighteenth-century fiction, popular culture, and book history.

KATHERINE BINHAMMER is Assistant Professor in the English Department at the University of Alberta where she teaches women's writing and eighteenth-century literature and culture. Her current research project studies the interconnections between gender and sexuality in political discourses of the 1790s. Previous articles on the 1790s have appeared in *The Journal of the History of Sexuality* and *Eighteenth-Century Fiction*.

CATHERINE H. DECKER is an English instructor at Chaffey Community College in California. She has published work in *Romanticism on the Net* and *The Wordsworth Circle* and also has presented papers at such conferences as NEASECS and ASECS. In 1995, she edited *The Aphra Behn Newsletter*. Her *Regency Page* on the World Wide Web (*http://locutus.ucr.edu/~cathy/reg.html*) is a large educational site dedicated to understanding fashion, literature, and culture from 1790–1829.

CARL FISHER is an Assistant Professor of English at Austin Peay State University. He received his Ph.D. from the University of California, Los Angeles, has published on Defoe and historical fiction, and is currently working on a book about crowd scenes in eighteenth-century novels.

LINDA LANG-PERALTA, Assistant Professor of English at The Metropolitan State College of Denver, earned a doctorate in comparative literature at the University of California, Irvine, where she wrote a dissertation on Frances Burney and Germaine de Staël. Her article "'Clandestine Delights': Frances Burney's Life-Writing" is included in *Women's Life-Writing: Finding Voice/Building Community* (Bowling Green, Ky.: Bowling Green University Press, 1997). Currently, she is working on African literature as a result of a Fulbright Seminar in Kenya in 1998.

SHAWN LISA MAURER is the editor of a modern critical edition of *Nature and Art*, published by Pickering Women's Classics in 1997. An independent scholar, she is the author of *Proposing Men: Dialectics of Gender and Class in the Eighteenth-Century English Periodical* (Stanford, Calif.: Stanford University Press, 1998).

CLARA D. MCLEAN is a doctoral candidate in the Department of English and Comparative Literature at the University of California, Irvine, writing her dissertation on elements of the Gothic in American modernism and postmodernism. Her most recent publication is "Wasted Words: The Body Language of Joyce's 'Nausicaa,'" in *Joycean Cultures* from the University of Delaware Press

GLYNIS RIDLEY, a graduate of the Universities of Edinburgh and Oxford, is now assistant professor at the University of Huddersfield in Yorkshire, England. She is currently completing a book on the relationship between the rhetorical tradition and the development of prose fiction in the eighteenth century. She serves as editor of the *Bulletin* of the British Society for Eighteenth-Century Studies and as a regular reviewer for the Society's *Journal*.

ELEANOR TY, Associate Professor of English at Wilfrid Laurier University, is the author of *Empowering the Feminine: The Narratives of Mary Robinson, Jane West, and Amelia Opie, 1796–1812* (University of Toronto Press, 1998) and *Unsex'd Revolutionaries: Women Novelists of the 1790s* (University of Toronto Press, 1993). She has edited *Memoirs of Emma Courtney* and *The Victim of Prejudice* by Mary Hays. She has published articles on ethnic and minority women writers, such as Joy Kogawa, Jamaica Kincaid, and Amy Tan, on reading romances, and on post-colonial politics in *Miss Saigon*.